TENNIS
2000

ALSO BY VIC BRADEN

Vic Braden's Laugh and Win at Doubles (with Bill Bruns)

Teaching Children Tennis the Vic Braden Way (with Bill Bruns)

Vic Braden's Quick Fixes (with Bill Bruns)

Vic Braden's Mental Tennis (with Robert Wool)

TENNIS
2000

Strokes, Strategy, and Psychology
for a Lifetime

VIC BRADEN
AND BILL BRUNS

LITTLE, BROWN AND COMPANY
Boston   New York   London

REVISED EDITION

Previously published as *Vic Braden's Tennis for the Future* in hardcover in 1977 and in paperback in 1980 by Little, Brown and Company. This edition is completely revised and updated.

Unless otherwise noted, the photographs in this book were taken by Vic and Melody Braden.
Special photography by John G. Zimmerman
Drawing on page 114 by Willy Paul and Mary Reilly
Other instructional charts and drawings by Moe Lebovitz and Mary Reilly

LIBRARY OF CONGRESS CATALOGING-IN-PUBLICATION DATA
Braden, Vic.
    Tennis 2000 : strokes, strategy, and psychology for a lifetime /
Vic Braden and Bill Bruns. — Rev. ed.
        p.   cm.
    Rev. ed. of : Vic Braden's tennis for the future. c 1977.
    ISBN 0-316-10503-1 (pbk.)
    1. Tennis. 2. Tennis — Training. 3. Tennis — Psychological
aspects. I. Bruns, Bill. II. Braden, Vic. Vic Braden's tennis
for the future. III. Title.
GV995.B6857   1998
796.342'2 — dc21   98-12795

10   9   8   7   6   5   4   3   2

MV-NY

Printed in the U.S.A.

*To my beautiful wife and best friend, Melody, and to
our wonderful children, Kelly, Troy, Kory, Kristen, and Shawn*

VIC BRADEN

*To the three men who were inspiring mentors during my high
school and college journalism days: Ralph Curtis at the
Encinitas* Coast Dispatch, *Ralph Alexander, cofounder of the
Scholastic Sports Association in Los Angeles, and
Howard Hurlbut, the adviser of our student newspaper at the
University of Redlands*

BILL BRUNS

Contents

Preface

N 1976, when I completed my first book with Bill Bruns, we decided to call it *Tennis for the Future*. After a lifetime of playing the sport, listening to other coaches, and studying the top players, I was beginning to do scientific research at my tennis college that was not only confirming many of my beliefs about how to hit a tennis ball but was also puncturing some common myths that hold players back. I felt there was so much for all of us to learn about biomechanics and the immutable laws of nature shaping successful tennis strokes that my book would lay the groundwork for playing the game properly well into the future.

Back then, white tennis balls were not yet obsolete, metal rackets were coming into vogue (though Jack Kramer's wood racket still reigned), topspin groundstrokes were gaining favor, and the top players in the game were Chris Evert, Bjorn Borg, and Jimmy Connors. More important, the tennis craze was in full bloom across the country: public courts were jammed, private indoor courts operated day and night, and Tim Galwey's book *The Inner Game of Tennis* was a national bestseller.

Like Galwey, I was interested in the psychological aspects of tennis, and I featured them in my teaching, but I had a more scientific objective. My tennis college at Coto de Caza, south of Los Angeles, was built specifically as a teaching facility — complete with an array of ball machines and TV cameras for video replay, but also special teaching courts, individual instruction lanes, and sophisticated classroom equipment — and I wanted to pull all the strokes and strategy together into one book.

Happily, when *Tennis for the Future* was published, a reviewer at *Time* magazine deemed it to be "the Wimbledon of tennis instructionals," and it subsequently went into eight printings in hardback while inspiring a twelve-week PBS series. I went on to write four other books about the game, but as we approached the year 2000, I wanted to go back to "the Future" and bring out a thoroughly updated version of the classic, taking into account the changes brought about by high-tech equipment — for example, longer rackets, stronger but lighter frames, expanded head sizes, and larger sweet spots. I also wanted to acknowledge the influence of stars who had played out their careers during that twenty-year interim, including the likes of Ivan Lendl, John McEnroe, and Martina Navratilova, as well as today's top players, from Martina Hingis and the Williams sisters to Pete Sampras and his cast of challengers.

Yet as I transformed the original book into *Tennis 2000,* and as I continued to travel around the country giving clinics and watching tournaments at every level, I realized that at its very heart, stripped of all the emphasis on outright power in the pro game, tennis still comes down to how well you can hit a target under stress. Today when I sit and talk with pros in the locker room, I still hear the same challenges and sense the same fears: "Can I serve well? . . . Can I return serve? . . . Can I hit my passing shots?" At the club level and in league play, there are more good players who can hit the ball harder with less effort today, but the game they play is still ruled by the net, the length and width of the court, and physical laws that can't be violated. I teach people from all parts of the country and from around the world, and they have the same questions, the same hang-ups, the same misconceptions, and the same hurdles to improvement that I have always enjoyed dealing with as a coach. And, of course, there's invariably somebody back home they want to beat.

Thus I'm always interested when I read articles or hear the experts talk about the "resurgence of the Australian tradition in tennis" or "the neglected strategy established by Jack Kramer," who emphasized the all-around game and getting to the net rather than simply camping on the baseline.

For, in all honesty, Kramer's approach to tennis — and the style of play epitomized by the great Australian players of the 1950s and 1960s — represented the heart of my original book. *Tennis for the Future* still lives! Jack was not only the best player I've ever seen, he could analyze the game better than anyone, as I learned firsthand when I began working for his four-man pro tour that barnstormed from city to city in the late 1950s. But I'm getting ahead of myself here. Let's move on to the Introduction and Chapter 1, and I think you'll soon realize why the approach to strokes and strategy I emphasized a generation ago still remains fresh and viable. "Good strokes last a lifetime," I wrote many years ago, and that is still my bottom-line approach today, for whether you play the game recreationally or on the tournament level, the basic question — and goal — always remains: Under pressure, do you have the consistent strokes you need to hit the shots you want?

And don't lose sight of my motto, "Laugh and win," the heart of my teaching philosophy. Some of my Type A students tell me, "I'll laugh after I win," but I like to think that you can work hard in practice and play hard during a match but still have a sense of humor about the crazy bounces and bizarre opponents in this game. If you can get wrapped up in self-improvement, making a strong effort and having some fun when you're out on the court, winning will take care of itself.

Jack Kramer, Vic Braden, writer Curry Kirkpatrick, and Billie Jean King. Jack Kramer and Billie Jean King did most for men's and women's professional tennis in the history of the game.

Acknowledgments

THANKS to all the students who have taught me how best to teach them. And to all of my fellow teaching professionals, I salute you for your investment in helping people and I thank you for your lasting friendship. To the most gentle, wonderful, and toughest woman in the world and, quietly, my inspiration, Annie Ruth.

To the scientists who have helped with my research over the past forty years: Dr. Gideon Ariel, Dr. Paul Braden, Dean Brittenham, Dr. Howard Brody, Dr. Ray Brown, Dr. Charles Dillman, Dr. Bruce Elliott, Dr. James Fallon, Gayle Godwin, Dr. Jack Groppel, Dr. Richard Haier, Dr. Robert Hintermeister, Dr. Michael Holden, Dr. Hans Hornung, Dr. Patrick Keating, Mary Ley, Dr. Hans Liepmann, Dr. Arnold Mandell, Dr. Rainer Martens, Jon Niednagel, Dr. Ann Penny, Dr. Frank Pollick, Dr. Charles Ribak, Dr. Richard Schmidt, Dr. Andrei Vorobiev.

To the professional players who took time to answer my questions over the years: the late Arthur Ashe, Tracy Austin, Don Budge, Owen Davidson, Roy Emerson, Chris Evert, the late Pancho Gonzales, Billie Jean King, Jack Kramer, Rod Laver, Ken Rosewall, Pete Sampras, Pancho Segura, Ted Schroeder, Stan Smith, Fred Stolle.

To Richard Curtis, our original agent; editor Susan Canavan, who skillfully maneuvered this book through editing and production; copyeditor Betty Power, who improved our manuscript with a professional's touch; designer Barbara Werden, who pulled the photographs and text together with inviting layouts; and Bill Phillips, our wise and loyal editor, who was a rookie at Little, Brown when our collaboration began and is now vice president and editor in chief.

Finally, my thanks to Bill Bruns for decades of fine writing and to John Zimmerman for his photographic wizardry.

TENNIS

2000

Introduction

TENNIS SEEMS innocently simple to those who are outside the fence looking in. There are no sand traps to worry about, or moguls, or blitzing linebackers, or 7–10 splits. The court looks so huge and the net seems so low that people tend to think, "Heck, this game's a piece of cake."

Yet those of you who have played tennis, and who have tried to improve, know how difficult it is to advance beyond the stage where you're just happy to get the ball back over the net without any special "sauce" or a particular strategy. Even professional athletes from other sports admit that tennis can be downright humbling. They can't understand how they can be strong, fast, and coordinated — yet miss the ball. Or that a ten-year-old kid can yo-yo them around the court and show no mercy, except to say afterward, "Gee, mister, you're getting better."

The truth of the matter is that you can laugh your guts out in tennis from the first day you pick up a racket, but once you try to keep the ball inside the boundaries — under pressure — this game can also produce a great amount of stress. The court starts to shrink, the "low" net seems to catch your best forehand drives, and there's no place to hide your ego if you hit the ball into the next county, miss it completely, trip over a crack on the court, or smash an overhead into the net as your opponent prays on the other side. Plus, you're out there with very few clothes on; if you lose, you lose half-naked. Students often tell me they wish they could wear a football helmet or a long robe so they could hide from their mistakes.

Basically, a good tennis player can be defined as one who is able to hit a target area while under stress. But that's the problem. Stress does strange things to people. The longest service toss I've ever witnessed went over the back fence, 12 feet up and 21 feet back. In singles I see people run to the net and get so mixed up that instead of hitting the ball they yell, "Yours!" Others will run nicely to hit a volley — but

Harsul is wearing the Eye Mark Recorder. We use this device because it actually tracks on film where the player is looking. It also tells us where the player first picks up the ball heading toward him.

catch the ball instead of swinging at it. Then there are those players who simply freeze up when their opponent prepares to return a shot. They're so afraid to make the wrong decision that they just stand there poised in their ready position thinking, "Is it going to be to my backhand or to my forehand? . . . Son-of-a-gun, it was to my backhand."

The goal of this book, therefore, is to help you handle this stress and perform well under pressure by helping you develop the right strokes, a confidence in these strokes, and a no-frills approach to strategy. Your basic swing on each stroke is my main concern because that's what tennis boils down to: do you have the weapons? You can have unbelievable anticipation, fancy footwork, and a brilliant mind, but if you have a crummy swing when you get to the ball, you're not going to win. Conversely, you can have slow reactions, lousy footwork, and get caught late, yet still make a good hit if you can effect a perfect swing. So work hard to develop proper strokes and, if we have to, we'll call a cab to get you to the ball in time.

Lefthanders, there's a place for you here, too. You may think that tennis is tougher for you to learn, but remember: your stroke patterns are identical to those used by righthanders, but in reverse. In other words, your forehand is exactly the same as a righthander's backhand, and your backhand is the same as his forehand. Physical laws dictate where the ball goes and these laws remain the same no matter which side you swing from. Still, I have great empathy for lefthanders because I know they are always being discriminated against in instruction.

When I first started coaching, I got an early lesson in how easy it is to forget that not every player is righthanded. There was a young boy in my group who was a natural athlete — but a crummy tennis player. He was hitting righthanded and he really had me baffled, so finally I said, "Gil, I can't understand it. You have all the moves, you look terrific, but you can't hit the ball at all. I must be doing something wrong."

"Yeah, man," he said. "You let me hit lefthanded and I'm terrific." I had directed the entire lesson to righthanders and he was simply doing what I asked him to do.

Not only will good strokes help you relax as you play, so will a sense of humor. I want you to have fun as we go along because I've always felt that learning to play a better game of tennis can co-exist with laughter if you will base your self-critique not upon how many matches you win or lose but upon your own self-improvement. When I see a student at my tennis college who can laugh at his mistakes, I know he's going to go home an improved player. He's having more fun and he's apt to try some of the new things that can help his game. The uptight people only get worse. As you will see later in this book, there is scientific evidence to prove that when you're having fun, you're more apt to recruit the right muscles to hit the ball well . . . and when you worry, you're more apt to send the wrong electrical messages to your muscles. That's why my motto has always been "Laugh and win."

Levels of proficiency take a long time to achieve, but your enjoyment can be immediate. Thus I try to be as entertaining as I can, while realizing that a coach can't humor people into playing good tennis — you and I eventually have to get down to nitty-gritty details about technique in order to make any real headway. Therefore a second objective of this book is to help make you self-reliant out on the court, no matter what your level of play. I want you to understand how to execute a particular stroke, why you want to swing that way, and where you want to try to hit particular shots. Not until tennis technique and strategy make sense to you will you have the confidence and willingness to develop the right strokes or to change your swing to overcome specific weaknesses.

A qualified professional can get you started on the right road, but after that, the answers to this game are in your head, not locked up with a local pro, to be dispensed in 30-minute lessons. That's what's beautiful about this game. You can teach yourself good, sound strokes and you can learn to detect errors in that technique. Independent thinkers, not dependent thinkers, make the biggest gains in tennis, so quit looking outside the gate for help — the solutions to developing sound strokes aren't far-out theories, they're inside you.

In order to help you help yourself improve at a faster rate — with or without the aid of a teaching pro — I present self-evaluative drills and checkpoints throughout the book that will enable you to analyze your own strokes during a match, while rallying with a friend, or while swinging your racket in the living room. I'll give you ideas for a do-it-yourself tennis lab, so that you can practice perfect strokes at home, while strengthening the muscles you need to make these strokes effective. With court space often at a premium, and few people willing to use such time simply to practice, you'll be way ahead of your rivals if you can learn to coach yourself, even while waiting for a court.

If you are already working with a qualified teaching pro, this book should increase the value of your lessons, and enrich your relationship with that pro. If you read this book and then take lessons, you will know exactly what the pro is trying to tell you about your game and what he is trying to achieve. You should even be able to detect unqualified pros.

This book is not for you, however, if you are shopping around for a revolutionary approach, trick shots, gimmicks, or a get-rich-quick theory that will "unlock" the secrets of the game. I don't believe that any pro — myself included — has a unique theory on how to play better tennis. All good strokes are supported by sound physical laws, not a pro's theory, and these laws reduce tennis strokes to a common denominator: people can approach the ball in any kind of unique fashion they want, but to produce identical results on two different shots, they must hit the ball exactly the same way both times.

The pro's job is to make you understand the forces that are at work when the racket contacts the ball, and to help you develop a swing to accommodate them. Unfortunately, most people try to fight reality by clinging to their same old swing and making "adjustments" with their racket face. These adjustments are the reason they keep finishing second in a field of two.

Some of the techniques I emphasize in this book go against the grain of certain tennis instruction and well-established myths. But I simply try to teach all strokes based upon what I have learned from respected physicists and through high-speed photography. Over the years, I have worked with several hundred pros at my tennis colleges around the world and I try to keep in touch with those who are interested in the latest research. Anyone can reach me at my e-mail address: vicbraden@vicbraden.com. People have told me that I have "an interesting system," and they often ask if there's a pro in their area who teaches it. I have to tell them that I simply base my approach on the basic physical laws which dictate the action of the racket, its impact on the ball, and the movement of the body. In addition, we're all governed by the realities of the court and the net.

For example, let's begin with the fact that tennis is a lifting game. The net is a high barrier — much higher than most people envision — and this means that you must try to produce topspin on your forehand and backhand if you want to hit the ball hard and still bring it down deep in your opponent's court. No matter what your ability or your strength — or what you've been told — you can learn to hit topspin. It doesn't take a strong arm or a powerful wrist, but it does require the ability to get low with your body and the racket head so that you can contact the ball with a vertical racket face that is moving from low to high.

I also place a lot of emphasis in my teaching on the all-around virtues of topspin because I want you to play this game right. With topspin — as opposed to underspin or anything hit on a horizontal plane — you can hit the ball harder, with greater safety, short or deep; thus you can beat an opponent who camps at the baseline or one who likes to rush the net. You cannot hit hard swinging on the horizontal unless you have unbelievable accuracy, and without speed on the ball you severely limit your opportunities against good players.

Everything in this book has been tested in special research or experiments at my tennis college since 1972 or through my association with the great players in the game over the last 50 years. Despite that, I know that if what I say doesn't make sense, you won't try it. So sit back periodically and think about what I'm saying. If

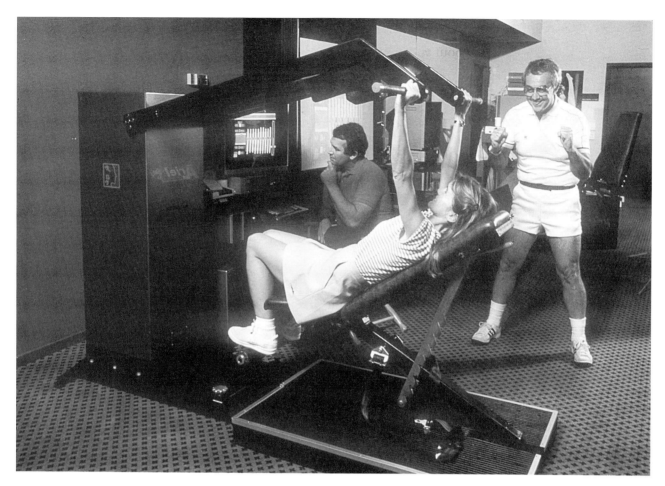

my rationale for a certain stroke sounds far out, then put me to the test out on the court. If you're thinking, "I don't need to work on my forehand — it's terrific," see if you can hit a target area (a three-foot radius around your intended target) while under stress.

Try the following test. Since the goal on forehands, when both players are at the baseline, is to land the ball within five feet of your opponent's baseline, lay a piece of rope from one singles sideline to the other, five feet inside the baseline. Then stand at the baseline and have a friend start hitting balls to your forehand. Play against yourself and see if you can win by giving yourself a point when your shot lands inside the target area, a point against you when it doesn't. Even by yourself, when you bounce the ball and hit a forehand, you'll have a hard time winning one game in a set. A similar drill is to lay rope across both courts (five feet inside the baseline) and rally with your friend. Catch any ball that falls short of the rope and start over. You'll find you're catching more balls than you're hitting.

On the serve, you may have the weirdest-looking motion in the world, but it's your own creation and it works in Pismo Beach, so you're not about to give it up despite what I might say. That's fine by me. I never insist that people change their crazy strokes, only that they put them to the test. If you can serve with a windmill motion and still hit the ball into your opponent's backhand corner 8 out of 10 times,

*Aerial view of
Vic Braden Tennis
College in Coto de
Caza, California, in
1974.*

I won't laugh — I'll just want to know your secret. But if you have a cannonball serve that only goes in once every other April, then think about changing your swing and your concept of the serve. You can take an individual approach in this game, but you can't fight physical laws if you expect to play well.

Just be fair with yourself. Learn to have fun playing tennis because you can't do all the things on the court you think you can do, nor is there much room in which to do them. When you really study your game, and learn which shots you actually "own," that's when you begin to place less emphasis on strategy and fancy shots, and much more attention to working on your strokes.

A final warning about this book: If you've finally grown tired of losing to the same people week after week, year after year, and you want to gain a little respect for your tennis game, you might be thinking, "I'll read Vic's book, schedule a match with Bertha next Tuesday, and blow her off the court with my new strokes." I wish I could promise you that kind of quick success, but as I'll discuss further in Chapter 1, when you start tinkering with your tennis game you often regress before improving. Instead of losing to Bertha 6–3, 6–3 as you usually do, you may lose 6–0, 6–0 for a couple of weeks, and I can hear you telling friends, "I just read Vic Braden's book, tried out the new concepts, and now I couldn't even beat my grandmother." Obviously I don't need that kind of endorsement.

So try to give what I say a chance. I'm confident I can help you make some pretty sizable gains if you will put these theories to the test with an open mind and a willingness to make key changes in your swing. Remember, tennis is a game you can play from age three to ninety (and beyond) — and good strokes will last a lifetime.

Common Myths
and Key Fundamentals

F YOU'RE LIKE MANY TENNIS PLAYERS, the chances are good that you can't control the shots you brag about in the locker room, nor are you likely to master those shots you see the pros try to hit — sharply angled cross-court drives, topspin lobs, underspin drop shots, service returns at your opponent's feet. So let's be honest. Cut out the fancy thinking and just concentrate on mastering the basic fundamentals. Learn to hit the same old boring winner and you'll beat most of the people who now beat you.

If you can learn to hit the ball deep and down the middle — and keep it in play — that's all the strategy you'll need to know to beat 99 percent of the players in the world. Trying to play this way may sound a little dull —"I want to do something big out there"— but believe me, you'll never get bored with winning. I've never heard anyone complain, "Nuts, I won again."

Before I delve into specific stroke production, I feel it's important to provide an overview of the game that will help make my approach to these strokes — and strategy — more meaningful. First, I will explore some of the physiological and psychological reasons why people don't improve. Second, I will try to refute entrenched myths that keep people from playing better tennis. And third, I will present the fundamentals that I regard as crucial to a sound tennis game.

LEARNING BLOCKS

Parents often ask me how competitive they should be when they play tennis against their children. I tell them, "You don't have to rush the net and kill every shot, but at least refrain from making intentional errors to help your youngster feel better. If you keep winning, don't worry. In fact, enjoy it now because in two or three years they'll be murdering you and you'll want to have something nice to remember." Most youngsters who get hooked on tennis are not afraid to make changes that will improve their games. But adults are thinking, "Gee, I've been playing all these years — I shouldn't mess around with my swing." They work desperately not to look bad by sticking with what is comfortable, rather than pushing through that awkward, frustrating period of making corrections that will eventually help them look good and win.

Thus, when you begin to work on a different grip or a new stroke, you will learn to play a much better game of tennis if you can remember one thing: try to feel good about feeling crummy because the crummy feeling that accompanies new and accurate strokes is going to make you famous.

No matter how uniquely you may swing, making changes in that swing is always painful because you must break motor programming patterns; you're going against what has become comfortable for you to do and what is ingrained, even if you've only played the game five or six months. Basically, you're attempting to change the software package, and your brain doesn't like to do that very quickly. It normally likes the old system even though the new one might be much better for you. We have people at the tennis college who give us 185 moves on their forehand, but when we try to make one basic correction that cuts off 110 extraneous moves, they say, "Boy, that is really awkward." Yet the uncomfortable feeling that accompanies the correct swing is what you must adopt if you hope to correct a bad habit. Even a slight grip change requires a whole new set of muscles. A person will come to the tennis college who has played for 25 years, but when we alter his grip an eighth of an inch he gets blisters.

Believe me, I know how grooved a habit can become. When I was giving lessons at the Toledo Tennis Club, one of my adult students had a bad habit of stepping forward with the wrong foot as he swung. I had only been teaching full-time about a year but I figured I knew it all. So I nailed an old tennis shoe to a piece of wood, and pounded through eight-inch spikes to anchor it into the clay court. Then I had the fellow put his back foot in the shoe and take a swing. I wanted him to get the sensation of leaving that foot stationary as he stepped forward with the other. Well, he took one swing and yanked the board right out of the clay court. He also pulled every ligament in his right leg. He was in a cast for a long time, and it just about ruined his tennis game. But both of us learned how strong motor programming really is. Fortunately he didn't sue me.

Interference by your ego is another hindrance to effecting important changes in your swing. When the pro starts tinkering with what you feel is comfortable, the natural tendency is to think there's something wrong in his method rather than in your swing. Furthermore, every good teaching pro has heard the complaint "Jeez, I was better before I took lessons." Very often this is true. No matter what the sport, when you are trying to make corrections, there's always a force trying to bring you back to your old comfort levels. Dr. Joe Sheehan, the late UCLA psychologist and speech therapist whose research work related to stutterers, termed this phenomenon the approach-avoidance conflict: you want to do something the new way but you want to maintain some of the old, and thus you get caught in the middle, vacillating between the two. This can be murder on your tennis game.

For instance, people will spend a week at the tennis college and try hard to solve basic problems in their swing. But when they return home to play their old rival, they may lose 6–0, 6–0, whereas before they lost 6–3, 6–3. It's only natural for them to think, "Boy, I can't wait to get back to my old form and lose 6–3, 6–3." Their ego takes such a beating over the next couple of weeks that unless they have patience and really work hard at grooving these new stroking sensations, they will soon retreat to their same old comfortable swing. The reason they get worse before they get better is that by working on new things, they no longer have a good handle on their old game nor do they have control of their new, and thus they have very spotty performances.

What it really comes down to is this: if the pain you are suffering in losing to people is greater than the pain you suffer making a change, then you'll try like heck to make the change. You'll experiment, you'll have an open mind, you'll concentrate, you won't try to avoid your weaknesses as you polish your strengths — and you'll have a much better future in this game than the average person. Believe me, most people tend to stay the same once they reach a certain level of performance, and you'll be amazed at how quickly you move up to higher playing levels if you can hang in there until the new software package is comfortable.

Another deterrent to acquiring good strokes is the myth in tennis that you should "Do what feels natural," since everything that's right feels comfortable. On the contrary, my experience with thousands of students has been that nearly everything that's natural in tennis turns out to be less desirable. I can't think of any change in your swing, or even your grip, that will feel natural to begin with. In fact, if I ask a relative beginner to try something new, and he or she does it right on the first or second try, I'm absolutely shocked, for I've only seen this happen two or three times in a 52-year career of coaching. (This doesn't mean, however, that you can't take a much more relaxed attitude toward a game that's unnatural.)

The reason tennis is such a difficult game to master is that it's natural to roll your forearm over on the forehand instead of keeping it fixed; it's natural to swing on a horizontal plane rather than from low to high; it's natural to play people instead of the ball; it's natural to watch your opponent's shot and to try to confirm your decision about which direction the ball is going in rather than react instinctively the instant the ball leaves the racket. If tennis were a natural game, we would have far more people swinging correctly, right from the beginning. Instead, people are flocking to teaching pros because the accurate movements in tennis, in my opinion, are not natural; seemingly strange software packages from the brain to the muscles have to be learned as old habits are broken down.

Of course, this doesn't mean that if you're unnatural in the beginning you will be awkward in the end. You can learn to play the game with fluid, easy strokes when at first you were stiff and uncomfortable. Yet when somebody tells me immediately after the first trial, "Hey, I tried your stroke — it's fantastic," I know that person probably hasn't really made a change, because if it feels good, it's usually what that person has been doing all along. That's why good pros won't teach

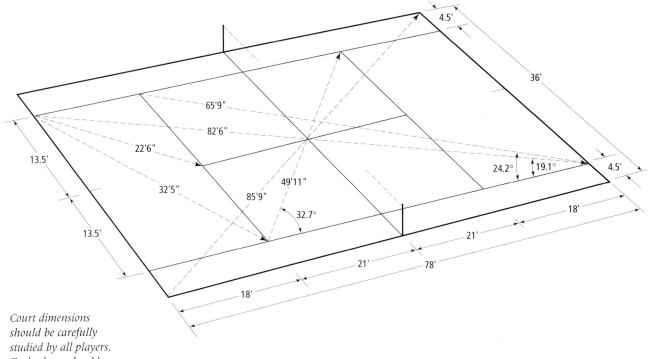

Court dimensions should be carefully studied by all players. Each player should know the precise distance his or her shots normally travel and make appropriate adjustments.

"comfort." They won't keep telling you, "If it feels good, keep doing it," unless what you're doing is correct. When people are changing a software package, there's temporary learning, and it takes several weeks of intensive effort to achieve permanent learning. After that is achieved, the brain seems to forget the old software package.

MYTHS AND MISCONCEPTIONS

Nearly everybody brings to the tennis court a great many incorrect impressions about how the game is played — and how well they play. But don't think lightly of these impressions, for they have everything to do with your attitude about the game, your future progress, and even the internal battle with your subconscious.

Believing the Court Is Gigantic

When you stand on the baseline, it's only natural to envision the court as a gigantic expanse, with plenty of leeway for your wrap-around follow-through. Instead, you should try to visualize playing on a long, narrow sidewalk with a follow-through that takes your racket out toward your target. Stand on the right baseline/sideline corner and see for yourself how little you can vary your follow-through when hitting from the baseline. Point your racket down the singles sideline to a righthander's backhand corner, and then to his forehand corner, and you have moved the direction of your follow-through only 19.1 degrees. From the

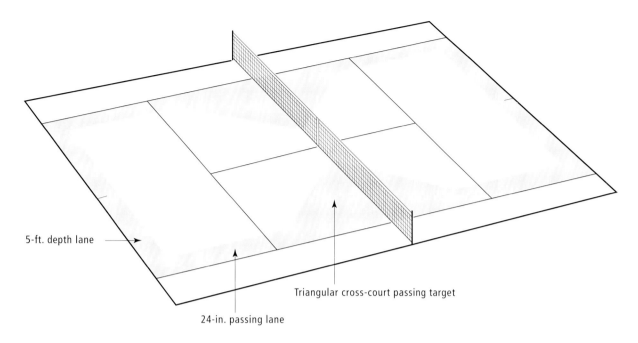

5-ft. depth lane

Triangular cross-court passing target

24-in. passing lane

The world's top players must be able to hit down-the-line passing shots inside a 24-inch lane, cross-court passing shots into the triangular shaded area, and groundstroke rally shots and lobs from their baseline into a 5-foot lane at their opponent's baseline.

Tennis players are often shocked when they discover how narrow a court actually is. When contacting a ball coming "down the line," a hitter's racket face, at a baseline corner, need only change 19.1 degrees at the ball-racket impact point to run an opponent from one baseline corner to the opposite baseline corner.

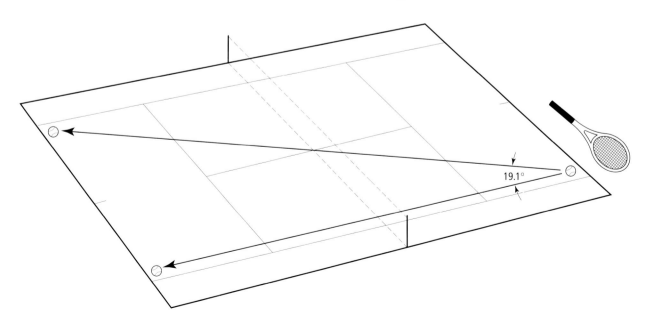

19.1°

center stripe, pointing from corner to corner, you still have just 19.6 degrees to play with.

Unfortunately, even though the follow-through for a shot down the line (passing shot) must virtually resemble the follow-through for a cross-court drive, this isn't the way most people swing. When they get their opponent in one corner they think, "Now I've got him!" and they proceed to take a 180-degree swing that pulls the ball 10 feet wide. I try to tell them, "You seldom get a chance to play your opponent on the next court."

The Concept of the "Low" Net

People love to talk about the low net. Yet you always see them going up to the net and retrieving their last shot with the cry "One more inch, Bertha, and I would have killed you!" What they don't understand is that in terms of hitting a tennis ball on a horizontal plane, the net is actually very high. When you stand at the baseline, you must be at least 6'7" tall in order to look over the net and see your opponent's baseline. This means that 99 percent of us never really see our opponent's court when playing from the baseline; we spend our lives looking through those little squares in the net in order to see the ball land.

Therefore, to play this game correctly you must think about lifting the ball up over a high barrier. Picture a volleyball net rather than a tennis net, and concentrate on elevating your shots — with a degree of topspin — so that the ball lands deep in your opponent's court rather than always catching the tape. (See Chapter 2 for a detailed description of topspin.) I've found that an interesting thing happens, psychologically, when you put up a solid net. People suddenly start bending their knees and elevating the ball because they can't even see their opponent's feet, let alone the court. But when you put up the regular net again, they say, "That's better," and they go back to their old horizontal swing. Pretty soon they start taking that 39-foot trip to the net to pick up the ball.

The Fallacy of Believing in "Net-Skimmers"

Players who continue to visualize a low net simply reinforce one of the most prevalent myths destroying good tennis everywhere: the concept that tennis balls should be hit on a horizontal plane, with hard, line-drive shots the ideal. Interestingly, the pros have an entirely different approach. They know that tennis is not just a driving game, but a lifting game; that to hit the ball hard and still make it come down inside their opponent's court, they must develop an ability to hit topspin while elevating the ball four to six feet over the net when both players are at the baseline. The pros also know that balls hit on a horizontal plane begin to drop sooner than balls hit at the same speed but elevated with topspin.

Thus I'm always amused at the paradox illustrated by the average player who says, "I can't wait to play like a pro and hit those nice low net-skimmers," and the pro who goes into the locker room after a match and moans, "Jeez, I'm playing so crummy. My ball's going so close to the net it's a joke."

The Theory of the Fallible Racket

I've always stressed the point that a tennis ball is really your pal, not your enemy: most tennis balls are round and they go exactly where you hit them. Unfortunately, if you take the ball on as a pal your ego needs an out, and so your racket becomes the target for all your frustrations and excuses. Tell me it's not true that often when you hit a truly lousy shot your first instinct is to blame your racket? You pluck the strings or give it the knee test, while muttering, "That doggone guy really sold me a lemon." Sporting goods dealers have told me that people actually come in and complain, "I'm returning this racket because it has no backhands in it at all."

Let's be realistic. Even at the pro level, it doesn't matter whether you use graphite or titanium, gut or nylon — the racket will go well beyond your ability level. I saw Bobby Riggs beat a good player with a broom, and if there's that much resiliency in straw, then gut or nylon is not your problem. In fact, all the great players I've known have only talked about their inability to effect the right stroke pattern. They've never said, "I failed to win the tournament because I had a crummy racket." Sure a $250 racket may give you a little extra juice and make you feel good, but it's not going to help you win matches if you continue to swing improperly. Almost any racket will do what you ask of it if you place it the right position at the right time. Yet most people place the racket in the wrong position at impact and expect it to produce a winning shot.

"I'm Not Smart Enough to Play Good Tennis"

In talking about the intricacies of technique and tactics for the more advanced player, I sometimes unintentionally scare people off. They start thinking, "I'm not smart enough to do all that. I just want to stay at the baseline and try to get a suntan." Thus I always try to assure my students that it doesn't require any exceptional intellect to grasp the basic concepts that can help them beat 95 percent of the tennis population.

I once gave a battery of personality and psychological tests to 20 successful tournament players, hoping I could isolate some of the psychological variables that help make a champion. I thought, for instance, that tennis demanded a lot of high-level intellectual functioning and that the top players were really smarter than we normals. But when my test results came in, IQs ranged from 88 to 144 — from educable mentally retarded to gifted. So I start with the assumption that nearly all the readers of this book are in the range, and that you have the ability to understand the most complex, but logical, theory ever promulgated about the game of tennis.

In my view, sophisticated theories about technique and strategy normally have little relevance in tennis. The game ultimately comes down to the basic question: do you have the weapons? If you are at the baseline and the ball is hit to your backhand and your opponent rushes the net, you normally have only four options — lob over his head, drive a passing shot down the line, hit the ball crosscourt, or try to give him a new navel. You don't need a Ph.D. in tennis to know that whatever option you choose, the real question is: can you hit a backhand?

Furthermore, physical laws dictate where the ball goes, not your IQ or a coach's "unique" approach. To hit the ball hard and make it land in a particular zone with a certain speed, you must hit with the same speed and ball rotation as everyone else, whether you are Rod Laver or Bertha Finkenbaum. If the racket is placed perfectly and contacts the ball properly, then the ball is going to be on target regardless of your IQ. Better to have quick reactions and an ability to coordinate body movements. For you can be the smartest person in your club, but if you're at the net and the ball is screaming at you 100 miles an hour, you can forget your swing, your name, everything.

"Okay, Then, I'm Too Uncoordinated"

One of the most common fears in tennis is the feeling by some people that they can't play the game, or they'll never be very good, because they don't have the co-ordination or an athletic background. Thus I tell all my students, "If you can walk to the drinking fountain without falling over, you have the physical ability to play this game pretty well." I'm always honest about the difficulty everybody will encounter, but I point out that enjoyment and "success" certainly don't need to be measured by how many matches you win or lose. Taking part in a physical activity and striving to improve your strokes — that's what counts. The list of the relatively uncoordinated people who have become fine players simply because they had the desire and the hunger to learn to play the game properly is endless.

A lot of adults who come to the tennis college claim they have no athletic ability whatsoever and give us the impression that if they buy an ice cream cone they'll stick it against their forehead on the way to their mouth. But when they get out on the court they are terrifically coordinated and they have tons of fun. When we talk to them about this, we usually discover that ever since high school they have been suffering from a delusion that they were athletic failures. "I never made the high school team," they will say, almost apologetically. But they've been comparing themselves with the super jocks — the upper 2 percent of the population — when they should have compared themselves to the average person.

It's tragic to see people who live in mortal fear of looking bad athletically, who think that nobody can have fun playing with them, or that they have to hit the ball well in order to really enjoy the game. I try to tell these people, "So you lose? So you don't play as well as you want to play? So what — you're still running around, you're getting some sun, you're meeting new people, you're having fun. That's what the game is all about."

FUNDAMENTAL CONSIDERATIONS

The following are some basic precepts of the game that never change, no matter what kind of shot you are hitting or what the circumstances, whether it be the first round at Wimbledon or the finals in Pismo Beach. I like to think of it as "non-technical technique."

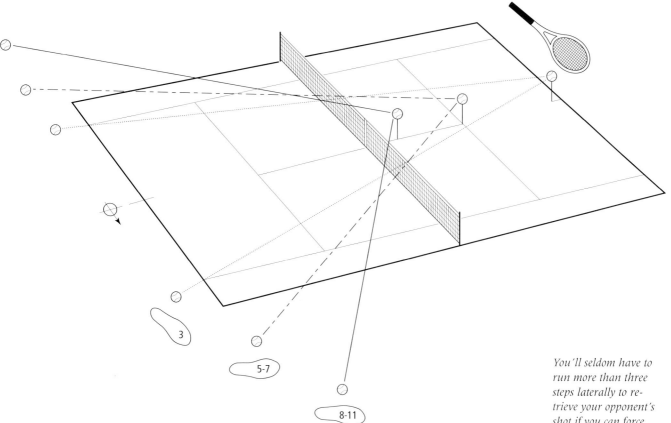

I. Keep the Ball Deep

The main goal in good tennis is simple: *don't hit the first short ball.* Keep all of your shots deep and in play, and you will be famous by Friday. By pinning your opponent behind the baseline you (a) give yourself more time to react to his return shot, (b) prevent him from moving in to do his in-fighting near the net, and (c) reduce the angle at which he can hit. For example, the most he can run you, hitting from the baseline, is normally three steps to your left or three to your right. If your shot lands short, near the service line, he can stretch you five to seven steps with his next shot. And if he is volleying at the net, he can move you eight to eleven steps, right off the court.

That's why you always hear the good players say, "Keep the ball deep," and why Jimmy Connors and Chris Evert — and now Pete Sampras and Martina Hingis — almost always reached the finals and semi-finals. They got such great depth on their shots that it was difficult to penetrate and gain the net against them. In fact, after one of his victories at Forest Hills, Connors's first response to newsmen was, "I was hitting the ball with a lot of depth." And Harold Solomon commented, after losing to Connors, "I hit too many short balls."

You'll seldom have to run more than three steps laterally to retrieve your opponent's shot if you can force him to hit from behind his baseline. If you hit short shots and allow your opponent to hit from midcourt, you have to run laterally as many as five to seven steps. Be ready to run all the way to the fence if you allow your opponent to hit while close to the net.

2. Give Your Opponent One More Chance to Take Gas

A lot of people, especially men, envision tennis as a game in which they can push people around. This isn't to say you can't run your opponent from one side of the court to the other, up and back, with an assortment of calculated shots. But the reality in tennis is that you beat yourself or the other person loses to you. As Jack Kramer liked to say, "Tennis is giving your opponent one more chance to take gas." And Chris Evert told me that her dad always emphasized, "Let your opponent make the mistakes."

In beginning and intermediate tennis, errors outnumber placements 20 or 30 to 1. Even in the pros, forced and unforced errors end the point much more often than outright winners. In fact, in all my years with the pros, I've never talked to a player who could remember having won a single match where he (or she) hit the ball so hard and so well that his placements outnumbered his opponent's errors. Gonzales, Kramer, Laver, Billie Jean King — all they could remember was people losing to them.

So reconcile yourself to the fact that the day is never going to come when you can play an opponent of comparable ability and just yo-yo that person around the court by hitting with wild abandon and unbelievable accuracy. Your goal must be to play the high-percentage shots, get the ball over the net and inside the boundaries, and let your opponent take the crazy chances.

This is what the dinker does so well. He (or she) takes three steps to the right, hits the helium ball and says,"Here's one more. Why don't you take it?" And if you get it back, he says, "Here's another one. Why don't you take that?" He keeps throwing up "moonballs" while you sit back there with all your fancy moves, cracking off net-skimmers. The dinker has never hit a hard ball in his life. He just keeps tightening the noose until finally you get so frustrated that you try to end the point with a fancy shot, which of course goes into the net.

No one likes to play dinkers, because they drive you crazy. You're always saying to them, "Why don't you stand up and play like a man?" But as I'll point out during the book, dinkers win for good reasons. They have mastered several basic physical laws and psychological ploys which make them winners in the Ds, the Cs, the Bs, and two rounds of the As in almost every tennis club around the world. You may make jokes about the dinkers, and they may have few friends, but their living room shelves are lined with trophies.

3. Learn to Buy Time

One of the basic mistakes made by most beginners and intermediates is their failure to buy time on every shot. Instead of beginning their appropriate backswing the instant they determine the direction of their opponent's shot, they delay until the last moment. Suddenly the ball is on top of them or they have to lunge to make the hit, and thus they seldom feel comfortable or in charge of the situation. They can't understand how the pro makes it look so easy.

If this is your problem, you must concentrate on turning your body and your racket back the instant you see the ball leave your opponent's racket, then quickly get into position so that you can step into the ball properly. You want to work hard getting to the ball early so that you can be absolutely calm as you take your swing. It's too late to yell, "Help!" when you're hitting the ball. I've found that when you take your racket back early, your brain has time to focus upon directing the ball to a target. But when your racket goes back late, the tendency is just to be content with any kind of hit possible.

One bad habit that leads to timing problems is to subconsciously wait for the ball to clear the net, or even to land on the court before you get your racket back. You have to break this hypnosis by telling yourself to take the racket back before the ball passes your opponent's service line. That's how quickly you should react. Think about your opponent's baseline as position number one, his service line number two, the net number three, and your service line number four. Then strive to get your racket back by the time the ball has reached position number two.

Another warning: whether you're playing singles or doubles, never let your feet fall asleep. They've got to get you to the ball in time to allow you to look great. Some people develop fantastic strokes but unfortunately they're 15 feet away from the ball when it bounces. Even a player as great as Arthur Ashe admitted that he wrote notes and put them under the umpire's stand to remind himself to keep his feet moving.

I have to warn you, however, that getting to the ball in time and good stroke production are not synonymous. If you know how to swing properly, then extra time is very beneficial. But if you've developed a lousy stroking pattern, arriving early only gives you more time to hit a crummy shot. Some people are uncomfortable — even fearful — when they have too much time; they don't know what to do with it. Thus they often fall into an unconscious rhythm trap: as the ball slows down, they slow down proportionately so that they are out of position no matter how fast the ball comes. If they are slightly late when they play against a person who hits the ball hard, they are slightly late against someone who hits softly.

4. "Keep Your Eyes on the . . ."

Like everybody else since the infant days of tennis, you've been told to "Keep your eyes on the ball." You may even be guilt-ridden because you can't read the writing on the ball or see it hit the strings, and your friends say they can. But don't let them fool you, for the ophthalmologists tell us that nobody can focus their eyes that well. Still, the effort to focus attention on the ball is important in two ways. First, this keeps your eyes off distractions such as your opponent. After all, tennis is a game in which you hit the ball, not your opponent. Second, this helps ensure a hit on the center of the strings by keeping your head still and eyes fixed on the point of contact.

You may be thinking, "If it's so important to keep your eyes on the ball, why do I see pictures of the pros hitting with their eyes focused out ahead of the ball?"

Well, several years ago, after realizing that nobody can actually see a ball in focus at or near impact, I started telling students to keep their eyes on the blur. Then I was told by an ophthalmological researcher that people with accurate vision can't even see that much. The eyes can follow a ball in focus until about five to seven feet before racket impact, and then they lose track, due to a sudden head shift. That's why tournament players subconsciously learn to take their cues for a stroke while the ball is still far from the point at which they intend to hit it.

Trying to get people to keep concentrating on following the ball into the racket for as long as possible is doggone tough. For one thing, a tennis ball is a lot smaller than most people think. The golf ball is tiny but the clubhead is small, too, and you know you have to stand there and really concentrate on making contact. In tennis, however, you feel like you have a big war club in your hand and you can't possibly miss, so your attention begins to wander.

Furthermore, people tend to be opponent-oriented rather than ball-oriented. In fact, I have a theory — as yet unproven — that some players think there are two balls in play simultaneously. Just as they start to swing, they subconsciously think their opponent is also hitting a ball, and thus they try to rush their own stroke to begin to chase their opponent's mysterious shot. I try to cure this syndrome by reminding people, "If you're worried about your opponent's next shot, don't bother, because your shot isn't going over in the first place." *Remember, there's only one ball in play and you have it — your opponent can't hurt you until your shot lands on his side of the net.*

Another way to help you take a good look at the ball is to relate to cues on your follow-through. For example, on the forehand don't look up to see where the ball is going until your upper arm or shoulder touches your chin. On the backhand, wait until the arm is extended upward before you let your eyes go to your opponent. Don't worry; you can "re-track" the ball before it reaches the net and you will have plenty of time to prepare for your next shot.

5. Take Good Care of Each Shot

Most players have a tendency to think there are a tremendous number of shots on every point. People will talk about how they like to set their opponent up with a variety of shots, or they'll be thinking to themselves as they play, "I know I'm crummy now but on the eighth shot I'll be great." Unfortunately, a point rarely lasts that long. The tendency is to remember the rally in 1978 when the ball went over the net 25 times, while forgetting that in club tennis most points end after the serve, or the service return, or one or two shots after that. That's why I tell people, take good care of the shot you're on — it's probably your last. If you approach tennis with this in mind, you'll find yourself developing far better concentration and stroke production.

6. The Basic Law of Tennis: Learn to Hit the Same Old Boring Winner

What tennis actually comes down to — stripped of the trick shots, the weird, sensual body movements, the best in equipment and clothes, the search for the latest theory — is a dedication to those fundamentals supported by physical laws. You may think, "Yeah, but I want to have fun out there, I want a little variety. I want to try lots of different shots, move the ball around, keep my opponent guessing."

Well, losers have tons of variety; their shots fly all over the court — and often beyond — simply because they fail to swing the same way twice in a row. Champions are those who take great pride in just learning to hit the same old boring winner.

The only problem with playing a "straight down the middle and deep" system is that you need a high frustration-tolerance threshold because you're not trying anything fancy to end a point quickly. Most people don't have the patience to try to outsteady their opponent. They say, "Jeez, the ball's gone over the net three times. I've got to come in and do something big." So they try to hit a drop shot or they go for the lines and that's when they die. It's not easy to hit those big-time shots, so just be happy to keep the ball in play. Stick to the fundamentals and try to master them first, then you can get fancy. But you'll probably find an interesting thing happening along the way: the better you play, the more simplistic you become in your approach. You find that you don't need to get fancy. It's usually the players who just can't win who feel they have to showboat. This type of player hangs around every club in the country, scoffing at regular forehands and backhands, while saying, "Man, I just want to serve, volley, attack, and hit the overhead smash." He glories in hitting the cover off the ball and has very little respect for the common shot. But that "common shot" is what made Chris Evert the queen of them all. She didn't try any fancy stuff. She was patient. She took care of simple fundamentals — hour after hour of practice, getting the ball deep. She rarely was the first to hit a short ball, so nobody could really hurt her consistently until Martina Navratilova came along; when they did try to come to the net, she could thread the needle with her passing shots. She didn't have a big serve or the world's strongest volley, but she showed that a forehand and a backhand could take you right to the top.

Just as Chrissie raised the level of the women's game, so did Jimmy Connors on the men's side. Whether you liked his style or not, he made his challengers develop good strokes on both the forehand and backhand because he kept dogging them and dogging them until they missed. And he forced better serving because he had a murderous service return.

7. Go for Form, Not Touch

Obviously, to hit the same old boring winner you must develop an efficient and consistent stroking pattern. My goal is to have you master a swing that will hold up when you have Excedrin headache number 38: you may feel crummy, but if your strokes are grooved you're still going to play well. That's a nice feeling to have going into a match. Possessing the basic weapons and an ability to use them is a great leveler against an opponent who has an advantage in size, strength, and/or age but who is erratic in stroke production.

This is why I want you to learn what at first may seem to be a rather rigid game. I'm a stroke-production fanatic. I teach form, and learning to keep the ball in play, rather than a "touch" system. Thus I want you to try to swing with a fixed wrist and a short, controlled backswing on your groundstrokes, volleys, and approach shots. Loose, free-flowing swings might look nice but they have too many extraneous movements that can break down under pressure. Connors had literally less racket-head movement than any player I've ever seen. There was little or no whip or roll in his swing — he just locked that racket in and left it fixed, then turned with the body. That's why you saw him in the finals or semi-finals of nearly every tournament he played during the height of his career.

In my opinion, when you play with floppy wrists, you're playing with a dynamite fuse. In fact, laying the wrist back on the backswing or rolling it over as you come into the ball destroys more good groundstrokes than any other single factor. This is why I feel that the person who plays with his wrist must be much more coordinated than the average fixed-wrist player. He has to rely on touch, and thus he's only as good as that touch on a particular day: when he loses it, he loses everything. He might beat the top player in the club on Saturday — when his game is finely tuned and he's in the right mood — yet turn around and lose to a dinker on Sunday.

You need a much more dependable game than "touch" if you ever hope to win a tournament by lasting through four, five, or six rounds, whether on the club or international level. So cut down the size of your swing, don't try to add a lot of extra sauce on the ball, don't horse around with your wrist, and be patient. Winning will loosen you up. If you don't win, keep working on basic fundamentals and learn to accept responsibility for your own strokes. Remember, in the end the ball goes exactly where you aim it. Titanium rackets and color-coordinated sweatbands can't bail you out. But a sense of humor will keep you sane.

2

"What the Heck Is Ball Rotation and Who Needs It?" You Do.

W HEN YOU LEARN to control ball rotation, you can make the ball do funny things — to your advantage. You can make it jump high for little people who hate to hit the ball at shoulder level, or you can make it stay low for tall people who don't want to bend their knees. You can slice it to the left or right to force your opponent to stretch wide for the return, or you can curve it into his body and give him a new navel. Just as the baseball pitcher uses ball rotation to throw a curve ball and win games, you can use spin to change the pace of the ball and vary the rhythm of a match. But to do all these things you must have a clear understanding of ball rotation, and why the ball behaves the way it does.

This is where some beginning and intermediate players start to get a little hostile at my tennis college. They start off by thinking, "Why study physics? That's for the pros to worry about. I just want to learn how to hit the ball right." I'm the first to admit that you can go a long way in tennis without having a clue about what actually happens to a ball when it's hit, provided you can master the stroking styles that produce the spin you want on a particular shot. But when you understand the basic principles of ball rotation, and clear away the myths, you're far more likely to dedicate yourself to learning how to hit the ball with spin, particularly topspin. Why limit yourself to a flat, horizontal game when ball rotation can help you defeat opponents?

GENERAL CHARACTERISTICS

Every time the ball is hit, some spin or rotation of the ball is produced. There is no such thing as a perfectly flat groundstroke or serve. A ball that is curving generates

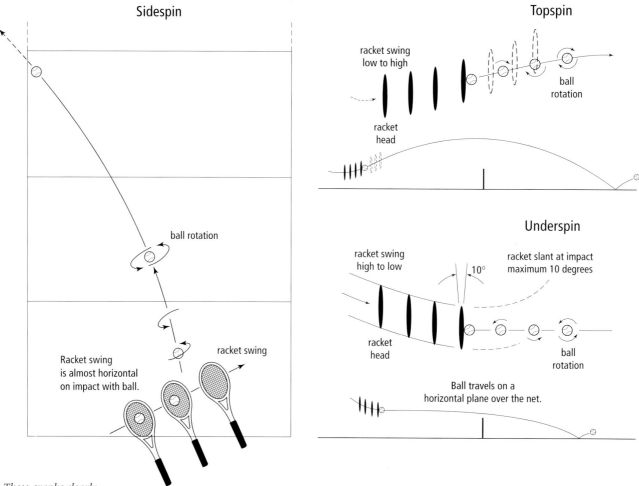

Sidespin

Topspin

racket swing
low to high

ball
rotation

racket
head

Underspin

racket swing
high to low

10°

racket slant at impact
maximum 10 degrees

racket
head

ball
rotation

Ball travels on a
horizontal plane over the net.

ball rotation

Racket swing
is almost horizontal
on impact with ball.

racket swing

*These graphs clearly
illustrate the charac-
teristics of topspin, un-
derspin, and sidespin.
You need to know
how, when, why, and
where to use each type
of ball rotation.*

air pockets, and that air friction makes the ball do certain things. Good tennis players deliberately control this ball rotation and use it to their advantage. There are
four major variations:

1. **Topspin** refers to a ball which is spinning from low to high on a vertical axis.
(Imagine a dot on the front side of the ball that moves forward and down toward
your opponent, or a dot on the back side that is moving low to high.) Topspin generates downward force, so that the ball's path will generally resemble the arc of a
rainbow.

2. **Sidespin**, or slice, refers to a ball revolving on a horizontal plane. Sidespin generates a ball which curves to your left or right and carries away from, or into, an
opponent. It is used mostly on the serve, though Jack Kramer sometimes hit an approach shot with a little sidespin and it curved into his opponent's backhand alley.

3. **Underspin**, or chip, refers to a ball where the imaginary dot on the back side
moves toward you from high to low; the dot rotates away from your opponent
while the ball moves toward him. Underspin generates an upward force until gravity takes over, but that gravitational pull is so great that the ball travels on an almost straight line, rather than in an inverted rainbow arc opposite of topspin.

4. On the typical **spin serve**, the racket brushes the ball about halfway between a full vertical (topspin) and horizontal (slice) spin — i.e., when traveling at a 45-degree angle at impact.

HOW TO HIT TOPSPIN — AND WHY

When I wrote the original edition of this book in the mid-1970s, I stressed the fact that I had always been fascinated by the misconceptions that had given topspin a bad image within the general tennis public, particularly the belief that underspin is the easier stroke to learn and to control. On the contrary, it's been my experience over the years that underspin is far more difficult to teach to the average player because it demands more talent and timing. I feel that topspin is much easier to impart, more reliable under pressure, and much more valuable to players of every ability level. (The major complaint about topspin is that it requires a little more energy to hit, while underspin shots utilize gravity in a high-to-low stroking motion.)

Beginners, for instance, should try to hit the majority of their groundstrokes with moderate topspin because it is safer, and it will lead to a stronger all-around game. (I'm not suggesting severe topspin, but a nice 30-degree upward swing with a vertical racket face.) With topspin from the baseline, you can hit the ball hard while hitting it safely over the net by four to six feet, and the rainbow arc will bring the ball down deep in your opponent's court — thus keeping him away from the net. It's almost impossible to hit a horizontal (flat) shot hard and deep into an opponent's backcourt; you must play the ball so close to the tape of the net that you take all the gamble. With underspin, you can hit the ball deep with ease, but you can't hit the ball with great speed as it will float out. Also, an underspin shot can be hit quite high over the net . . . but softly.

More advanced players should heed the words of Jack Kramer, who told me, "The more I see of the great champions, the more I feel they have two common denominators: (1) great speed afoot, which gets them into proper positions, and (2) the ability to hit topspin off the forehand and the backhand sides." Indeed, over the past 25 years, the champions have won mainly with topspin. We've had the topspin forehands of Billie Jean King, Martina Navratilova, Steffi Graf, Arantxa Sanchez Vicario, and Martina Hingis on the women's side — and even Monica Seles can hit with topspin when she chooses. Graf hits an underspin backhand, but her topspin

Here is what happens to a tennis ball when it is hit properly with slight topspin.

Slight Topspin

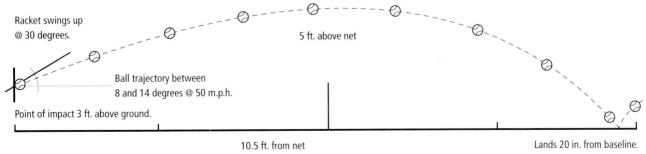

Racket swings up @ 30 degrees.

5 ft. above net

Ball trajectory between 8 and 14 degrees @ 50 m.p.h.

Point of impact 3 ft. above ground.

10.5 ft. from net

Lands 20 in. from baseline.

forehand is her weapon. Among the men, the standouts have been John McEnroe, Bjorn Borg, Ivan Lendl, Andre Agassi, Boris Becker, and Pete Sampras. Even Thomas Muster, the clay court king of the world at one point, hits with severe top-spin on both sides. Chris Evert and Jimmy Connors hit relatively flat on the fore-hand but could hit topspin when necessary, and both had topspin backhands.

Only with topspin can you play an offensive game. Not only can you drive the ball deep with topspin, or bring it up short, you can pass an opponent who has come to the net, whether down the line or cross-court. Thus you have beautiful flexibility: you can always hit the shot that is called for, depending on where your opponent is positioned.

The Stroke

To impart topspin on the forehand or the backhand, you must contact the back side of the ball with a racket head that is vertical at impact and traveling from low to high in the direction of your target. When the racket face brushes against the ball, the ball is lifted up until air pockets begin to generate the downward force that produces a rainbow arc.

On the forehand, for example, take the racket back and then lower your arm and fixed wrist to place the racket at least 12 inches below the intended point of impact. Then come up at about a 30-degree angle (using the court as the measuring line) and strike the ball going from low to high, with the racket head vertical to the ground at impact. Follow through with your arm high and pointing in the general direction of your target.

Topspin is responsible for that familiar, if seldom understood line "Bend your knees." The reason the knees are so important is that if a ball arrives at waist level or below, and you try to maintain a fixed-wrist position (which is crucial), you can't get the racket 12 inches below the ball without bending your knees — unless you simply loosen the wrist and drop the racket head. But when you stand erect and let the racket head fall in this manner, the tendency is to scoop your back-hand — and sometimes your forehand — harmlessly over the net. So to ensure a vertical racket head at impact, bend your knees sufficiently to allow your racket head, hitting hand, and fixed wrist to lower together. By getting low in this man-ner you can generate power from the lifting action of your thighs and hips as you move into the ball. If you hit stiff-kneed ("Sorry, Coach, this is as far as my knees will bend"), then your arm is your only source of power.

Another common myth about topspin, which has been perpetuated by some of the greatest players in the game, is that you should use the wrist to roll the racket over the ball at impact in order to impart topspin. You'll hear a player com-plain, "I couldn't get over the ball with my racket face as much as I would have liked," or a tennis commentator will say, "Notice how so-and-so rolls over the top of the ball." Even Rod Laver talked about hitting his forehand with "quite a lot of wrist" and "coming over the ball with a snap of the wrist."

Pros may have this rolling-over sensation but the question remains: if you really get the racket over the ball, how the heck is the ball going to go over the net? By rising up through the strings? My research has shown — filming at 12,000

frames a second — that even if the ball is standing still, suspended on a thread, or somebody is hitting the ball to you, it is physically impossible to roll over the ball and maintain racket-ball contact. The ball just goes straight down or into the net. Instead, you must brush the back side of the ball with a racket face that is vertical or nearly vertical at impact and moving from low to high. Remember, we are all controlled by the same physical laws.

Okay, now you want to take a shot at me. You've seen some of those wristy pro players and they're imparting heavy topspin. How do they do it?

It is true that some pros use a lot of wrist in hitting topspin, but it's actually forearm action because the wrist has no separate set of muscles within the wrist. These pros will drop the racket head below the intended point of impact with the ball, then bring it up with a big flick of the forearm. However, if the shot is successful, the forearm does not roll over — it is generally fixed at impact and the racket head is vertical, exactly like the player who hits with a solid forearm and lifts his arm up to brush the ball. The key thing to understand is that relying on "wrist" action to hit topspin does not mean rolling the palm over and facing it down to the court. Instead, the racket face and the palm of the hitting hand must remain on the same vertical plane, facing the opponent, with the palm moving up and finishing across the left shoulder, for some players.

For example, people always commented about how the great Pancho Gonzales got his racket "up and over" the ball on the forehand. This was the reason, they felt, that he could hit the sharp forehand angle shot. But when I studied his stroke on high-speed, stop-action movie film, I discovered that his racket head never rolled over the ball. He appeared to roll the racket over after the initial im-

All that talk about how the racket face "rolls over" the top of the ball to impart topspin is a myth. In this photo (the first of this nature ever recorded), the hitter tries desperately to roll the racket face over the top of the ball — but to no avail. The racket face is vertical at impact as it moves from low to high. High-speed motion pictures also substantiate that the ball leaves the racket face long before the racket face begins its rollover.

pact, but he actually imparted topspin with a vertical racket head that did not roll over until near the end of his follow-through . . . long after the ball had left his strings.

I'm also challenged occasionally by people who have been told that topspin requires a lot of strength, and that its constant use can wear you out. The first myth is perpetuated by playing pros who have convinced themselves that the wrist and forearm are critical in producing topspin. One pro has even written, "You should work on strengthening your wrist if you intend to use much topspin." Putting aside the fact that you shouldn't be relying on wrist action in the first place, I would agree that a strong wrist/forearm is necessary only when you're late on the hit and you need a sudden burst of racket speed to impart hard-hit topspin. But I'm not teaching anybody to be late. Skinny eight-year-olds can bomb the ball with topspin when they learn to move into position quickly and then coordinate their body and racket arm as they stroke the ball.

Meanwhile, early in his career in the mid-1970s Bjorn Borg was commonly cited as a player who got worn out by his reliance on heavy topspin from the baseline. What critics overlooked is that hitting topspin didn't wear him out, it was the fact that he whacked the ball so hard on every shot, even when he knew he couldn't put the ball away. I felt then that if he could learn to "soften up" and conserve his energy, he would be just as effective at one-third the speed from behind the baseline, and I always told my students, "I'd like to do what Borg does and hit all that topspin and be crummy and tired out — and worth $300,000 a year." Imagine the millions he would be worth today after winning five consecutive Wimbledons! Borg now mixes speed better on the Senior Tour.

The Uses of Topspin

Remember that tennis is a lifting game, and to hit groundstrokes hard — with the greatest depth and safety — it will be in your best interest to build your game around topspin. If you try to slug the ball with an erect body and a horizontal, across-the-body swing, you have almost no margin for error between the tape of the net and the baseline. It's scary how accurate you have to be. When you try to drive the ball deep, it never seems to come down in time — if only the court could be three feet long, you'd be sensational. But then when you try to hit "net-skimmers," the net seems to stop every other shot; you "own" the tape of the net and you can't understand why you can be so unlucky. The reason, of course, is that a ball hit on a horizontal plane begins to drop sooner, just like a bullet that is shot off in a physics lab vacuum. In a vacuum you must aim the gun at a 45-degree angle to make the bullet travel the greatest distance. Aim the gun parallel to the ground and the fired bullet begins to drop much sooner. A tennis ball is no different, except that outdoors the air is denser and the ball must be aimed at about 50 to 55 degrees.

When I point out these facts to people, some get all pumped up. They think I've unlocked the secrets of this game. All they have to do is drop their arm and racket together below the ball, maintain a fixed wrist/forearm, swing low-to-high, and aim four to six feet over the net. "Piece of cake," they think. Unfortunately, when they go out to play, they can't get their knees to bend or their racket and racket arm down below the level of the ball. Instead of swinging on a low-to-high plane they simply bevel their racket under (meaning the bottom edge of the racket is turned up) and the ball goes over the back fence.

Remember, the body — as well as the racket — must move from low to high, and the racket face must be vertical at impact.

Some dinkers get around this problem by going plunk . . . plunk . . . plunk. They hit "moonballs" high and deep with very little energy output. By letting gravity do their work, they never get tired while you wear yourself out trying to slug the ball harder and harder from a deep position. I'm not suggesting that you should play like a dinker, especially if you enjoy having a lot of friends, but they do apply some sound physical — and psychological — principles in their approach to the game, which I will detail in Chapter 8.

Besides giving you a greater margin for error, a second reason you want to hit groundstrokes deep and with topspin is that topspin produces a high bounce and gives your opponent a difficult shot to handle behind the baseline. Deep, high-bouncing balls up at chest level drive everybody crazy, pros included, because it's difficult to get your body into the shot; the only alternative is to try to take the shot on the rise, shortly after it bounces, and this takes real skill. In recent years, several pro players have developed a new weapon by learning to attack high balls inside the baseline — one of the few major changes in the game in the 1990s. On the other hand, those low, hard net-skimmers that look so nice will bounce short and come up waist high, making it easy for people to just throw their rear end into the shot and crack off a winner. Furthermore, topspin shots which land near your opponent's baseline may drive him to the back fence and leave him vulnerable to short returns up near the net.

Third, if your opponent likes to come to the net when you hit a short ball, your ability to hit topspin passing shots close to the net will help nullify his tactical advantage, and will make him hesitant about even coming to the net. These shots, hit down the line or cross-court, will give your opponent trouble even if he reaches them in time to make a return volley. The reason for this is that balls hit with topspin dip down after clearing the net, making the volley more difficult to execute: your opponent must now hit up over the net instead of down. Hard, flat, horizontal drives can also pose problems for a person at the net, but the pressure is on you to thread the needle: if you elevate the ball too much, your opponent can simply let it go past, and out of bounds. But he has to make a play on topspin because he knows that even a high ball may come down near the baseline. A ball that is sinking fast as it approaches the volleyer causes him to make sudden new calculations on the racket-head position, and these changes can be catastrophic. That's why it's easier to volley a hard line drive because there are relatively fewer calculations to make.

SIDESPIN

The sidespin, or sliced shot, is achieved by brushing across the back side of the ball, with the racket continuing on to the right. (One exception was the sidespin of Jack

Kramer, whose racket moved right to left on his forehand approach shot.) It is used primarily on the serve to pull an opponent "out of court" or for outright aces, and on "peel the orange" volleys where you want to sharpen the angle on your volley and help slow the ball down. Although I tell students to visualize peeling an orange when they make this type of volley, this is only to give them the right imagery. The face of the racket never goes around the ball, but moves left to right for a righthander. The angled racket travels on a horizontal plane and makes a direct hit on the back (right) side of the ball, which then makes a very sharp angle and dips.

UNDERSPIN

Despite my emphasis on topspin, never accuse me of not teaching underspin. When properly mastered, it can be used effectively on the following shots:

1. Underspin is a basic ingredient of the good approach shot, which you use to take the net when your opponent hits a short ball. Since underspin is hit with a lower trajectory than topspin, the ball stays low instead of bouncing high, thus forcing your opponent to hit up from a low position. If you are coming to the net, this guarantees a rising ball for your volley.

2. A ball hit softly with underspin (or backspin) tends to "die" when it hits the court, thus making it invaluable for drop shots, stop volleys, and softly hit short-angle shots that are designed to fake out your opponent when he is deep, not when he is at the net.

3. On volleys, you can use underspin to reduce the speed of the ball. Pros who have the touch will also use it on service returns to take the speed off their opponent's serve. But many people raise the ball up when they try this.

4. On the backhand it gives you a nice defensive shot from the baseline, providing you can learn to control it under pressure. You'll often see the pros hitting underspin backhands from baseline to baseline, since without swinging hard they can hit the ball deep while slowing it up. This gives them plenty of time to get in position for their next shot, and by slowing the ball up they can sometimes upset their opponent's rhythm. The ball will also bounce low because of its flat trajectory.

UNDERSPIN VS. TOPSPIN

No matter what some coaches and pros may preach, hitting the backhand with underspin is a tough play. Only talented players can hit the shot well with any consistency, and then only through experience, practice, and concentration. The reason for this, physicists tell me, is that the minute you begin to favor underspin, by bringing your racket from high to low, you not only must make corrections with your wrist/forearm, you must manipulate five variables: (1) the speed of your opponent's shot, (2) the ball rotation that your opponent has hit, (3) the angle at which you must come down on your swing, (4) the angle at which you must bevel your racket, and (5) the speed at which you must swing down with that beveled racket.

Little wonder that people have a tendency to lose control on underspin. If they hit the ball up, or hit it hard on a horizontal plane with underspin, the ball

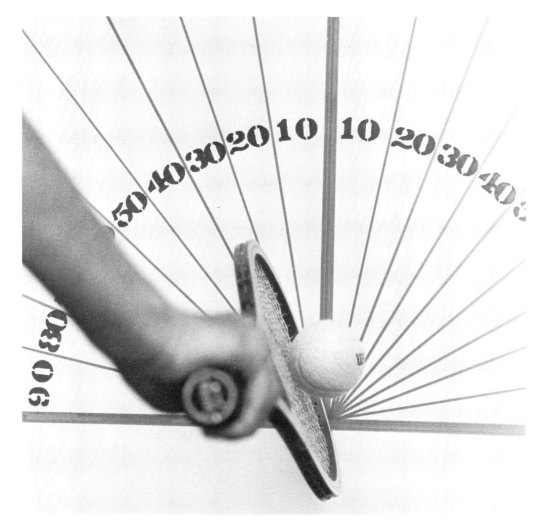

Just as there's a myth that you must come over the ball to hit topspin, some people believe that the racket must come under the ball to impart underspin. This, too, is incorrect. Notice in this photograph that even with the racket beveled 30 degrees, the ball is clearly not contacted on the bottom. When hitting a severe "chip" backhand, one should think of the racket face meeting the lower back side of the ball, just below the equatorial line, to produce underspin.

has a tendency to sail and keep on going until gravity takes hold. (Research shows that this is especially true when hitting in the wind.) Thus, when you hit with underspin you must calculate — under pressure — how hard you should hit the ball and how much you should bevel your racket so that the ball will come down in time to land in your opponent's court. Most people can't make these decisions with any consistency because they seldom practice. So when they try to hit the ball hard with underspin — trying to win a point — they usually have to walk out the gate, pick up the ball, and come back for the next point.

On the other hand, if you just concentrate on hitting your backhand (and of course the forehand) with topspin — by swinging from low to high with a fixed wrist — you can hit the ball almost as hard as you want and still be safe. No matter what your opponent hits, or what pressure you're under, you can take his shot and return it with topspin. Instead of five variables, you only have to deal with three — the rackethead speed, the vertical angle at which you are going to elevate the ball, and the forward and upward angle of the swing. You fix the racket and leave it alone, then go back, down low, and come up through the ball. Sure it's tough to get that racket head and the racket arm down low, as well as the knees, but as I'll discuss (in Chapter 3) this is more of a mental barrier than a physical problem: people can bend their knees to sit in a chair at home, but they just can't seem to do it on the tennis court.

Another problem with relying on an underspin backhand arises when your opponent rushes the net. You can't drive a backhand past him with underspin, nor can you hit cross-court just over the net with power. Underspin shots hit hard enough to pass a person at the net tend to travel 70 feet or more. The court is 78 feet long, but if you want to pass your opponent with a cross-court shot while he's waiting to volley, you must be able to break the ball off inside of 65 or 66 feet. You just can't do that with hard-hit underspin. You can try, of course, but the ball will either go out or so close to your opponent that he will have an easy volley. (Some old-timers cite Kenny Rosewall's "underspin" backhand, but our studies show that he actually hit the ball flat.)

My approach to tennis tries to minimize every possible chance for error. I want you to build a game based on taking the percentage shot, and knowing how to execute that shot under pressure. That's why, in my opinion, when you rely on topspin rather than underspin, you have a much more dependable ally. The crucial question with topspin is: "Can you get it over the net?" If you can, then it works in your behalf. Very few people have ever hit the ball with topspin and watched it go over the fence. Intermediates seldom have this confidence with underspin when they try to hit the ball hard. Oftentimes it goes over the net and just keeps heading north.

Topspin is the only stroke in tennis that allows you to slug away and get rid of frustrations without worrying about losing the ball. I've noticed over the years that many people tend to choke because they can't hit the ball hard. They're naturally strong, or frustrated, and they want to hit all-out on the ball, but if they've learned an underspin game, they aren't allowed to do this; they have to baby the ball. You rarely have to finesse topspin.

Though everyone should learn to hit underspin for the right moment, I'm convinced that every young player coming up in tennis — boys and girls alike — had better learn to hit topspin off both the forehand and the backhand if they expect to remain competitive in the coming years. The great young players in the mid-1970s — McEnroe, Borg, and Guillermo Vilas — were topspin artists on both sides, and the youngest U.S. Open champion in history, Tracy Austin, had used topspin since she was five years old. It could easily be said that the players of the '80s and '90s rose to the top with topspin, notably Martina Navratilova, who started playing her best tennis when she began hitting her forehand with more topspin. Years earlier, after being ranked in the world's top ten for practically a decade, Françoise Durr admitted the deficiency of her game to *Sports Illustrated* (in 1971): "If I had my life to do over," she said, "I would be a topspin tennis player — instead of playing the flat game I do now."

If you have the feel for underspin, and you can mix it in with topspin, terrific — you'll be using both in the finals. But when you lose that feeling on underspin, you usually lose your confidence because the variables are so difficult to control.

This was once pointed out to me by Rod Laver, who attributed a great deal of his success at Wimbledon to his ability to topspin off both sides. He talked about the intense pressure at Wimbledon, and the pageantry that preceded every match: being driven to the stadium in a black limousine; hundreds of people pounding on the windows wanting your autograph; going to the locker room and then to the waiting room — just you, your opponent, and one official — and finally out on the court, where you bowed to royalty and then began to warm up. The grass could be bad and the ball could take bad hops, but you realized that in spite of everything, this was the most important tournament in the world; if you could win here just once, you were home free.

Knowing what that pressure could do to players — he once saw Bob Mark serve a ball up into the grandstands as he warmed up — Laver's strategy in warmups would be to start hitting into his opponent's backhand, since many of them would underspin that shot, instead of using topspin. Rod knew that underspin was only defensive, and required touch, which was hard to come by at Wimbledon because you were so nervous. Plus, it's tough learning to control underspin on grass right away when the ball is taking bad hops. As a result, Laver's opponent might be questioning his confidence before the match even began. But Laver would immediately start off hitting topspin on both sides as his way to combat the pressure. He would flail away, and at first the ball wouldn't go exactly where he wanted it — but boy, the doggone thing would go in. Pretty soon he would have the nervousness worked out of his system, and then he would go to work on his underspin shots. But by this time his opponent would be praying, "Dear God, please let this be my day," because he had already lost his touch.

Not that Laver really needed a psychological edge when he was in his prime — he won Grand Slam titles — but that's how important he felt topspin was to his game.

The Forehand

O NE OF THE CURIOSITIES of tennis is our love affair with the forehand. Most people regard it as their biggest weapon, the one they can rely on under pressure. On the forehand there seldom is the sense of panic that occurs when the ball is coming to the backhand side. Yet when I wrote *Tennis for the Future* in the mid-1970s, I pointed out that in all my years in tennis, I hadn't found one pro player who could quickly name ten great forehands in the history of the game. "But there have been dozens of great backhand hitters," I said back then. And by "great" I meant someone who, while under stress, could place the ball near the intended target.

Since then, I'll admit, improved forehands represent one of the biggest changes in the game, and I can now name quite a few outstanding forehand hitters, including Pete Sampras, Michael Chang, Steffi Graf, Chris Evert, Thomas Muster, and Boris Becker. But for most players the disparity between the two strokes still exists. Psychology is one factor, but basically it's physical: the forehand is simply a more difficult shot to hit accurately than the backhand. On the forehand, when you swing at a ball which is even with or slightly in front of your body, the hitting arm starts to pinch against the body. Anticipating this pinch, most players relax the hitting elbow and wrist a little too early — before impact — and then wrap the racket around their body on the follow-through, instead of going out toward their target. In fact, many times the racket arm ends up around the neck, leading me to wonder why I never read the headline "Man Hangs Self on Forehand Follow-Through." But of course, today, many pro players wrap the racket around their neck after making a nice stroke and the purpose is to relax the muscles.

Follow-through aside, your goal should be to effect a low-to-high stroke pattern that produces topspin and allows you to follow through out toward your

This is the loop forehand used by most male and female professional players. In this photograph, the initial backswing has already been effected, so that you can observe the continuous motion of the loop swing once the racket begins its drop. Notice the spaces between the racket images: the wider the space, the greater the racket's speed. Thus, the greatest racket speed is recorded two to three feet before the racket meets the ball. Also observe how small an arc the hitting hand actually makes. There's very little hand swing to a good stroke.

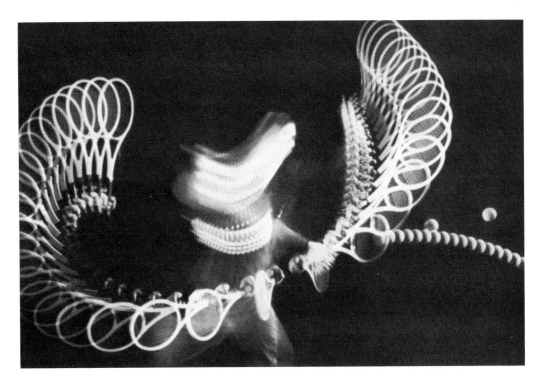

target — instead of the adjacent court. If you're thinking, "I don't need to work on my forehand — it's terrific," just be honest with yourself. What are you comparing it to? Many people claim to have a strong forehand, but when we get out on the court I discover that they've simply been comparing it to their backhand. Their backhand is crummy, but their forehand is a shade better than crummy, so they have a real "weapon." Don't let this kind of reasoning keep you from developing a good stroke on both sides.

I also want to reemphasize how difficult it will be to change your current stroking pattern or make important little improvements. Your brain simply does not want to change these comfortable patterns and, as a result, it seems as though you're in a war against yourself. If a new stroke will make most players much better, why do they continue to keep the old one? The answer is, the brain likes the old one and keeps reverting to it under stress. So you must be patient while developing a new stroking pattern. Achieving a permanent change takes considerable time (several months or longer) and practice. Until one can hit consistently with the desired new pattern, under stress, the changes are only temporary. Most players are not content with temporary learning and easily revert back to old habits. Thus, I advise players not to expect too much, too soon. If you refuse to experiment and you continue to lose with your same old forehand, perhaps you're a little masochistic. In that case, look around for a sadist to play each week and you'll always have a grand time.

THE GRIP

Those of you who scoff at the importance of the grip need to realize one thing: no matter how many adjustments you might make in your swing, a proper grip will last for the rest of your life. That's fairly crucial, so don't think you can go out and hold the racket any way that feels comfortable. Furthermore, your grip dictates the position and comfort of your wrist, knees, and body.

Thus, it is important here to discuss the concept of efficiency. My definition of an efficient stroke is: hitting the ball where you want to hit it, with the speed and spin you desire, with the least amount of muscle recruitment. Except for underspin shots, the racket face should be vertical to the ground when it meets the ball. Thus, you want a grip that will necessitate the least amount of wrist motion in order to produce a racket face that is straight up and down at impact. Whatever grip you adopt will place some amount of awkwardness or stress upon the forearm and wrist, but the Eastern grip, in my opinion, demands the least adjustment and produces the most consistency.

Special names have been given to the forehand grips based upon the position of the palm against the racket handle.

When the palm sits primarily upon the top right side, the grip is called the Continental. It requires a strong forearm and perfect timing and is used by many professionals for both forehand and backhand strokes. I still have trouble naming great forehand players who used a Continental grip. I've often been told that the late Ellsworth Vines was a great Continental forehand hitter. Yet, when I interviewed him in the early 1980s, he told me that there were days when he didn't have a clue where the ball was going. That's an amazing statement for Ellsworth to make, as Jack Kramer told me that Ellsworth was a more natural athlete than Pete Sampras.

When the palm sits mainly on the back side of the handle, it's called the Eastern grip. The palm and the racket face are on the same plane, which gives the sensation of hitting the ball with the palm of your hand. This is the most common grip and, in my opinion, requires the least amount of muscle activity and critical timing.

When the palm rests primarily on the bottom of the handle, so that the palm points at the sky, it's called a Western grip. This is the least common grip, although some players use it to great advantage (especially those who compromise by holding a semi-Western). An important fact about Western players is that the grip makes it nearly impossible to volley well and therefore Western grippers normally change grips when they go to the net. However, most of them seldom go to the net.

The Eastern

If you are righthanded, start by holding the throat of your racket with your left hand so that the racket face is vertical to the ground. Then hold the racket at waist level with the right palm vertical and your fingers pointing slightly downward at approximately a 45-degree angle. The thumb should overlap and lie next to the middle finger, with the index finger spread. Now hold the racket out away from you and look at the top edge of your racket and the top edge of your right palm to see if they are both absolutely vertical. Test yourself by placing the racket on edge on a table to see what it means to have the face straight up and down. Remember, if you play this game right you'll rarely hit a shot that requires the racket to vary more than 10 degrees from this vertical position.

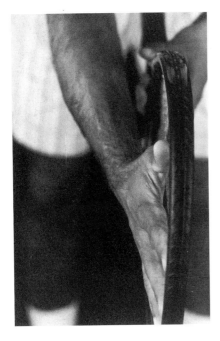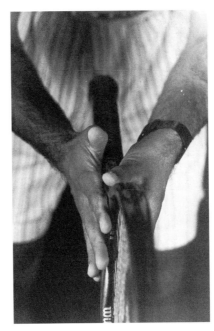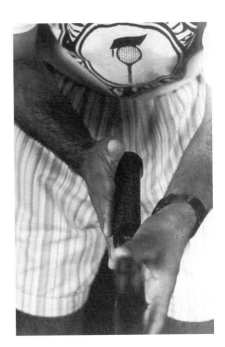

Harsul demonstrates a typical approach to finding the Eastern forehand grip. He starts by placing his palm flat against the racket face and begins to slide his hand down the racket to the grip. However, you will see that the approach actually promotes a different grip.

Harsul is halfway down the racket handle.

He has now reached the grip and his palm appears to be perfectly vertical, as is the racket face.

Many people discuss "shaking hands" with the racket in order to achieve the proper grip, while others suggest putting the right palm against the strings, then sliding the hand down the racket to the grip. But I find that many people shake hands differently, while others achieve a unique position with their palm as they slide it down from the face of the racket.

In the early 1980s, I made a major discovery in one of my research projects on the grip. That is, when some people place their palm on the racket in a "shake hands" mode — in which the thumb is wrapped around the grip — this often pulls the palm closer to a Continental grip and away from the Eastern grip. So the secret is to place the palm slightly to the sky and then grip the racket. This will place the palm in the correct position.

Everybody wants to know, "How can you tell if your grip is right when you are playing a match?" A good pro can detect a quarter-inch flaw in your grip from 50 feet away, but it gets a little expensive having him watch your match from the bench. Short of that, all you can really do is learn through repetition and by "feel" when your grip is right. You can check your grip between points to see if the palm and the racket head are indeed vertical, but "feel" is all you can rely on as you play, especially if you switch grips between the forehand and the backhand, which I advocate. So begin to think kinesthetically. Close your eyes and try to achieve the perfect grip, then open your eyes and see if you are right. Even when you buy a new racket, test the grip with your eyes closed. (Don't feel you're alone with this problem. I'm always amazed by the number of good players who begin to lose their "grip" on occasion.)

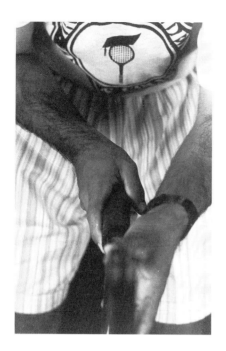
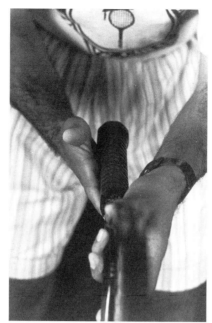
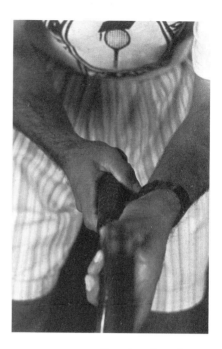

The Continental

The Continental brings the palm of the hand an eighth turn higher on the racket handle. But this requires you to change the wrist position as you hit in order to effect a vertical racket head at impact, and I don't like anything that forces you to play around with the wrist. (If you're holding a racket, try the Continental; get that sensation I'm talking about.) In my opinion, by forcing greater wrist play the Continental is destructive to consistent play for 95 percent of the people who use the grip. Jack Kramer is even more adamant. He feels the Continental grip has done more to destroy good groundstrokes than any other single factor.

Yet the battle goes on. In the mid-1970s, one of the arguments for the Continental, for example, was its use by many of the top players — especially the Australians. But that is the point: you have to be extremely talented to use the Continental and play a winning game (and even then, nearly every Australian player I watched carefully in the '50s and '60s had weaker forehands than backhands, except John Newcombe). Or, put another way, you must be more coordinated. Even then you leave yourself vulnerable. If you hold the Continental you tend to pull across the body in a big way. Thus, every time you reach out in front to hit the ball — especially on the forehand volley — you tend to hit cross-court because that's where the face of the racket is automatically pointed. You have to make a difficult adjustment in order to hit down the line. That's why when pros like Pancho Segura and Jack Kramer played Pancho Gonzales, they would run like heck for the cross-court return when he had a forehand volley. They knew that when he volleyed out in front, his racket face pointed to his left naturally. Kramer states that he was able to build 14 courts and 5,000 square feet of clubhouse on the Palos Verdes Peninsula (the Kramer Tennis Club) because Gorgo — as Gonzales was

But when Harsul finally grips the racket, his palm is placed slightly toward the top of the grip, which promotes a semi-Continental grip.

Harsul demonstrates a more precise manner of locating the Eastern grip by starting with the palm slightly open.

Now when he grips the racket, his palm is squarely on the back side of the grip.

Mary demonstrates a Continental grip (which shows her palm slightly on top of the grip…then an Eastern forehand… followed by a semi-Western (with the palm almost under the grip)…and finally a full Western (with the palm completely under the grip). This grip is used by many successful players from Spain who stay primarily on the baseline to defeat their opponents.

known — had a bad grip on the forehand side when they played their head-to-head tour in 1949, which Kramer won, 97–26.

The Western

This grip, which places the palm partly under the racket handle, was used by more male French Open champions in the 1990s than any other grip: specifically, Thomas Muster, Sergi Bruguera, Jim Courier, Andres Gomez, and Gustavo Kuerten. Players using the Western grip are normally more successful on clay courts as there is relatively little volleying on the slick surface. And on clay courts, the balls tend to bounce high, which is an easy shot for Western grippers. Hold the grip yourself, and notice how easy it is to produce a vertical racket head at impact when the ball is chest high. But when the ball bounces low — especially on grass — the Western places such a severe strain on the wrist and forearm that it's difficult for players to hit with any authority. Western grippers are seldom seen in the final rounds of Wimbledon because the ball skids on grass and stays low longer, making it more difficult to handle with this grip. But those with semi-Westerns are faring well.

THE IDEAL STROKING PATTERN

Before breaking down the forehand into specific elements, I will explain the stroking pattern I seek. I like to have people see the complete stroke and how the pieces fit together. Then I work backward, filling in the details according to how much students can grasp and assimilate.

Starting out, all players should know why they want to get the racket back as soon as possible. The brain and the central nervous system work together to make the most intelligent swing possible. We have found that when one gets the racket back quickly, there is more time to spend recruiting the right muscles to direct shots from corner to corner. But when one is late, there is only sufficient time to get the ball back.

Therefore, from a ready position, your backswing should begin the instant you detect the direction of your opponent's shot. Tell yourself, "It's a forehand!" and rotate both shoulders back simultaneously to begin your backswing pivot. This turns your left side toward the net. Using the loop swing (analyzed later), take your racket back at eye level and away from your body until it points to the back fence. Pause here until the ball approaches, then step out with your front foot and bend your knees so that you can drop your racket and racket hand approximately 12 inches below the intended point of impact. Stepping out on the front foot and lowering the racket and racket arm should take place simultaneously. This enables you to transfer your weight forward and up as your racket moves from low to high and strikes the ball with a vertical face. Try to have your eyes follow the ball as far as you can into your racket strings and leave your head down, in a fixed position, so that you will not disturb your stroking pattern. Don't lift your head until your upper hitting arm touches your chin on the follow-through. Your head weighs more, inch for inch, than any other part of your body, and if you look up before you've hit the ball, you're apt to pull your upper body open to face the net. Your upper body houses large muscle groups and when they turn too early, they change the racket's flight pattern to a "straight across" swing which normally forces the ball to go into the net. You should finish with your hitting arm pointed skyward and directed at your target, while the racket itself is facing to your right. If you prefer to relax your muscles and wrap the racket around your neck, make certain it's long after you've contacted the ball.

If you can visualize your follow-through "reaching toward the sky," this will give you a greater respect for getting the racket down at the lowest point of your backswing, in order to swing from low to high. No matter how low the ball is coming, fight to get your racket head below the intended point of impact and lift up, so that your body can supply power along with your arm. (Our research has shown that you can drop the racket head on the forehand swing and still keep the racket face vertical, but the one-handed backhand requires more knee bend because dropping the racket head produces an awkward wrist position.) Don't forget: tennis is a lifting game. A person 6'6" tall, standing behind his own baseline and looking over the net, cannot even see his target areas on the other side. (Caution: On forehands and backhands, whenever I talking about getting the racket head 12 inches below the intended point of impact in order to hit with topspin, don't get the impression that you simply drop the racket head by loosening the wrist. Your arm can be pointed down, but the wrist is still in the same fixed position. You must lower the hitting arm, the wrist, and the racket as a fixed unit, so that your hitting hand is also 12 inches below the oncoming ball, on the same level as the racket head.)

Now, with an overview of the forehand in mind, strive to make your body accommodate the ideal swing. You can have your body twisted crazily, your legs crossed, and a finger in your ear, but if the stroking pattern is perfect, and the racket head is vertical at impact, you can make the play. Conversely, you may have very sensuous and beautiful body movements on the court, but if your racket head is crooked at impact you'll seldom get the ball in. Certainly you want to be relaxed out there, since excess muscular tension inhibits free movement. But never let your entire body go so loose that you change the position of the racket head. People who try to tell themselves, "Relax, dummy, relax," tend to let their racket wrist go floppy and they generally finish second in a field of two. Instead, learn to keep your racket arm fixed (but not in a death clutch) and your racket face in a steady position as you take your swing. You may feel a little stiff at first, but the more you keep the ball in play — and win matches — the more you'll find yourself loosening up.

One of the biggest reasons for the change in forehands has been the "prestretch" stroke pattern. Although Jack Kramer once used this system, Andre Agassi and Boris Becker popularized it in the 1990s. This particular forehand utilizes a short backswing with a racket layback while the forearm is going forward. This stretches the forearm muscles and causes the racket to play catch-up with great speed, in effect creating a rubber band out of the muscles in the forearm. The short swing allows players to take balls on the rise and, more important, to hit service returns with an attacking style.

THE LOOP SWING

What I'm advocating in this book, on both the forehand and the backhand, is an identical loop swing, as opposed to "straight back." This is a controversial issue among teaching pros, yet I find it interesting that most of those who teach "straight back" use the loop when they go out to play — as does virtually every player in pro tennis, with the exception of Jimmy Connors and John McEnroe.

Advocates of the straight-back swing argue that the average player can understand it more easily, and other pros state, "I teach straight back because the loop takes too long." Yet I've found that the loop can be learned by nearly everybody, and a test at my tennis college showed that both swings reach the same impact point at about the same time. I allow my students to use a straight-back swing if they prefer, but I remind them that the loop will produce better results in the long run.

To visualize the loop swing, try to think of a little hairpin turn taken in two parts. First, bring the racket back at about eye level and wait for the approaching ball. Then, in a continuous motion, drop the racket and your hitting hand 12 inches below the intended point of impact, and come forward and up through the ball, toward your target. On the backswing, remember to keep your hitting shoulder raised until the racket is pointed to the back fence. Try to get the feeling of a little lift going back, as if you were taking your racket hand back, down, and around a large beach ball. One important movement that will help you to get down is to lower your hitting wrist and the butt of your racket to your right thigh (if you are righthanded) so that you can have a natural lifting motion. Some pros will literally brush the butt of their grip against that right thigh on a low ball, and then follow through like a bowler. This allows them to stay on a natural line to the target.

One reason I advocate the loop over straight back is that the loop is more rhythmical and produces significantly more power and control. My friend and physicist Dr. Pat Keating has found that on the free-falling loop, the racket head gains approximately 5.5 m.p.h. on the first foot of the drop; then multiply 5.5 times the square root of the height of the drop. The result is the speed of the racket due to gravity. This increased racket speed has a multiple effect on the speed of the ball, and it helps explain why little kids who use the loop can hit the ball so hard. In contrast to this, the person who goes straight back to the low point of his backswing has gained zero miles an hour as he starts to move into the ball. He must use a lot more muscular effort to gain sufficient racket speed in a short period of time. I often have people tell me that gravity isn't that powerful and my answer is, "Look what it does to our face."

A second virtue of the loop is that the stroking pattern you effect is identical for both the forehand and the backhand. By always getting your racket and racket hand 12 inches below the intended point of impact (at the farthest point of your back-swing), you groove the same stroke for every height of the ball. Your stroking pattern will always look the same, except for extremely high or low bounces, and you will find it easier to conceal shots from a person at the net, since he or she can't detect whether you are going to drive or lob.

Third, those instructors who teach a straight-back swing will argue, "If you want people to get down lower than the intended point of impact, they're already down with straight back." Unfortunately, I've found that most straight-back players fail to do what they think they do. They swear they lower their racket 12 inches below the intended point of impact, in order to hit with topspin, but their racket actually remains waist high or above. Thus, when they lean into the shot, their hitting arm goes up even farther and raises their racket higher than the oncoming ball. This forces them to make last-second adjustments in their swing just to contact the ball on a horizontal level. These "adjustments," of course, are what cause them to look different from the successful pro.

Those straight-back hitters who learn it right — by taking the racket back at waist level and then dropping it to about knee level — are actually using a modified loop swing. Far more often, however, those people who get the racket low do so by taking the racket straight down on a diagonal line to the lowest point of the back-swing, which of course costs them a power-producing loop.

If you're a successful straight-back player, don't change. But I encourage the rest of you to go out and watch the pros hit their forehands and backhands. Nearly all of them will have basic loop swings, unless they're intentionally hitting with un-

Mary Ley takes her racket back quickly, her hand at shoulder level. Some players prefer a slightly higher or lower starting position with the hitting hand.

Mary allows her racket to fall 30 degrees below the intended point of impact with the ball. She stays relaxed at the shoulder in order to gain the effects of gravity.

She contacts the ball slightly ahead of the front side of her body with a vertical racket head.

Mary finishes her follow-through toward the intended target so that she stays on course.

Some players like to have an "around the neck" follow-through, which relaxes the muscles but also causes a slight delay in getting to the net.

derspin. Sometimes, the exception to this rule is the two-handed forehand hitter who relies more on a body uncoiling upward rather than on an independent arm swing upward.

THE OPEN-STANCE FOREHAND

Over the past decade, a giant controversy has raged in tennis circles about the best way to stand when hitting a ball. The racket doesn't care which way you stand as long as you make the racket do the right thing, so the real issue is whether or not you intend to go to the net. The player who steps into the ball and has his center of gravity ahead of the front foot is already in a position to attack the net. The player who hits facing the net and carries the racket around the neck is normally heading back to the center of the court. This means that the player facing the net will probably have great difficulty gaining the desired net position as, or before, his opponent strikes the intended passing shot. In the 1980s and 1990s, players from Spain made great inroads in professional tennis. Spain produced many stars, but their greatest success has been on slower courts where long baseline rallies dictate play. Their biggest weakness has been on grass courts where shorter swings and quick movements to the net are crucial.

I receive many calls and letters each year asking, "Why not have everyone hit with the open stance?" If I had my choice, I would teach people to hit from several balanced positions. However, the most desired technique would be to step into the ball, whenever possible, since any shot one hits which places an opponent in a vulnerable position should be followed with a net-rushing effort.

Another question I get is, "If open-stance players can hit so hard facing the net, why does one need to coil the body?" This question intrigues me. When we measure the body coil of the open-stance player, he or she usually coils much more than the closed stance (or side to the net) player. And that's why they can hit the ball hard from the baseline. But this is the opposite of what most viewers actually see. When you watch an open-stance player on television or at a tournament, study his front shoulder. If the back of this shoulder is showing to the opponent, the open-stance player has coiled a minimum of 90 degrees. A closed-stance player showing his front shoulder to the opponent will have coiled approximately 45 degrees.

The bottom line is that if you have no intention of going to the net when your opponent is in a vulnerable position, there's no sense in working hard to get your front foot out toward the net when hitting a forehand groundstroke. But if you want to "collar" your opponent's neck when you have him out of position, you must learn to step into the ball for a fast start to the net. I've seen Pete Sampras hit both ways, but seldom do I see him face the net when he intends to rush the net. On the other hand, before the United States played the Netherlands in the Davis Cup in 1997, Andre Agassi admitted that he simply was not going to go to the net. That's fine, if you have Agassi's forehand — the best I've ever seen, on the days he's right — but the pros took advantage of his baseline style and handed Andre his worst defeats in years in 1997. He was not "on mark" with his great groundstrokes and he had no backup plan to gain the net. So, he lost one early-round match after another. I think Andre Agassi has accomplished more from the baseline than almost any player in history, winning three Grand Slam titles, and I love to watch him play. In fact, I've liked him from the first time I held him on my knee for a television interview when he was six years old. But I die a thousand deaths watching him play and knowing what he could have done with a strong net game to back up his penetrating groundstrokes. His style of play normally produces good wins and bad losses.

THE TWO-HANDED FOREHAND

Playing two-handed off both sides, Pancho Segura had one of the greatest forehands in the history of the game, but it took Monica Seles to bring the two-handed forehand into prominence in the 1990s. In the television era, Monica received a great deal of publicity and more and more young people are now giving the two-hander a try.

The racket doesn't care what you use as long as the hitter makes the racket's flight pattern honor the physical principles. However, the two-handed hitter requires very stable footing to be able to turn his/her upper body into the ball. We have found that many players are ineffective at coiling the body and are thus rendered almost helpless with a two-hander. (We will cover the two-hander in greater depth in the backhand chapter, as there is relatively little difference between the two-handed backhand and the two-handed forehand.)

Rich Ley shows the effects of an open stance "around the neck" forehand follow-through which pulls him toward the middle of the baseline while Mary has completed her closed-stance follow-through and is well on her way to the net.

THE FOREHAND IN DETAIL

Now that you have the desired forehand stroke in mind, I'll go through the entire swing in more detail. Only by concentrating on these specific details can you hope to develop a stroke that keeps the ball in play under pressure. You may wonder why I seem to be so obsessive about grooving the proper stroking patterns. My reason is based on a simple physical law, translated here into tennis terms: "Any extraneous movement by the racket which deviates from the ideal stroking pattern demands a corrective measure in the middle of the stroke to bring the racket back to its original position." In other words, an incorrect movement by the racket — such as that caused by a floppy wrist — is really a twofold error, and two errors actually add four extra movements. So when you keep making seemingly minor "adjustments" in your swing on every shot, all you're doing is making corrections. My object is to to eliminate as many of those corrections as possible.

Ready Position

Many people become enamored of the ready position because it's one of the few things they can master early. They don't have a forehand or a backhand but they've got the best ready position in the club and you can spot them a mile away.

Mary demonstrates ready position at the beginning of an open-stance forehand. The racket parallel to the net in her left hand will be used to calculate the amount of body turn used in an open-stance forehand.

Mary shows the amount of body coil used with an open stance and it's almost 100 degrees, explaining the extra power one gets with an open stance.

Nevertheless, I've never been too concerned about a standardized ready position because some people can make fast exits from unique stances. Besides, many top pro players assume a different type of ready position before the ball is struck by their opponent. The idea, therefore, is to find that stance which will produce the fastest first step toward the ball and the fastest turn of the body in order to get in position for the shot. To test for this, go out on a court and have a friend time you with a stopwatch. Face an imaginary opponent, racket in hand, while straddling the center stripe. When your friend says "Go!" turn and run to either singles sideline. Do it over and over again to both sidelines until you find the ready position which gets you there the fastest. Remember that when your opponent is about to strike the ball, you don't know if your next shot will be a forehand or a backhand, so be ready to pivot for either stroke with equal ease.

The Backswing Pivot

The more I teach this game, the more I emphasize a proper backswing. I want my students to realize that "As the preparation goes, so goes the stroke," because once you're in the middle of your swing you're locked into that shot. It's a myth to think you can "guide" the ball or control it with last-second adjustments in your swing. In fact, unless your opponent's shot is traveling at an unbelievably slow rate of speed, there can be no adaptive behavior in the middle of the swing that can be positive in nature.

Therefore, keeping in mind that your ultimate accuracy on groundstrokes traces back to your initial backswing, learn these two key points as you try to develop a strong forehand: (1) react quickly to your opponent's shot and (2) rotate both shoulders together as you turn your body to take your racket back.

It's impossible to be too early on your backswing, since your goal is never to be rushed on any stroke. The more time you can buy with quick reactions and a quick but fluid backswing, the more easily and rhythmically you can stroke the ball. Remember, too, that the loop swing is not continuous but is taken in two parts. So the moment you see the ball coming to your forehand, turn your body and start the racket back — but save the racket's fall and the drop of your body until you are ready to step into the ball. Even when you run to get into position, have the racket head back at about eye level and pointed upward. If you wait until you get to the ball to take the racket back, you'll always be rushed and you'll produce an erratic pattern of shots. A late backswing, as we shall see, also leads to wrist layback — one of the most damaging errors you can make.

Just as it's crucial to have an early backswing, never let your racket arm take a solo. Turn or coil your shoulders simultaneously with the racket so that you can unleash this energy at the ball, for it's the unwinding of the body that supplies the added power at impact to go with the power generated by the forward movement of the hitting arm. When you pull the racket back alone, you get an isolated arm movement going forward, and this demands a much stronger arm. But by coiling the body in sync with the racket, you can turn into the shot and hit the ball very hard with less energy input.

Preparing early and rolling the non-hitting shoulder inward on the backswing is such an elemental — yet often overlooked — factor in good tennis that Jack Kramer hated to even rally with players who didn't have this grooved into their stroke. He'd say, "Jeez, kid, if you don't turn your shoulder, how in the heck do you ever expect to play this game?" To force his own front (left) shoulder to turn inward, Jack would hold his left hand up by the throat of the racket, which pulled his left shoulder back as he made his turn. On the follow-through he would catch the racket again, so that his racket was never far away from his left hand.

Another way to help yourself turn back, on both the forehand and backhand, is to imagine that your initials are on the back of each shoulder blade and you want to turn and show people who you are. Little kids get the idea quickly and some of them will turn that shoulder back and say, "Hi, I'm Allison."

The Racket, the Wrist, and the Palm on the Backswing

Throughout my discussion on the forehand and the backhand, I want to emphasize that it's not how hard you swing, or the strength of your arm that will make you famous. It's how well you keep your body and your racket moving in sync, by coiling back together and uncoiling forward together and then up together. Thus, you don't want to do anything that will destroy the proper relationship between your body and your racket arm. Easy to say, hard to do, but there are ways you can minimize breakdowns under pressure.

To begin with, my observation over the years has been that the body seems to have an innate ability to turn into the ball at the proper time. I'll hit balls to absolute beginners and tell them to "Swing when you think it's time." If I just watch their bodies move into the shot, I think, "Terrific." Yet they rarely hit the ball properly because the racket is out of sync: it's either too high or too low, too early or too late, too open faced or closed face, or a combination of those factors. And the culprit, of course, is the racket arm.

The Racket

Let the pivoting of your shoulders turn the racket back, with the racket head raised substantially higher than wrist level, at approximately a 45-degree angle. If you pivot the upper body, the racket should travel no farther than pointing straight at the back fence, and that should happen automatically if there has been no wrist movement. In fact, some of the better forehands on the pro circuit do not even come back this far. By shortening your backswing in this manner, (1) it's easier to keep the racket arm moving in synchronization with the body, and (2) you get the racket head on the ball consistently because the racket has a shorter distance to travel to meet the ball. (Some pros urge average players to swing "straight back" to avoid a common error on the loop: starting the backswing too high. That's why I teach loop swingers to simply bring the racket back at eye level and maintain a short backswing.)

Modern tennis equipment is so good that it has speeded up the game. Shots are traveling faster and there's less reaction time. As a result, strokes are forced to get shorter. Physicist Dr. Howard Brody states that a decent formula to measure ball speed is 50 percent of your opponent's incoming speed, plus 1.5 times your own racket head speed. That means that the harder your opponent hits the ball, the easier you can swing to produce the desired speed.

Another advantage to a shorter swing is the fact that it is normally more in sync with the uncoiling of the body than a longer swing. The key is to keep the racket on the front side of your body and not allow the racket to continue way around your backside. What most good players do to ensure this is to raise the elbow slightly on the backswing, making it virtually impossible to lay the racket back too far.

The Wrist

Unless you're trying to hit with the "pre-stretch" forehand described earlier in this chapter, and if you hope to produce a vertical racket head at impact, your hitting wrist must be kept firm and must not change its original position on the backswing or forward motion. No matter how fluidly you swing, if you allow the wrist to "lay back" on the backswing, the racket head will go out of sync with your shoulders. Believe me, you'll save yourself tons of grief as a tennis player if you can prevent this from ever happening. For when you lay the wrist back, you not only have the initial error, you must now make an excess movement to get the wrist — and the racket — back in sync with the body.

The problem, of course, is how to keep your wrist from laying back. First, don't take your racket arm back in isolated fashion. Have your body do the work by rotating with both shoulders while your wrist remains firm.

This shows the body coiling for a closed-stance forehand. Notice in the second photo that the initial upper-body coil is less than 30 degrees, as indicated by the racket in Mary's left hand.

Second, as you take your forehand backswing, lead with your hitting elbow slightly raised and bent as you draw the racket back, instead of maintaining a straight arm. Try this yourself by placing your back foot up against a line and then seeing that your elbow passes the line slightly before the wrist and racket on the backswing. The more you tend to lay the wrist back, the more you will have to raise and bend the elbow. Experiment to see what it takes to keep the wrist in its original fixed position.

Third, remember to regard the loop as a two-part swing and not one continuous motion. Get the racket back quickly, then save the drop for when you step out on your front foot. When you start your swing too late — either with the loop or straight back — you might think that you can recover by suddenly stopping your racket arm on the backswing and moving quickly into the ball. But research shows this doesn't happen. When your arm suddenly decelerates, the racket accelerates and keeps going back, producing wrist layback. Only by getting the racket back early enough to recover from this deceleration-acceleration, and by leading with the raised elbow, can you keep the racket moving in sync with the body. Once again: the success of your forward swing is almost completely dependent upon your backswing.

The Palm

Remember, you want to keep the face of your racket and your palm moving together in their original position, since direction and accuracy are best controlled by your palm. If you keep your palm and the face of your racket lined up in exactly the same manner, then all you have to do is keep your palm moving toward the target and you're home free — if you supply the right elevation. In 1996, Dr. Gideon Ariel, Dr. Andrei Vorobiev, and I completed a research project on Andre Agassi's forehand. We were quite surprised to find that he had no wrist action (displacement) in his forehand swing just before impacting the ball. His wrist was fixed and his palm was pointing to the target before and while impacting the ball. However, when you watch Andre on television, it looks as though he is snapping at the ball with a "wristy" motion. True, his racket actually lays back on the backswing because his arm is going forward while the racket is forced backward, which stretches the forearm muscles that serve as a rubber band. But on almost all of the forward motion of the racket, there is not even one degree of wrist action.

In order to produce a vertical racket head at impact, your palm (and racket) must be turned down or faced down slightly at the end of your backswing. You can test this for yourself right in your living room. First, if your racket face is straight up and down at the lowest point of your backswing, and you keep the wrist fixed as you move into an imaginary ball, you'll find that your racket is facing upward at impact.

To correct this, place your racket with a vertical face at the point where you normally contact the ball. Now lock the wrist at that point. Without moving your wrist position, slowly allow your racket arm to creep backward in a natural motion, retracing your forward movement. At the lowest point of your backswing you will notice that your racket face is not vertical, but is pointing to the ground. You will think, "If I swing like this I'm going to hit myself in the foot." But then move the racket forward, without changing your wrist position, and bring it to the impact point. The racket should now be vertical again. Repeat the drill and take a good look at each stage of the swing. Even close your eyes and try to feel what it means to have that racket and the palm pointed down toward the court. If the racket face is not ending up vertical at impact, experiment with the palm until you discover how much you should face it down on the backswing. Leading slightly with the elbow on the backswing will also help keep the palm down.

Tetiana is an open-stance player with a super forehand and little desire to attack the net.

When you try this drill, remember to start and end with the racket where you actually contact the ball. For instance, don't make the mistake of lining up the ball

straight off your right hip. The racket face may be vertical at this point, but you actually contact the ball approximately 12 inches later, which means that the bottom of your racket will come under.

Pros like Rod Laver and Bjorn Borg really push that palm down on the backswing — without changing their wrist — when they plan to hit with topspin. Try it yourself and see how "clean" and how solid your stroke feels when you contact the ball properly. If the ball keeps hitting the net, or even your own side of the court, don't be discouraged, and don't bevel the racket face to adjust. All you have to do is bend your knees so that you can hit properly from low to high.

Bending Your Knees and Getting the Racket Low

We tell everybody going through the tennis college that we can make them famous by Friday if they can get to the ball and learn to do three "simple" things: get the racket head 12 inches below the intended point of impact, contact the ball with a vertical racket head, and follow through up under their chin on about a 30-degree angle from the court. Unfortunately, we have to practically beat people over the head to get them to bend their knees and drop their racket head below the ball — all in the same motion.

One problem is that it's an unnatural feeling to get the racket low and maintain that position on the backswing. When some people get lower than the object to be struck, they feel as though they're going to miss it; others are handicapped by their memory of hitting a baseball with a level swing. Another hang-up is that most people haven't bent their knees since 1958. I'll see a woman in the restaurant sitting down to eat lunch, and an hour later she'll tell me out on the court, "Honest, Vic, my knees really don't bend." Furthermore, people often have an image of themselves which is very different from that revealed by our videotape cameras. I once had a man tell me, in all seriousness, "You know, I think something's wrong with your TV camera. It doesn't show me bending my knees."

Then you have the corporation president who sits in the classroom the first day

and gets all stoked up. He's thinking, "I manipulate planes and trains every day. If all I have to do is control three little variables in tennis, I'll be famous by 2:30." So he rushes out on the court, takes a couple of swings, and asks expectantly, "How am I on this backswing?" Even though he thinks his racket is low, it very often is higher than his own head and we have to say, "You're still a little high." Intelligence tells the guy he has to get lower, so he really bends his knees, but the doggone racket stays up around his head. "I've got it!" he thinks. But we could use his racket for a hat rack.

Remember, it's easy to visualize getting low but quite another matter to actually do it. You have to fight through an invisible barrier to bend the knees and bring the racket down together. Try to realize that you probably can never get low enough. Exaggerate, because even when you think you are low, you probably are still too high — until you've grooved the proper swing. I've seen Rod Laver touch the court with one knee to hit a ball just above knee level, yet most people won't even bend down for a ball that "high." They simply say, "No problem, I'll just make this little adjustment in my swing," and instead of almost scraping the court with their racket and racket hand, they simply loosen their wrist, drop the racket head, and bevel the racket face. This usually produces an exceptionally high shot over the net, or the back fence.

Every time you fail to get your racket and your racket hand lower than the approaching ball at the farthest point of your backswing, you must alter your stroke in order to produce a correct, vertical racket face at impact. If your goal is to play a consistent, topspin-oriented game, then failure to get low on every groundstroke will force you to have a different stroke for every height of the ball — and that's a losing formula in good tennis.

Timing the Drop on the Loop Swing

Unless you are late arriving at the ball, don't take a continuous loop swing. You'll develop a much more consistent, error-free swing if you turn your shoulders and get the racket back quickly — pointed to the back fence — and then delay the drop of the racket and racket arm until you step into the ball. Even from a dead start, this drop generates significant energy and thus greater power in your swing than if you simply take the racket straight back down to about knee level before moving into the ball.

The problem is to learn when to bend the knees and to let the racket and racket arm drop as the ball approaches. Try my "sit-and-hit" drill (see page 60) to learn the right coordination of movements, then get out on the court to develop the proper timing when a ball is in play. Try to find a ball machine or a friend who can feed you dozens of balls in the same area so that you can concentrate solely on lowering the racket with a fixed wrist as your thighs start down and your front foot goes out. Remember, your weight is equally distributed over both feet at this point, and now your racket arm and thighs are free to come forward and up as you uncoil your body segments. The result is maximum rhythm and power from your swing. Remember, you only have to bend enough to comfortably get the racket a foot or so below the

Abi demonstrates the number one error in most forehands—a swing that is too long and will cause the racket to come through long after the body links have uncoiled.

intended point of impact with the ball. This drill becomes even more important for the one-handed backhand.

If you drop the racket too fast, you have to wait on the ball at the bottom of the loop, and thus you may as well eliminate the loop, since you've just lost the potential energy gains of a continous motion from the top of the loop through impact. If you're late with the drop, you suddenly have to cut across your body in order to meet the ball in time. One argument I often hear is that it takes too much "timing" to use the loop. But it turns out that the exact same mental process is necessary whether or not you take a loop swing or go straight back.

Contacting the Ball

If you step into the ball, the ball should be contacted when it is even with or slightly in front of the side of your body closer to the net, while the hitting elbow is approximately six to ten inches away from your body in a slightly bent position. The farther away from your body the ball is at contact, the more power you get from the same expenditure of energy, providing you can maintain a firm wrist and still feel comfortable. (Remember: as you stand sideways to the net, "away from" means the direction your belly button is pointed in, and "in front of" means the side closer to the net.) In the 1990s, several pro players have hit forehands similar to a person throwing a discus. Their bodies uncoil way ahead of the hit as though they are pulling the racket through the shot. Spain's Conchita Martinez (the Wimbledon champ in 1994) and

Arantxa Sanchez Vicario (who won the French Open in 1989) both hit in this manner. But again, their center of gravity is always heading back to the center of the baseline and they find it almost impossible to get to the net in singles. As a matter of fact, as younger, more versatile players came along, their records began to slip.

There are two other important considerations about the ball and the racket at impact. First, learn what it means to actually have the racket face vertical at impact (which is a prerequisite of topspin). Most people don't have this feeling. I'll ask players to take a practice swing with their eyes closed and stop their racket where they normally meet the ball. Then I ask, "How does it feel?" They say, "Terrific." But their racket face is generally pointing to the sky and their shot is on its way to the next county. Then I ask them to keep their eyes closed and I adjust the racket to its proper position at impact. Again I ask, "How does this feel?" They say, "Crummy." But I tell them, "Remember this crummy feeling . . . it will take you to the finals."

Second, it's a myth that any player can "feel" the ball on the strings or "guide" the ball toward the target. Research has shown that the ball is on the strings for only four to six milliseconds before it releases; when you feel the ball touch the strings, it's already gone and on its way. This doesn't mean you can contact the ball and then go anywhere with your follow-through. On the contrary, the racket contacts the ball for such a brief instant that you want to develop a "straight to the target" low-to-high swing that enables you to meet the ball within a 6- to 18-inch span. This allows you to mistime the ball and still be good. A swing that is horizontal, and in an arc, makes timing much more difficult by allowing you only one point where you can contact the ball and make it be successful.

Play the Ball, Not Your Opponent

Remember, you don't play people in this game. The only thing that's going to make you a great tennis player is your relationship to the ball, so take good care of it. Keep your eyes on the ball for as long as you can, and concentrate on the point of impact until your upper arm or shoulder comes up and brushes your chin. Then lift your chin and let your eyes track the ball out over the net. When you leave your eyes down that long, you get a panicky feeling that your opponent's return shot is going to hit you in the ear. But in reality, when hitting from the baseline in this manner, your shot will not even reach the net by the time you raise your eyes to follow the ball. Try it! You'll find that you have plenty of time to stay over the ball and still get ready for your opponent's return.

Since our eyes can't track the ball all the way into the racket, I tell my students, "Keep your head down and try to see the racket pass in front of your eyes." Try this drill: rally with a friend, and whenever one of you doesn't watch the racket pass by your eyes at or near impact, that person yells, "Stop." At first your rallies will end after one or two shots, but they will lengthen out as you learn to concentrate on watching the ball as it approaches you, and then the racket.

Keeping your eyes down on the point of impact is also a guarantee that you will not lift your chin early, and thus disturb the relationship between your head and the racket. If the center of the strings of your racket is about to strike the ball, and you suddenly lift your chin, this is going to lift your racket and cause you to hit off-center. That's one important reason why you occasionally — perhaps frequently — hit "metal" shots off the edge of your racket.

Some coaches argue that when you leave your eyes down until your arm touches your chin on the follow-through, your shoulders "freeze" and you cannot move them properly as you contact the ball. But I can't buy that concept. Leaving your head and eyes down is also one key to a good golf swing, and it certainly doesn't stop your shoulders or hips from moving efficiently through the ball in that sport.

Remembering the proper follow-through will also help keep your head down as you stroke the ball. It's like shooting a camera: some people have a tendency to think they've taken the picture before they actually release the shutter, and thus they pull away at the wrong moment. In tennis, if you fail to realize how important it is to go all the way up and out on the follow-through, you have a tendency to pull off the ball at or before impact. I watch people all the time who lift their eyes and pull their head up before the ball even reaches the racket, yet they swear they actually see the ball hitting the strings. Therefore, don't be in such a hurry at impact; "hang on" to the swing for as long as possible, even though the ball is here and gone in an instant. It should be of interest to you that as the speed of the ball has increased, the length of rallies has decreased. So I say, take care of the shot you're on, because statistically it's probably your last.

Go After the Ball

Not only on the forehand but all your strokes, always strive to play the game out in front (toward the net) and away from your body (toward the sidelines) — never up close. Be aggressive and go after the ball. Don't let it come to you. There are two critical points to be made here.

First, when you take the ball on the rise, you reduce your opponent's response time by 50 percent. Our studies indicate that you don't actually get more speed by contacting the ball early, but you give your opponent less time to reach the ball early, set himself, and hit the desired spot. The player to watch here is Monica Seles. Even against Steffi Graf in her prime, the harder Steffi hit the ball, the faster it came back from Seles — again, the key is not the speed of the ball, but how quickly Monica ripped it back over the net and kept Graf on the move. Of course, most club players have a major challenge taking the ball on the rise because their swing is too long and they get caught late. But if you can keep the racket on the front side of the body and not let it go behind your body, then you can begin to attack short balls with greater confidence and success.

Second, stepping into the ball doesn't produce more power, but it does normally place your center of gravity ahead of your front foot and speeds up your approach to the net. Don't hit with your weight on your back foot and don't back up unless you are absolutely forced to by a deep shot.

The farther out in front you can step, and still maintain good balance, the longer you can keep your palm and racket going to the target. A long step forward gives you a greater range in which to meet the ball and still produce a successful shot. The shorter your step, the shorter your follow-through will be, and thus the more you will tend to pull across your body. A horizontal swing is similar to a spin-

Pooja uses a chair to demonstrate the proper knee bend for a low shot. She moves from a "racket back" quickly ready position to a knee bend and back up again as she strikes the ball.

When hitting groundstrokes with topspin, it's your knees that will allow you to lower your body so that you can hit with a natural lifting motion. Stiff knees, especially on balls bouncing waist high or lower, generally lead to a dropped racket head and ineffective stroke patterns. So if your knees seem chronically stiff on the tennis court, try the following drill to give yourself an idea of just how much they should bend on most groundstrokes, and what it feels like to coordinate the body and the racket arm on the loop swing. (This drill is actually more useful on the backhand, since one can stand a little taller on the forehand and still have the racket head in a vertical position at impact.)

Stand with your back to an average-sized chair or even a park bench as you wait for a court, and imagine that a ball has just been hit. Pivot your body and take your racket back in a loop swing. As your racket and racket hand

drop to brush your thigh, lower your rear end and step forward simultaneously with your front foot. Your rear end should touch the chair or bench as your front foot finishes the forward step. Think of making a brief three-point landing with your racket, rear end, and front foot. You're now ready to come forward and up with a low-to-high motion. (On the backhand, do the same thing.) Also remember to practice keeping your head fixed and eyes down on the point of impact as you come up. If you get in the habit of looking up to see where the ball is going as you lift up, you may disturb your stroke pattern.

Most people refuse to bend their knees as low as I ask because they're afraid they won't have enough strength to come back up. But if you stick with this drill you're going to get your thighs in shape while your stroke improves.

ning top, which must keep its balance over the center point. That's why people who swing on a horizontal plane take shorter steps: when they try to take a long step into the ball they have a hard time judging their swing.

After the hit, you can let your back foot come up to meet your front foot but don't let it come off the ground in a forward step, for this spins the body on a horizontal plane and usually effects a somewhat horizontal swing.

Swing Inside-Out, Like a Golfer

If you are turning from golf to tennis, and you have a good golf swing, you should be the happiest person alive. All that money you spent on lessons is now going to pay off in dividends because the efficient golf swing and the proper forehand share many important similarities, such as: (1) the head must be kept down and eyes fixed on the point of impact, (2) the shoulders must rotate in sync, slightly before the ball is met, (3) the real power is derived from the movement of the hips and the thighs as you contact the ball, and (4) there is an "inside-out" movement of the body and arms before impact so that the club or racket makes solid contact with the ball.

Most tennis players, especially those who swing on a horizontal plane, have difficulty in grasping the inside-out concept. They are accustomed to starting their swing out away from the body, and moving into their body with the forward motion of their hitting arm. This swing pulls the ball cross-court and with less power. Hitting inside-out, however, means the hitting arm is fairly close or "in" to the body on the backswing and the forward striking motion is away from the body. At first you get the feeling that you're going to hit the ball off to the right of your target. That, in fact, is the feeling you want. But if you can get your racket and racket hand lower than the ball on the backswing and swing inside-out, your palm and racket face will point to your intended target at impact, and will often be parallel to the net.

The inside-out motion contributes to a successful forehand in many ways. First, it leads to greater control and consistency by allowing the racket face to remain on target with the ball much longer than does a horizontal swing. If you can develop a stroke that keeps your palm going toward your target even before you strike the ball, you increase the distance in which you can make contact and still make a good hit. Second, inside-out keeps you from pulling across your body. Third, it forces you to contact the ball out away from your body, which lengthens the radius of your stroke and thus gives you more power with the same energy input. And fourth, since your energy flow is out toward your target, you can pull off one of the game's toughest plays: the passing shot down the line when your opponent is coming to the net. Yet swinging inside-out does not restrict you from hitting cross-court.

Assuming you get down properly with your thighs and your racket, the movement of your hips is the key to the inside-out movement. As you shift your weight forward into the ball, rotate your hips slightly ahead of your upper body (as in golf) so that your right hip turns in toward the target. Think about rolling your hips into the ball and directing your body's inertia out toward your opponent's backhand (assuming you are both righthanded). Knowing when to turn the hips is a tricky little maneuver, and some people find it easier to visualize their palm swinging out toward the right net post, instead of trying to relate to their hips. But remember, use your arm more to perfect the stroke pattern, and let your body generate the power. Relying on your arm to supply the power will only lead to a greater number of errors.

One reason most tennis players have trouble swinging inside-out is that they simultaneously try to swing on a horizontal plane. You may think, "I'm so accurate that I can swing horizontally, hit the ball out toward my target, and then follow through across my body." But if you can do that, I'd like to get it on film, because I've never seen it happen before. You can't fight physical laws. When you swing horizontally, your hips want to bring you around like a spinning top and it's virtually impossible to snap them forward and out toward your target. You are swinging from outside-in, across your body, and your racket face can only stay pointed toward the target for an instant. This doesn't allow you much margin for timing errors.

The Real Power Comes from Uncoiling as You Lift

People often tell me that they've read, or have been told, "Stay down with the ball" on groundstrokes. This always baffles me, since I've only seen one pro player stay down after contacting the ball, and that was Françoise Durr on the backhand. But I have seen great players get down to the ball and then lift their bodies in synchronization with their forward and upward stroke. Many pros have told me that they stay down with the ball, but when we film them in super high speed and digitize their movements, their center of gravity makes close to the same forward and upward movement as their swing. When Drs. Ariel and Vorobiev and I digitized Andre Agassi's body and hitting arm, his center of gravity made the same loop as his patented forehand swing. The same thing happened when we did an analysis of Jimmy Connors's strokes for a shoe company. His body would lift at approximately the same angle as his swing on the backhand, which often pulled him off the ground. He didn't do it as much on the forehand and he normally made ten errors on the forehand for each error on the backhand. It turns out that the lifting doesn't give one as much power as it does to provide the same directional forces between the body and racket arm while freeing the body segments to uncoil. When the two don't make the same movements, they can actually oppose each other.

The Importance of Your Palm

You can have the greatest footwork in the world and beautiful, sensual moves, but if you're holding an Eastern grip and your palm is not vertical at impact and pointing straight toward your target, you're going to die young. For example, if you can make the palm go straight down the line, the ball will follow, providing you have the proper stroke and the right elevation. But if the ball hits the net post, you'll know that your palm was pointing there at impact.

Watch the top players. When they are having trouble, or they feel their swing is out of kilter, they often will take their palm and start swinging it toward an imaginary target, trying to regain the proper sensation. Even at Wimbledon you could see Kramer and Laver shadow-swinging with their palms. So "think palm" and you'll be on the road to a trusted forehand.

PRACTICE TIP: SELF-EVALUATION ON THE FOLLOW-THROUGH

A teaching pro is certainly not the only person who can detect flaws in your swing and suggest remedies that can lead to good tennis. If you know the basic elements of a good stroke, and some of the common errors, you can evaluate yourself while rallying before a match or while practicing. One excellent method is to simply freeze on your follow-through and look for the following tip-offs:

1. Is your weight forward on your front foot?

2. Can you lift the back foot off the ground and maintain your balance on the front foot? If not, you haven't shifted your weight and you are failing to utilize the body segments; the chances are excellent that your body hasn't lifted two inches.

3. Is your upper hitting arm under your chin and pointed out toward the target?

4. Are your eyes still fixed on the point of impact?

5. Has your head remained in precisely the same position as when the ball was contacted?

6. Your belly button should be facing your opponent and should not have gone beyond that point.

7. If you have hit with an inside-out mo-tion, your right knee will have come up close to your left. Ideally, the back foot should not have moved forward, but if it has, then no farther than the front foot.

8. Bring your hitting arm back to the point of impact and see if the racket face is still vertical. Or has your wrist rolled — over or under — or shifted dramatically?

Some players will even freeze and take a look at their follow-through while actually playing a match. They know they have a full second with which to take a quick look at their body before they need to prepare for their opponent's shot. Yet when we ask people to try this at the tennis college, they just can't bring themselves to do it. They're so worried about not having enough time to handle their next shot that they don't want to see if they are actually taking a good swing. Their only criterion is whether the ball lands in or out, irrespective of how crummy their swing might be. All I can urge you to do is: don't delay solving your problems. Eventually you have to check out your swing and see what you are doing wrong if you want to start making improvements. So don't keep waiting until "the next shot."

The Crucial Role of a Fixed Wrist and Forearm

One of the major goals of this book is to convince you how important it is on groundstrokes to get your hitting wrist and forearm in perfect position, and then leave them fixed throughout your swing (unless you are hitting the "pre-stretch" forehand described earlier in this chapter). If you can hold the proper grip and form the proper wrist/forearm position — and hold them firm — you can mistime the ball yet still effect a shot toward your target. But if you lay the wrist back on the backswing or roll it over as you come into the ball, then you throw everything out in favor of the touch system. Even if, at times, you have the coordination and the talent to play with your wrist and hit a target area under stress, you'll probably be an erratic player forever. You'll be famous one day, a toad the next. For when you lose your "touch," you lose everything. Instead of adjusting and coming close to a good hit, you don't have a clue where your next shot is going. That's why I'll guarantee you: if a person can snap his wrist well — on groundstrokes and volleys — and still be successful, he's on the pro tour.

Hitting with a lot of wrist/forearm action not only demands concentration and super timing every day, it leaves you nowhere to turn for advice on technique. A coach can't teach "touch"— he can only ask you how you feel. Wristy players are always coming through my tennis college and saying, "Jeez, I'm trying to work on your strokes but I just don't have the feel today." Well, they probably haven't had the feel since they started playing tennis, because the wrist play requires just too much from the average player. The person who rolls his wrist before impact, for example, reduces the range in which he can hit the ball on the money with a vertical racket face. He must time the inertia from the roll of his wrist and then he must curb that inertia so that the wrist doesn't roll over once it is parallel to the net. This takes perfect timing and control. Conversely, when you can fix the wrist and leave it alone, and swing on a low-to-high plane out toward your target, you have a much longer range in which to hit a good shot. Chris Evert has discussed playing with a quiet racket and that simply means leaving the wrist and forearm in a fixed position.

(A reminder here about terminology: Remember, the wrist joint area has no separate set of muscles, so we're actually talking about the wrist and forearm as a unit.)

The Follow-Through

In reality, the follow-through has nothing to do with guiding the ball; once the ball leaves your strings, you can do nothing about it. Nevertheless, the reason you want to develop a follow-through that stays on target is that you may not contact the ball at the right point. The correct follow-through simply guarantees your best chance to be off the mark and still be accurate. In addition, we have studied many shots and the ball doesn't always bounce the way one would think; it can hit a rough spot on the court and slow down a bit.

I find it interesting that when we ask players to demonstrate Andre Agassi's forehand follow-through, they are almost always wrong. His forehand happens so fast that it looks as though he is pulling across the ball in what is known as the Agassi "windshield wiper" shot. But in fact, his follow-through is quite long before

Travis attempts to keep his racket fairly close to the fence through the entire swing, which will be sufficient when he coils his body. This drill helps him shorten his swing, feel the inside-out follow-through, and generate his own feedback system.

he relaxes the muscles and allows the racket to come around his neck. The lesson here: try to see how long you can hang on to your follow-through rather than how quickly you can let it go, in order that you don't pull off the shot before impact.

COMMON FOREHAND PROBLEMS

Following are many of the common forehand problems and the prescribed treatment as already described in this chapter.

Your Shots Keep Going to the Left

The most common cause is that you are pulling across your body, which is usually caused by a horizontal swing and improper movement by the wrist/forearm. A second reason, though rare, is that you may be impacting the ball too far in front of your body. Your hips will have completed their turn at impact and you will be out of sync and hitting with less power. Andres Gimeno, in fact, is the only successful player I've ever seen who could contact the ball more than 12 inches out in front of his body. Why? His follow-through was so long that he was still heading in the same direction at that point.

When you swing on a horizontal level, centrifugal force drives you around and causes your follow-through to cross your body instead of going on a line to your target. To play tennis as dictated by physical laws you must get your body down and your racket below the ball so that you can swing naturally from low to high while maintaining forward movement toward the target. Rather than have your racket start and finish on the same plane, visualize it moving from low to high.

Other reminders:

1. When playing inside the singles sidelines, you have only 19.1 to 19.6 degrees variation on your follow-through from the baseline if you try to shift from your opponent's backhand corner to his forehand corner.

2. Develop an inside-out stroke so that your palm and racket can travel out as far as possible toward the target.

3. Don't let the ball get too close. Stride into the ball with your hips leading slightly, and transfer your weight to the front foot. This keeps you from pulling back or hitting from your heels or the back foot as you swing.

4. Keep your head fixed and eyes down on the point of impact until you have felt the ball hit the racket strings. If your head turns or lifts during the hit, your body will tend to move in the same direction and pull the racket with it.

5. When you reach the front side of your body on the forehand, there's a ten-

On a hard-hit shot, you can vary the ball 30 feet in any direction by moving your wrist just one inch during the swing. That's going to put you in deep trouble. The problem is to correct the error, but first try to discover where the racket is going astray, whether on the backswing or while moving into the ball. Fortunately, there are ways you can analyze yourself on the court or at home to see if you are achieving the correct wrist position to begin with, and to check if you are rolling your wrist or laying it back or otherwise tampering with what should be a fixed position.

- Stand sideways to a fence or a wall with your front foot angled against the fence. Achieve the proper forehand grip and place the racket face flush against the fence, where you normally contact the ball. The racket face should be vertical, parallel to the fence. If you want to measure the correct position, the bottom edge of the racket head should be at the same level as your index finger.

  Now, whatever wrist bend there is in your hand to keep your palm and the racket face parallel to the fence (and perpendicular to the ground) is the wrist bend you want to maintain for the rest of your life. Never change this bend at any point during the swing unless you become an extremely proficient player. Even then, remember that pros who use a lot of wrist action are playing seven days a week and wristy pros sometimes go sour.

- To practice the "feel" of keeping your wrist fixed on your backswing and through contact with the ball, swing very slowly, then stop just before the intended point of impact and analyze the surface of the racket face to see if it has remained parallel to the fence. Also try to swing with your eyes closed to keep yourself honest.

- If you are righthanded, place the thumb and middle finger of your left hand on the wrist of your hitting arm and feel exactly what it means to lay the wrist back or roll it over. You'll discover where your problem is starting, and what it takes to maintain a firm wrist.

- Stand with the toes of both feet against a line on the court and take a swing. If the racket crosses the line on the backswing, then you're taking it back too far. For a visual check in your living room, you want to see the entire racket at the end of your backswing. If it disappears behind your body, then chances are excellent that you're laying the wrist back.
- Attach a yardstick to the surface plane of the racket and try to keep the yardstick from laying back on the backswing. You actually want the yardstick and racket faced slightly down as you go back. The yardstick magnifies any wrist movement and thus helps identify the problem area.
- The next time you are rallying, freeze on your follow-through, then slowly lower your hitting arm back down to the hitting contact point and then stop. If the racket face is still vertical you know you haven't moved your wrist on the swing. But if the racket face is pointed up, then it was turned under when you hit, and whatever it takes to roll the racket back to a vertical position is the amount you have moved it during your swing.

dency to break the elbow and pull the ball to the left, unless you develop a low-to-high stroke and maintain a fixed wrist. Check to see that your initial wrist position is proper and that you're not laying the wrist back or rolling it over before or during impact.

Missing the Ball Completely

When you are swinging in a northernly direction and the ball keeps heading west, you are in deep trouble. One reason is that you very likely are watching your opponent instead of the ball. Even though your eyes cannot track the ball as it approaches impact with your racket, try to look at the seams of the ball, or read the writing, or watch the wool come through the back side of the strings — anything to get you to concentrate on making good contact. This also helps keep your head down so that your racket isn't pulled away at the last moment in your eagerness to see where the shot is going. A good drill is the "stop-rally drill" explained on page 58.

Finally, your only goal should be to hit the ball. Most beginners are thinking two things simultaneously: hit the ball and get it in the court. So just take one goal at a time.

Your Shots Keep Going to the Right

The cause of this problem is that your racket head is late coming through as you swing into the ball, and this difficulty can stem from a number of factors: you're late getting to the ball, you're starting your swing too late, your wrist is laid back, or your backswing is too long.

Learn to get that fast first step the instant you see the ball leave your opponent's racket. Turn your body and racket back simultaneously, instead of using an isolated arm motion — then delay the drop of the racket and racket arm until you're ready to step into the ball. Test yourself to see if your wrist is laying back on the backswing. One way to check this, as well as the length of your backswing, is to stand with your back against a wall or a fence. Take a practice swing and if your racket bangs against the barrier on your backswing or follow-through, you are taking the racket back too far, or swinging too far across on the follow-through.

The Ball Is Landing Too Short

1. One reason may be that you are hitting on a horizontal plane, which causes the ball to begin its drop sooner, unless hit harder. Instead, swing low to high, elevate your shots, and let the higher arc and topspin bring the ball down deep in your opponent's court. Refer to the "sit-and-hit" drill (page 60) to remind yourself how low you must get, even on a waist-high shot.

2. You may be "arming" the ball, which means an isolated arm motion and little input by the body. This is caused by hitting from a fixed open stance, which decreases hip rotation potential, and failing to turn your front shoulder as you take the racket back. Instead, try to show the back side of that front shoulder to your opponent, and then step in to the ball.

3. Your wrist/forearm may be rolling over. Work to keep the wrist fixed while increasing your body movements (i.e., turning the shoulders) to supply the power.

4. You may have a fixed wrist/forearm, but the top edge of your racket is leaning forward. Work against a vertical wall or fence to find the wrist position that produces a vertical racket head at impact.

5. You may simply be hitting too weakly, in which case you need to increase your hip movement, and the lifting motion of your thighs, to gain more power. Remember the inside-out golf swing.

6. You may even be hitting with excess topspin, which is a nice problem to have, especially when your opponent is at the net. All you have to do to hit deeper is to decrease the upward angle of your forward swing.

The Ball Consistently Goes Too Long

Either your shots have insufficient topspin — in which case you must increase the angle of your low-to-high forward swing — or the bottom of your racket is leading (which means the racket face is tilted up). For the latter problem, check your wrist position to see that it produces a vertical racket head at impact. If the racket is turning under, the reasons could be that you are hitting off the back foot, leaning back, lifting your head too early, or your palm may not be pointed downward (about 30 degrees) at the lowest point of your backswing. So work to maintain a steady racket head, and then get your body moving in sync with your swing. Concentrate on stepping into the ball and trying to take it more on the rise, instead of hesitating and letting the ball play you.

Overhitting

It just may be that it's more important to your ego to hit the ball as hard as possible than to worry about keeping it in play and winning a lot more often. If that's the case, I can't help you. But if you don't have the competitive temperament to slow down your swing, and you also want to win, then you must learn to increase the angle of your low-to-high lift so that you impart severe topspin. Then you can get rid of all your frustrations and still keep the ball in the county. In the finals of the 1997 U.S. Nationals, champion Martina Hingis continually changed the pace of the ball and it threw Venus Williams off track. It was a wonderful tournament for Venus, but her biggest lesson for the future was learning that you don't have to beat everyone with speed, nor will speed alone allow you to beat everyone if you make too many unforced errors.

PRACTICE TIP: FOREHAND DRILLS

1. You want to keep all movements out in front of your body, on the backswing and the follow-through. To test for this, stand with your back flat against a fence or wall and practice taking a swing. To keep from touching the fence you must have a nicely controlled swing that goes inside-out. You can test yourself on the court as well. Stand with your front side to the net and draw an imaginary line from that front side to your target area. Now try to keep your swing from taking the racket across that line, at least until the last possible moment.

2. Jack Kramer has always insisted that nobody can really develop solid groundstrokes unless he or she turns the non-hitting shoulder inward to start the backswing. I mentioned earlier how he would put his left hand on the handle of his racket in order to pull that shoulder back. Another drill you can use to help develop a "feel" for the proper loop swing is to stand sideways to the net and place the butt of your racket against your front shoulder, then take a swing. Turn the front shoulder, take the racket back at eye level, go down, forward, and then up. Taking your front shoulder through the same stroking pattern, in miniature, as your hitting arm will give you exactly the sensation I'm seeking.

3. Try the same drill using two rackets, one held in perfect hitting position, the other held against the front shoulder. Ideally, both rackets should stay the same distance apart throughout the swing, since your body — on the loop swing — must make the same movement as the hitting arm. If not, they will begin to spread apart and you (or a coach) can discover exactly where your trouble starts. Another benefit of this drill is that your knees are forced to bend properly if you hope to keep your rackets in sync.

4. To help steady your head and keep it from lifting too early during impact, use the "neck brace drill," in which you place your non-racket hand behind your head and then hold your head down as you swing.

The Backhand

KNOW I'VE TOLD YOU that the backhand is actually physically easier to hit than the forehand. But we all know that's not the way it is psychologically, right? If you're like the average player, you're pretty relaxed on the forehand, but when you see a ball coming to your backhand you cringe, "Dear God, it's a backhand!" and your racket goes up in defense. When rallying before an important match you try desperately to look good by hitting everything off your forehand, while hoping your opponent doesn't discover the fact that your backhand is a disaster. You may even be thinking, "I know I don't have a backhand, but I've got a terrific forehand and a great serve, so I can win anyway." And you probably will, too — as long as your opponent agrees to have a forehand contest. But good players will never give you a chance to hide a severe weakness. Instead of simply attacking your backhand at every opportunity, they will first drive the ball wide to your forehand, which opens up the entire court. If you manage to get the ball back, they will just hit to your backhand and you have no choice but to try to hit it.

So why continue to be defensive — and vulnerable — with a stroke that can be an offensive weapon? When you develop a good forehand and a good backhand, you make your strong side even stronger because you don't have to give ground. Instead of overplaying your strength, by running around a weak backhand to hit a forehand, you can stand where you should and thus conserve energy while forcing your opponent to hit better shots.

If your backhand is an obvious handicap, let's break down your swing and start over. And if you feel that you already have a good stroke, many of the checkpoints and drills in this chapter should help sharpen it up — and put it to the test.

A BIG DECISION: TWO HANDS OR ONE?

An overwhelming trend has hit the tennis world since my book was first published in 1977, and that's the two-handed backhand. At my tennis camps, about 50 percent of the adults are now hitting two-handed backhands. In junior tennis classes, we see more two-handed backhands than one-handed backhands. Just a couple of years ago, I listened to a debate between the great Bobby Riggs (1940s) and Jack Kramer (1950s), the best player I've ever seen play the game. Bobby was telling Jack that if he had it to do all over again, he would play with, and teach, a two-handed backhand. Kramer was astonished. He felt it would be much easier to beat the best two-handed backhand than the best one-handed player.

This type of backhand argument continues. The two players who have dominated tennis for most of the 1990s — Steffi Graf and Pete Sampras — are one-handed backhand players. But right behind them is a string of great two-handed backhand players, including Martina Hingis, Monica Seles, Arantxa Sanchez Vicario, Michael Chang, and Andre Agassi. In the 1980s, Bjorn Borg only went to the net to collect his check but won five Wimbledons with a two-handed backhand, while his archrival, Jimmy Connors, had a two-handed backhand and the most punishing service return in the game. Though Chris Evert helped popularize the two-handed backhand, her chief rival, Martina Navratilova, used one hand.

When making the decision about whether to start out with a two-handed backhand or convert from using one hand, keep in mind that, physiologically, there are definitely two types of players. One type seems to work more with the forearms and the second type likes to hit more with the body. Those players who can coil their body easily seem to be better suited for the two-handed backhand. Those who favor more forearm action appear to fare much better with the one-handed backhand.

Today, if I had to choose the current player who best demonstrates the backhand I teach, it would be Pete Sampras. But a generation ago my model for the one-handed backhand was Don Budge. At that time, old-timers agreed that Donald (the Grand Slam winner in 1938) had the greatest backhand in the history of the game. He was the only player I had ever seen who could take Pancho Gonzales's serve — in its prime — and pound it back off the backhand. Gonzales would serve and attack against everybody; he took the net easily against Rod Laver, and he defeated Ken Rosewall consistently by moving in on his backhand. Yet when Budge and Gonzales played in the early 1950s, and Budge had been out of the game for nearly five years, he still had such a lethal backhand that Gonzales literally could not come to the net when he served to that backhand, for fear of being passed.

I began studying Budge's backhand during my senior year at Monroe High School in Michigan when I hitchhiked into Detroit to see him play Bobby Riggs during their barnstorming tour in 1947. I took along a 3-by-5 card that was punched with different-sized holes, and all during the match I just followed Budge through one of those little holes, trying to focus on different aspects of his strokes and his body movements, particularly on the backhand. That's when it really struck home how important it is to swing from low to high with a lifting thigh motion, for I realized that Budge played with his knees, thighs, and hips, as well as with his arm. He would get his body and his racket low and then lift out toward his target, brushing the ball with heavy topspin that enabled him to get great depth and blistering speed. Years later, Jack Kramer would tell me, "The thing I always remember about Budge's backhand is his butt stretched up on the follow-through, his hitting arm extended high in the air, and the ball going by me at 120 miles per hour."

When I began giving lessons I added a few of my own interpretations to help my students try to swing like Budge. For example, I needed a gimmick to help them to keep the racket face going through the ball — out toward the intended target — and to finish high, instead of pulling it across their body in the Humble Harv fashion. Finally I came up with three initials which have always worked pretty well: A.T.A., for "Air the Armpits." You laugh, but today I have students all over the world telling their opponents, "A.T.A.!"

Another concept I emphasize today is that the knuckles on your hitting hand dictate the success of your backhand, just as the palm is your guidance control on the forehand. Try to see how long you can keep the knuckles pointed to the net, going out to the target, and skyward, for they are identical in purpose with the face of your racket.

Keeping "A.T.A" and the knuckles in mind should help you understand why a strong, accurate backhand is dependent upon swinging from low to high with a vertical racket head at impact, and why a horizontal swing is going to prevent you from making any real gains in this game.

THE GRIP

One-Handed Backhand

If you can perform two separate tasks simultaneously (and most people can with practice) you should switch grips when you turn from the forehand to hit a backhand. I advocate the Eastern backhand, with the palm moved to the top of the racket, the knuckle of the index finger riding the top right ridge, and the thumb placed at an angle behind the racket handle to provide a brace-like stability when the ball is contacted. Many people hold their thumb under the handle because they feel as though the racket is going to fall out of their hand, but this tends to take more strength to hold the racket steady at impact. Still, there are some very strong pro players who put the thumb under the grip.

When I get people to hold the Eastern backhand for the first time they think, "This shot is going to hit me in the foot," because the racket head feels like it is pointed down. But this grip position provides the most stability and requires the least amount of wrist adjustment in order to produce a vertical racket head at impact. You thus minimize your errors in hitting the ball.

The Continental — halfway between the Eastern forehand and the Eastern backhand — is the most common alternative grip, especially among the pros. Many top players hold a Continental for both grips, not because they think it is better on the backhand but because they feel there is insufficient time to change grips in a game where the ball is coming back at them at 90 or 100 miles per hour. Don't fall

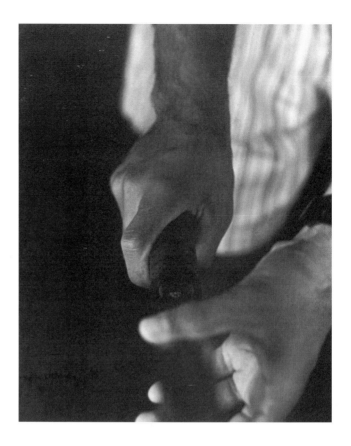

Harsul demonstrates the full Eastern backhand grip with the palm squarely on top of the grip.

for this myth. Research at my tennis college has shown that if you can perform two separate tasks simultaneously you can change grips faster than you can take a single step. See for yourself. Practice switching grips for five minutes every day as you step toward an imaginary shot, and in a week or two your hands should beat your feet every time. As Kramer has stated, "If people can change grips when receiving a 130 m.p.h. serve, why wouldn't they be able to change grips on normal volleys and groundstrokes?"

The Continental is made for the chip (underspin) backhand volley and is fine for the backhand chip or underspin groundstroke. But for basic topspin drives from the baseline it requires a strong wrist and a roll of that wrist to bring the racket straight up and down at impact. Mastering this wrist play is asking too much of just about everyone. Far better, it seems to me, to take the time now to learn to switch grips, and then build a winning game on something far more dependable than "touch." It should be noted that this is an issue which continues to be debated by teaching professionals around the world.

The Two-Handed Backhand Grip

I try to get righthanded players to think like lefthanders. In other words, use an Eastern forehand grip with the left hand at the top and a Continental grip with the right hand on the bottom. If the left hand can become the dominant hand, the player is simply hitting a lefthanded forehand with the right hand serving as a stabilizer. The righthander can't take a normal "palm on top" Eastern one-handed backhand grip because the right elbow is pulled too close to the body due to the left hand involvement. Bjorn Borg, winner of six French Open championships on clay, was quoted as saying that each arm should apply equal force on the grip. But when we looked at the muscle contractions on both arms, it was the left arm that appeared to be doing most of the work. As a matter of fact, I was once doing a telecast in Montreal and the coach of the Canadiens hockey team told me that Borg had worked out with his team. What amazed him was that Borg had an excellent slap shot from the left side.

THE SWING: AN OVERVIEW

The ball doesn't know you're hitting one-handed or two-handed. All it knows is how the racket meets it at the impact point. Thus, the flight pattern of the swing must be the same for both types of backhand if you wish to produce the same result.

One reason the backhand produces so many unhappy, contorted faces in contrast to the forehand is that people tend to regard it as some weird stroke, unique in itself, when the truth of the matter is that the forehand and the backhand should have identical stroking patterns and the same basic body movements. (The only real difference — and an important one — is that you must step into the ball and swing sooner on the backhand side because your hitting arm is much closer to the net.) Thus, as I describe the backhand, I will remind you of the similarities with the forehand while detailing those aspects of the swing that differ slightly from the forehand.

The instant you see the ball coming to your backhand, turn the shoulder of your hitting·arm and your racket back simultaneously so that your arm doesn't make an isolated movement. This places your side to the net and enables your body and racket to move in sync.

Just as on the forehand, I prefer to have you take a short loop swing. Start by bringing your racket back at eye level or slightly higher, and out away from your body. (Holding the throat of the racket with your non-hitting hand will help keep the racket head up on the backswing.) Maintain a straight, but not rigid, hitting arm and a fixed wrist, keeping in mind that your hips, thighs, and your upper body will supply most of the power you need.

When the racket is pointing to the back fence or slightly beyond, step out with your front foot and drop your racket, fixed wrist, and hitting hand approximately 12 inches below the intended point of impact. This will enable you to make a low-to-high forward motion as you shift your weight into the ball. When you lower your body, the throat of your racket should almost brush the back thigh going down to help ensure a natural lifting motion. The racket face should also be slightly turned down (approximately 30 degrees), facing the court, at the lowest point of your backswing.

Remembering that the loop swing must be continuous from the moment you begin the drop, come out of your low position by lifting up hard with your thighs and stomach muscles. Contact the ball 12 to 18 inches out in front of your body,

Rich in "racket back" position for backhand.

Rich drops his racket to 30 degrees below the intended point of impact with the ball. Normally the racket head is wrapped slightly around the back leg due to the bend in the wrist.

Rich shows the hitting point in front of the body, which normally finds the hitting elbow about a finger span from the body. Notice that the racket is parallel to the court and the racket head is perpendicular to the court.

The follow-through goes skyward, but in the direction of the intended target. We often call this position "A.T.A.," which stands for "Air the Armpits."

with your hitting arm fully extended and the racket face vertical. Then stretch your body out toward the target and up, while getting the feeling of your hips snapping into the ball and carrying out; don't let them pull you around. The lifting motion with the body is the subject of great debate, but when our research team digitizes the top players, it's quite evident that the most successful one-handed backhand players lift their body at almost the same upward angle as the racket is traveling. A major discussion point from the adversaries is that the body often arrives up ahead of the impact point. That is correct. When the body arrives slightly ahead of the impact point and abruptly stops, the racket continues on its same path with an even greater acceleration rate.

Your eyes should follow the ball as long as possible and remain fixed near the point of contact until your racket arm is pointed toward the target and skyward at about a 45-degree angle. You want to get down to the ball, and then stay over the ball as you come up — but don't stay down, or all the power for your shot will have to come from your arm. Lift up with your thighs and keep the racket going parallel (or in the direction of your intended target) to the net as long as you can. Though it's impossible to effect, think of hanging on to the ball — pretend that you're not going to let it off the strings — and this will help keep your racket face pointed toward the target. *Don't let anything pull you off on the horizontal.*

KEY ELEMENTS OF THE SWING

The Backswing

From a motor learning standpoint, it's important to note that when a player is able to buy an extra second, that same player's brain and central nervous system can unite to spend time focusing on placing the shot. When one is late, the result is simply an effort to get the ball back.

So remembering the forehand, react quickly and get your racket back immediately but don't let your hitting arm take a solo. Righthanders, cradle the throat of the racket lightly with the left hand as you turn back and this will keep both shoulders rotating as a unit. Leading with the left elbow going back — as long as you don't let the elbow drop — will also help keep the racket face on the ball.

If you turn your body properly, and maintain the appropriate fixed-wrist position, you don't have to make a big play on the backswing in order to hit with power. All you need is a short, efficient backswing with the hitting hand pointing no farther than perpendicular to the back fence. If your racket goes beyond that point, it should be due to your excessive body turn and not because you laid your wrist back. You can also bring your racket back farther, in order to conceal your shot or to apply excessive brush topspin. Thinking you can take a big backswing by simply playing with your wrist is one of the most common mistakes made on the backhand.

In fact, people worry so much about their backhand that they tend to increase the length of their swing instead of shortening it. When you take the hitting hand back too far, this pinches the racket against your body and you have to flick your wrist out to compensate. Your shoulder is a radial point and as you take the hitting arm back, the racket has a tendency to lift up, and even get higher than the approaching ball. Take a racket right now and test this for yourself.

Another persistent error on the backswing concerns the elbow of the hitting arm. When you bend this elbow at any point — instead of maintaining an extended arm — the racket face will suddenly point to the sky. This forces you to straighten out the elbow and use a lot of wrist action in order to get the racket into a correct position at impact. Most people, unfortunately, can't make this "adjustment," and thus their racket face is tilted back at impact, ready to produce a "sky ball."

Remember, too, how a quick, controlled backswing that allows you to wait for the ball will help prevent the problem of "deceleration-acceleration." Just as on the forehand, when the arm decelerates at the end of your backswing, the racket continues to accelerate. This produces wrist layback if you are not careful, and particularly if you are rushing to complete your swing. But when you "buy time" and fix the racket on the loop swing before letting it drop, then decleration-acceleration normally disappears.

Fighting to Get Low

Although I don't have the physiological research data to support this statement, I've found that the tennis racket does a funny thing to your legs: it locks your joints. How else to explain the fact that people can't bend their knees when they get a racket in their hand? They can sit down and eat lunch, and they can climb into the bathtub, but put them on a tennis court and their legs are like yardsticks. Even the racket seems to be held up by some invisible force. One voice inside keeps saying, "Get your body and racket down, dummy," while the other voice is arguing, "If I get lower than the ball, I'll miss it."

Nevertheless, you have to remember that making successful groundstrokes depends on your ability to bend your knees and drop the throat of the racket to your back thigh so that the racket head is below the intended point of impact. The lower you get, the easier it is to stay on line with your target, for you now have a natural pendulum movement, like the motion in throwing a bowling ball. Think, for instance, about getting low and bowling with the back side of your hitting hand.

Always try to get too low. Imagine that your hitting knuckles are falling and that they are going to touch the court. To realize just how much you must bend down, even for a ball at waist level, try my "sit-and-hit" drill, where you sit in a chair as your racket drops and your foot steps out to meet the ball (see page 60). Several other drills will help you learn what it means to get the throat of your racket down properly without simply loosening the wrist and dropping the racket head, as the average player seems to do. It is of great interest that in over fifty years of teaching tennis, I've never seen a player get too low on the backswing of the backhand.

1. Have a friend hold a stick at waist level or lower; then try to bring your racket under the stick as you make your move into the ball.

2. Righthanders, hold the back of your left hand against your left thigh and

Rich shows that you should seek the same flight pattern for a two-handed backhand as for a one-handed backhand.

Rich shows the most vulnerable position of the two-handed player who must hit on the run; he gains little support from the lower body to efficiently use the upper body.

stick out your fingers, then try to have the throat of your racket brush these fingers on the way down.

3. Righthanders, learn to make a perfect lefthander's forehand by cradling the throat of the racket with your left hand on the backswing. Then come down and have the left hand — still holding the racket — touch the back thigh. At this point release the left hand and the right arm will complete the swing.

Unfortunately, when people try to touch their back thigh going down, they cheat so much it's scary. They'll drop their racket two inches and ask expectantly, "Am I getting down?" That's why I've always wanted to invent a little sensor device that could be strapped to your thigh, so that when the hand cradling the racket on the backswing came down and touched the sensor, it would cry out, "You're the greatest!" and you would know that you were free to go forward and up. Plus, your ego would get a nice boost.

Timing the Racket's Fall

The idea of "working hard to swing easy" is even more important on the backhand than the forehand, since on the backhand you must contact the ball farther out in front of your body in order to hit with maximum power and accuracy. Therefore, the instant your opponent hits the ball, run to get in position with your racket already back. Even if the ball comes straight at you, get in the habit of turning back as fast as possible. Then it's only a matter of learning how to coordinate the lowering of your racket, your fixed wrist, and your knees.

When you bring the racket back you can delay the drop without any loss of power. But once you let it fall, keep the swing continuous, for the fall is what produces significant kinetic energy gains. If you drop the racket too soon, you'll lose the rhythm and power of the racket and body moving together into the ball; your only option will be to "arm" the ball over the net. If you let the racket fall too late, you'll be forced to swing horizontally just to get a piece of the ball.

Try to learn to time your drop by experimenting against a ball machine, or with a friend who will hit you 30 or 40 balls in a row. Only through repetition and

Isis uses a chair to check her knee bend. Note how she makes a three-point landing—her racket lowered, her body lowered, and her front foot out ahead to support her body's un-coiling. She then lifts up to contact the ball and provide the necessary lift. She completes her normal follow-through and feels what a real knee bend is like.

experimentation will you learn to sense where the ball must be before you can start your drop. One little experiment you can try is to hold your left hand behind your back as you swing at the ball. It doesn't matter what type of swing you use; eventually you'll have to encode a great number of variables to know when to begin the forward swing.

Contacting the Ball

Remember what I stressed earlier on the forehand, that to play this game with power and accuracy, you must go out to meet the ball. Be aggressive. Don't let the ball play you; don't back up out of hesitation or fear, because you will always be crowded and cramped trying to take your swing — and the closeness of the ball to your body will force a bent elbow, especially on the backhand. You can have the racket fairly close to your body and still make a hit. But when the ball comes closer than about three to four feet from your body (for adults), you're in deep trouble, my friend.

If you are always late contacting the ball, the most likely reason is an incorrect belief that you should hit the backhand the same distance from your body as the forehand. But the forehand can be contacted even with the front side because

the shoulder housing the hitting arm is on the back. In contrast, the one-handed backhand must be contacted farther out in front, when your hitting elbow is about six inches away from your body, because the hitting shoulder is closer to the net. This enables your hips to pull through on an inside-out axis while gaining the greatest amount of power from your thighs and rear end.

As your body moves into the ball, keep your head fixed and eyes down; try to see the ball at impact, even though this is visually impossible. When you feel the racket contact the ball, stay with your stroke — don't suddenly pull off the ball, or stop your follow-through, or jerk your head up to see where the ball is going. Remember, a fixed head serves two purposes: (1) it helps the hitter stop his upper body and causes the racket arm to accelerate, and (2) it helps ensure a consistent hit on the center of your strings. Some critics of the lifting motion argue that people tend to throw their head up or back when they lift, but you can keep it down and over the ball if you concentrate.

Footwork

Try to envision a baseball hitter striding forward into the ball, or a boxer stepping in to deliver his punch. You want to step out on your front foot as the racket drops, and then transfer your weight forward as you push your body up. If your front foot lands parallel to the net you'll risk twisting an ankle, and if you finish flat-footed you'll lose power. Nor do you want to let the back foot come past the front foot, for your hip will spin you around on the horizontal. Stepping across with your front foot also leads to a horizontal swing and a shot that is pulled off to the side. If you are righthanded, think of stepping toward the left net post with the toes of your front foot.

Generating Your Power with the Lift

Stand in an open area and watch how your body segments work when they uncoil. The knees will arrive first, followed by the hips, followed by the upper body and finally the arm and racket arrive. This is often called the "kinetic chain." Each segment contributes to the speed of the next segment up the chain. I have found that the lifting motion of the body is almost a reminder that there is an important uncoiling motion that adds to power. When the last large muscle segment arrives and abruptly stops, the racket arm speeds up, like snapping a towel. By themselves, the legs don't provide much rackethead speed, but when they're used to activate the kinetic chain, they play a major role.

In fact, you don't need a strong arm to hit a hard backhand. Your arm's job is to hold the racket steady in the proper position. If you can bend your knees and get your racket low, then the rising motion of your body will supply all the power you need. When your body uncoils in an upward fashion, the racket picks up speed. And when your body abruptly stops at the end of the lift, the racket arm and racket pick up even greater speed, due to the sudden deceleration of the upper body. When I worked with the Argentine Tennis Federation in 1967, I learned that you don't even need to hold the doggone racket to play this game. I had a metalsmith build me a belt holster that could hold my racket straight out from my thigh with a vertical racket face. Then I stood just inside the baseline with my arms folded and had somebody throw a ball to my backhand. I would go down, come up while uncoiling, and hit the ball over the net, just by using the power initiated in my legs.

This was the key to Don Budge's backhand. He played with his thighs, hips, and stomach while his hitting arm followed in sync with his body uncoiling abruptly. After watching him play in Detroit decades ago, I spent the next three or four weeks trying to emulate his stroke. I would go out on the court, stand in front of a fence, toss the ball up, and let it bounce. Then, keeping my racket arm stiff while bending my knees, I would just lift with my thighs and rear end and hit the ball into the fence. Gradually I would move back and strive for a little more rhythm, always using my body and doing little with my racket arm. Within a month I had my basic backhand.

You can learn to time your lift in much the same way. Hit against a fence, use a ball machine, or have a friend stand off to the side about 15 feet away and bounce the ball to your backhand. At first, just try to relax and get the feeling of the proper stroke in slow motion. Use your body to supply the power and see how slowly you can go and still lift the ball over the net. You'll find that you can swing very slowly and still hit the ball pretty darn hard — if you learn to utilize the power in the lower half of your body.

Let your swing flow and just get the rhythm. Don't worry about where the ball goes, or even that you keep missing it. Try to exaggerate. Come right off the ground when you lift — but don't lunge — so that you understand what it really means to lift. On your forward motion, turn your rear end into the ball, then lift out toward the net and up. Stretch those stomach muscles and come up on your toes as you hit through the ball; make the calves and thighs really work for you — feel them pull you up.

I can't emphasize enough how important it is to let your body come up as you hit. Yet people going through the tennis college are always trying to fake us out. They shout, "Lift! LIFT!" thinking they've really stretched out, when all they've actually done is step out and land flat-footed. Good coaches, however, won't be fooled by grunts and groans. They simply watch your rear end to see whether or not you lift. So don't get lazy down there. Get way down and then go way up. I once saw of a film of Budge in which he took a ball just inches off the ground, yet still finished up on his toes on the follow-through.

The more you insist on staying down, the stronger your arm must be. Françoise Durr was virtually the only top player I've ever seen who stayed down on the ball on the backhand, and she had an unorthodox grip to begin with. Plus, she was one of the strongest players off-balance I've come across. But nearly all the top players realize that you bail yourself out of a hole with your rear end, not your arm. They know that by learning to use the power in your thighs you can take a low-bouncing ball and still hit it over the net with power.

A final point to remember about timing your lift is that you must have your body and racket moving forward and up together. If they move in the same direction and in sync — and the racket head is vertical at impact — you can take a ball right against your body and still bang it over the net. Don't try to make last-minute adjustments in your swing; just pull the elbow back a little bit, shorten the radius

The hitter shows that the racket head can drop below the wrist level on the forehand while maintaining a vertical racket face. But the one-handed backhand player is wiser to keep the racket parallel to the ground, which requires more muscle recruitment. The ring finger can be used as a guide to direct the shot.

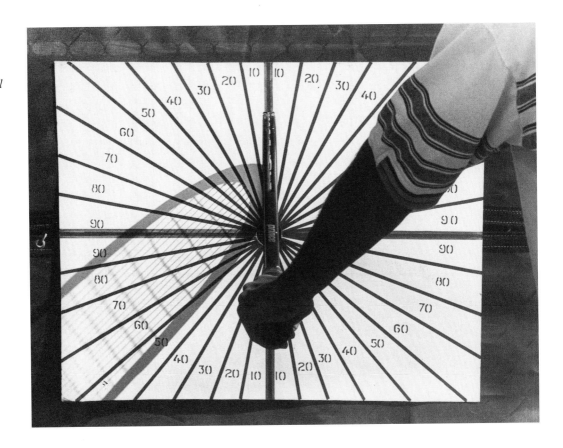

Learning to position the wrist correctly will place the racket in a vertical position.

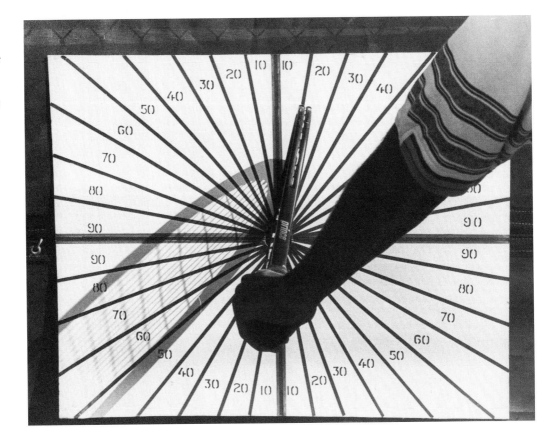

However, it only takes the slightest change in the wrist position to move the racket ten degrees from vertical. A ten-degree racket-face change can vary a shot by many feet.

of your swing, and thrust yourself up. But if your racket is up and the body is down, or vice versa, then you don't have a prayer.

All my tennis life I've heard the words, "Stay down with the ball." Yet when we digitize the body with a three-dimensional system, the best players lift their body. The engineers explain that when a body is going down, and an arm is going up, the effect is the resultant, which is a force somewhere between those two vectors. And when a body stays fixed while "down with the ball," only the arm is left to hit the ball.

The Inside-Out Concept

Getting low with your body and racket and lifting up with your thighs will be useless if you don't learn to hit through the ball with an inside-out motion that keeps the racket on line with your target. This is no less important on the backhand than it is on the forehand (see page 62).

To visualize what the inside-out motion means on the backhand, stand facing a fence while practicing the forward swing. Try keeping your racket a couple of inches from the fence as long as possible from the impact point. The feeling is that you're being pulled into the fence and that is the "inside-out" experience.

Also try to get the feeling of turning your back hip into the ball, and then carrying that hip out toward your target and up. With your body coiled at the end of your backswing, think about turning the hip "in and then out"— not in and around on a horizontal plane. Focus on your lower body and make your hips and knees do all the work. When the pros get caught on their back foot, for example, they snap their hips through and still hit with power. But this requires getting low and then pushing the hips forward while carrying them out toward the target. If you swing on a level plane, inertia is going to drive your hips around horizontally and it will be difficult if not impossible to keep the racket from following.

Another problem occurs if you pull your rear shoulder back, or lean back, as you are making your lift. This pulls the racket off-target. Instead, the rear shoulder must go out toward your target in sync with your hips and the knuckles of your hitting hand. Turning this shoulder inside-out enables you to lengthen the follow-through.

The Crucial Fixed Wrist

Just as with the forehand (except for the prestretch forehand), if you ever want your backhand to be a pal under pressure, don't horse around with your wrist. Leave it fixed and your arm extended throughout the swing, while your body supplies all the rhythm and power you need. Remember, you don't want to make any adjustments with the wrist in order to produce a vertical racket head at impact — unless you think that you can win by relying on "touch." But as I warned you wrist players earlier, most of you will never know from day to day what kind of player you are because the fluctuations in your game will be too great. There are simply too many variables as it is, and to add many more with a big wrist action is to make the game almost impossible to play.

If you buy my rationale for a fixed-wrist position, you first must know when you have the appropriate wrist position at the beginning of your swing. Using the same drill as on the forehand, stand with your right side against a fence. Place the racket flush against the fence, about waist high, with the racket head slightly higher than the level of your wrist. Then move away from the fence until your elbow is a finger's length from your body, and your arm is extended. Now leave the wrist alone because you're perfectly placed for a backhand. Get the sensation of how the wrist feels in this position because that's where you want to leave it on the backswing and through impact for the rest of your life.

When you take the racket back from this beginning position, the racket face should be pointed down at the end of your backswing (approximately 30 degrees) and you will probably think, "This crummy shot is going under the net." But if you keep the wrist locked as you complete your swing, you'll see that the racket becomes absolutely vertical at impact.

Thus, you want to concentrate on keeping the racket head slightly hooded (facing down) as you take it back, with your hitting knuckles pointed to the court as you reach the bottom of your backswing. The natural tendency is for these knuckles to be facing up on the backswing because the elbow bends, which is why many players end up adjusting their swing to hit with underspin. But your goal, on a drive, is to hit with topspin, which means you must push those knuckles down as you draw the racket back. Have the left hand help out by pushing down on the throat of the racket. You can lift with confidence and hit the ball as hard as you want with topspin if you know your racket is going to be straight up and down at impact, and your forward and upward swing is nearly vertical, as was true with Bjorn Borg. Playing with a fixed wrist and an extended hitting arm will give you this assurance. If the ball starts going past the baseline, just push the knuckles down more and lift on a more vertical angle.

Even though what feels wrong on the backswing is actually right, most people go for comfort. Their wrist is often perfect or just slightly off when they start their backswing. But then their wrist has a natural tendency to lay back when the elbow breaks, which causes the racket to turn under. These people must now snap their wrist forward in order to produce a vertical racket face at impact — a "touch" play that helps distinguish them from the champions. This inability to judge the amount of wrist roll is one reason why they also produce such an interesting variety of backhands — into the net, over the back fence, or bloopers to their opponent.

As you concentrate on maintaining a fixed-wrist position, don't forget to let your body turn the racket back. Most people are lazy with their bodies and thus they bring their racket back by simply bending the hitting elbow or laying the wrist back, which leads to a "slapping" motion as the elbow leads the way into ball contact. This is one of the most common problems on the backhand and can be corrected by maintaining an extended hitting arm while pivoting with the body.

Unfortunately, most losers will change their stroke to accommodate an improper racket head, rather than changing their body movements to accommodate a properly placed racket head. These players think they can stand stiff-kneed and swing with a low-to-high motion by simply loosening their wrist to drop the racket head, and then beveling the racket face — instead of getting their body low and lifting up with a vertical racket face that is level with, or slightly higher than, the level of their wrist. As a result, they must scoop the ball over the net rather than lifting it up and over with the power and accuracy of topspin.

Another example is the player who tries to lift with his body from low to high, but his shots keep going out because he has an improper wrist position. Yet instead of finding the correct wrist position to accommodate his proper stroke pattern, he immediately changes the nature of his backswing and swings from high to low to accommodate his incorrect wrist bend.

I want you to swing at a normal speed — with a low-to-high motion — and if your wrist position is proper the ball should land inside your opponent's court or very near the outside boundaries. You should be able to see the topspin arc effect take place and this should give you the confidence to make a slight wrist adjustment or grip change to give you the consistency you want. But if you don't have this confidence, and a willingness to experiment in making corrections, then you'll simply leave the racket alone — in its incorrect position — and try to change your swing. When you start to "choke," for instance, you will start leveling off your swing instead of lifting up from low to high.

So get the racket set perfectly, keep your arm and wrist fixed, and work on achieving the proper body movements. Your body can be absolutely perfect but if the racket is slightly off at impact, you take gas. If your racket is perfect, on the other hand, you can do a lot of crazy things with your body and still make the hit.

The Follow-Through

If you can remember "A.T.A." (Air the Armpits) and "knuckles" as you swing, this should help give you a greater respect and the proper imagery for developing the correct follow-through.

"Air the Armpits" reminds you to extend your hitting arm upward after you contact the ball until it's pointed toward the sky, not a side court. Don't hold the arm back — let inertia carry it up. Keep telling yourself, "The stroke is never over," and when you think you've gone far enough, go a little farther. You have all this energy input going forward and up, so don't suddenly let it end. Think about forming a little archway with your arm and the racket and literally walking underneath.

Moreover, "as your knuckles go, so goes your racket head." Thus, you want to try and carry your knuckles out toward the target and upward. Don't jab or cut across or swat at the ball, and don't fall back. Hit through the ball and go all the way up. If you can do this, and the racket head is vertical at impact, then you're going to come pretty close to an accurate placement.

Put me to the test on an empty court. Stand near the baseline, gently throw the ball up in the air, and let it bounce. Take your backswing and then keep your knuckles on an absolute straight line to the target and see how close the ball comes. Even after making contact, keep your knuckles going toward the sky. There are two basic variables on every shot: width and length, and if you can make your knuckles go inside-out and face your target all the way from impact on, you will control 50 percent of your backhand. All you have to worry about then is length.

Yet most people yank their knuckles off target by pulling across their bodies, and with only 19.1 degrees margin, they die young.

A third little guidance checkpoint can be the thumb of your hitting hand, if you hold the Eastern grip with the thumb placed behind the racket handle. Try to visualize the thumb following out toward the target, the same as with the knuckles. You may even want to make a dot on your thumb and then try not to let that dot come off the target line as you play.

A Follow-Through Checklist

Spend time testing your own backhand: when rallying or during a match, freeze on the follow-through and take a look at your body, not where the ball ends up. Here are some points to look for:

1. Can you lift your back foot off the ground without falling? If not, you haven't transferred your weight forward to the front foot.

2. If your front foot is perfectly flat or your knees aren't straightened out, you didn't lift up with your thighs and rear end.

3. You should be able to drop a plumb line from your front shoulder to your front foot.

4. Righthanders, your racket should be pointed slightly to the left of your target if you have swung properly with an inside-out motion.

5. Did you A.T.A.? On the forehand, a checkpoint is your arm coming up under your chin. But your arm is going away from your body on the backhand, so to see if you've really stretched your arm up properly, it should be pointed to about 1 or 2 o'clock. Some top players, in fact, will be literally vertical, with their arm pointed skyward.

6. Your upper body should finish with your front shoulder slightly facing the net, as your eyes remain fixed on the point of impact.

7. Moving only your shoulder joint, let your hitting arm fall back to where you think you contacted the ball, then see if the racket face is vertical. If not, you haven't maintained a fixed-wrist position, or you must correct your grip.

8. If you consistently pull across your body on the follow-through, the problem can usually be traced to either a high backswing or getting too close to the ball. By remaining too high on the backswing, you allow centrifugal force to drive you around on the horizontal, which makes it impossible to swing out toward your target. Letting the ball get too close generally forces the hitting elbow to bend, with the racket following the elbow around. When you swing on the horizontal or let the ball get too close, you must throw your front hip back in order to make contact, which results in a pulled shot.

9. If your racket head is vertical at impact, and you are hitting with topspin, but the ball keeps going in the net, then you must get your racket lower on the backswing in order to produce more of a lifting motion. If the ball is going too long, you need to increase the angle of your low-to-high motion so that greater topspin will bring the ball down quicker. The crucial point is: don't change your racket head to make these corrections — only the angle at which you swing.

The volleyer assumes a position midway between the potential range of an opponent's shot. The cross-court shot shown by the dotted line is 65'9" long and is a very difficult passing shot to hit.

Rich shows that there's only a slight difference (19.1 degrees) in the position of the racket at impact to hit a down-the-line backhand (left) and a cross-court backhand.

BACKHAND TACTICS

If your backhand is an embarrassment to you, even among loved ones, your first goal must be to focus on the problem and not try to hide it by always running around to play forehands. The longer you attempt to cover up a lousy backhand, the more you ingrain your fear of the shot — and fear inhibits learning.

You're probably thinking, "Yeah, but I see the pros run around backhands to hit a forehand all the time." This is true, except they do it for entirely different reasons.

First of all, when your opponent is rushing the net, you want to hit the ball

with topspin so it will go over the net and down at his feet. This forces him to bend low and lift the ball, which produces a defensive shot and thus an easier volley to handle. If you can topspin your backhand when an oppponent is attacking the net, great. But most backhands tend to produce high balls because most people tend to hit them with underspin. Forehands, however, have a more natural tendency to brush the ball and it's easier to keep the racket face on a vertical plane, which facilitates topspin. Thus, when top players have a choice they usually opt for their forehand.

Second, you can be late on a forehand and still hit with topspin. If you are late on the backhand — where the ball must be contacted farther out in front of your body — you can only underspin. That's why, on service returns especially, you will see the top players try desperately to run around backhands because they can be late and still whip off a topspin forehand that makes the ball dip down at the feet of the onrushing server.

Topspin vs. Underspin

Contrary to what some instructors preach, hitting the backhand with underspin (or "slice," as it is incorrectly labeled) is not only a tough play but, except for the approach shot, is a defensive weapon at best. Whereas topspin enables you to play aggressively on any surface, underspin is a delicate "touch" shot that only talented players can hit well with any consistency, and only then through experience, practice, and concentration. I don't underestimate the value of underspin, but the only aggressive player I've seen who consistently uses underspin effectively on the backhand side has been Steffi Graf. But if your goal is to simply get the ball back deep, with little muscular effort, then underspin is your shot.

If you concentrate on learning to hit with topspin, you can slug the ball almost as hard as you want and still be safe; when you start hitting long you simply increase the vertical angle of your swing to produce greater topspin. But the minute you begin to favor underspin, by bringing your racket from high to low, you not only must deal with the five variables I discussed earlier (page 32), you also lose some tactical advantages.

Still, people talk about underspin being a reliable shot. Even Jack Kramer used to get on me a little bit. He would say, "Work on that chip backhand, kid, because it's pretty safe to hit." But it's only easy if you have the touch. When people try to hit that shot hard under pressure, it often goes into the net or over the fence.

Another virtue of topspin is that you can hit short or long — on any court surface — and hit it hard. Underspin doesn't give you this flexibility. Very few people can drive underspin on the backhand, nor can they hit short-angled shots with enough speed to get them past a person at the net. Remember, balls hit hard with underspin have a tendency to travel 70 feet or more, and the distance from the baseline singles corner to your opponent's service-line corner on the diagonal is only 65'9" (see page 14). To "own" that shot you must be able to hit the ball with topspin and bring it down inside of 66 feet. Hard-hit underspin will simply not come down in time. You can try, but the ball will either sail out or come so close to your opponent that he has an easy put-away volley at the net. For years, most of us believed that Ken Rosewall had the world's finest underspin backhand. Yet, in the late 1970s when we did a three-dimensional study of Ken's underspin backhand, it turned out that he actually hit "flat" shots. I remember telling Kramer that we had just spent a lot of money analyzing Rosewall's underspin backhand and before I could finish the sentence, Jack said, "What underspin backhand? 'Muscles' hits flat!" Indeed, on Rosewall's best underspin shot of the day, the ball rotated only 12 times from one end of the court to the other.

Now, these figures may seem unimportant to you if your opponent simply plays from the baseline and never tries to rush the net. In fact, underspin enables you to hit the ball deep without swinging hard, and by slowing the ball up it pro-

vides you with more time to regain position while possibly upsetting your opponent's rhythm. However, if you try to improve and you begin stepping up in competition, you are going to play people who rush the net on every short ball and who try to hit an approach shot or volley to your underspin backhand. In that case you have only three options, and just two are sound: (1) lob over their heads, or (2) pass them down the line. An underspin backhand cross-court is not a sound option. Thus, you give away one-third of your opportunities.

I remember watching Stan Smith lose to Pancho Gonzales in Las Vegas about 1970. Stan's biggest problem that day was that he was chipping his backhand — hitting with underspin — and the wind was blowing his cross-court shots out. I thought, "Why doesn't someone teach Stan to topspin off the backhand? Then he could control the shot much easier and he could pass people like Gonzales instead of having to play the ball defensively."

Well, about three days later I was at the Los Angeles Tennis Club and Stan was out on the court like a beginner, throwing the ball up and working on a topspin backhand. He would let the ball bounce, take his racket back at eye level, then drop down with his thighs and lift up as he hit the ball. Once he had that shot under control, he had the final weapon he needed in order to become the world's number one ranked player by 1973. In fact, after Stan won the World Championship Tennis title in 1975, Arthur Ashe pointed out that he now hated to play him because Stan had learned to topspin his backhand cross-court, which made him lethal all over the court.

Wayne helps his sister Isis with her loop swing. She starts above Wayne's racket ... then goes behind his racket and down to approximately 30 degrees below the intended point of impact ... and then comes back up for the hit.

Developing a Passing Shot

Another technique that will help make you famous on the backhand is your ability to hit the ball on a straight line when you want to. If you can drive the ball down the line as your opponent rushes the net or when he (or she) has already gained control, you can take away his tactical advantage. You either win the point outright, or you pull him so wide that unless he volleys strongly you have a wide-open court for your next shot. Moreover, when your opponent knows that you can pass down the line, he must play you honestly: he can't "cheat" to the middle of the court to cut off the cross-court backhand that is virtually automatic if you can only swing on a horizontal plane.

Developing the vertical, low-to-high swing that enables you to pass down the line has been the main goal of this chapter. You have only a 24-inch margin of safety in order to hit a good passing shot between your opponent and the singles sideline, and you'll rarely ram it down this narrow alley by swinging horizontally. You may think you're talented enough to pull off this shot by just making a little "adjustment" in your swing, but first put yourself to the test.

This is my favorite drill to help you develop the proper inside-out swing, and to have you appreciate how difficult it is to hit backhand passing shots unless you swing from low to high with an inside-out motion. Mark off a 24-inch "alley"

down the singles sideline (with tennis ball cans, for example) and try to place every shot inside the lane. Be happy if you can manage to beat yourself in a little game where you bounce the ball and hit it down the line, giving yourself a point when your shot lands in the alley and a point against yourself when it doesn't. Drills like this will help you realize the importance of owning an inside-out motion where your hips, shoulders, knuckles, and hitting arm all follow through toward the target.

Hitting with Underspin

If after all my arguing you still want to pursue an offensive underspin backhand, let me clear up three common myths. First, nobody has a "slice" backhand. A ball hit with slice is actually rotating on a horizontal axis, such as in a slice serve. Second, you don't hit "under the ball." If the racket were under the ball at impact, the shot would go up into the sky. And third, the wrist is in a fixed position at impact if you take the proper stroke.

Most players who hit with underspin have less bevel at the impact point than we suspected. For most players, there was a bevel of 10 to 20 degrees, but what gave underspin to the ball was the high-to-low swing of the hitter. The only time you actually want to try to hit "under" the ball is on trick shots, where you want to impart such severe underspin that the ball will bounce backward when it hits your opponent's court. But first win the Nationals, then you can worry about this shot.

A final point to remember when hitting with underspin is that although you strike down on the ball with a high-to-low stroke, you must take the racket right back up after impact if you hope to be ready for the next shot. Generally, you want a stroke pattern that resembles the high-low-high curve of an archer's bow.

The Two-Handed Backhand

The first two-handed backhand I ever saw was in the 1940s and it was owned by John Bromwich of Australia. Chris Evert and Bjorn Borg helped start the craze we see today, with the world now about evenly divided between one-handers and two-handers.

We used to think that hitting two-handed was made for shorter and weaker players, but Jimmy Connors, Monica Seles, Michael Chang, and Martina Hingis have taught us a real lesson. Good two-handed backhand hitters can return hard serves with great accuracy and power as the second hand steadies the racket. Indeed, this stroke may give you the aggressive, reliable backhand you dream about — providing you understand your own physical capabilities.

What we coaches are finding is that there are individuals who will always have difficulty hitting with two hands and vice versa. Jon Niednagel's "brain typing" concept, which states that some individuals are wired genetically with a preference for fine motor movements and others are wired for gross motor movements, appears to have credibility. Those who are wired for natural gross motor movements seem to be quite comfortable coiling their large muscle groups and adapting to the two-handed backhand, while those with fine motor preferences seem to do better using primarily their forearm to hit a one-handed backhand. Coaches everywhere tell me that they have experienced a great deal of frustration trying to get a young player to coil his body for a sound two-handed backhand, only to find that the player can make a minimal coil and yet suddenly explode with his loose forearms. And then along comes another student who just loves to coil her body and picks up the two-hander in minutes.

Also, you need to have more than a little natural ability and coordination not only to play well with two hands, but to convert from one hand in the first place. The most important requirement is a supple and flexible upper body.

After becoming familiar with these factors, if you still want to try to hit with two hands, give it a try. Most players can't control the ball with one hand, so if you can learn control with two hands, I say great. When starting out, try to realize that what we're actually talking about is a two-handed lefthanded forehand on the backhand side (for you righthanders). The left hand and the left side are dominant as you strike the ball. Thus you should practice learning to hit a lefthanded forehand, for this is exactly what you need to achieve with a two-handed backhand.

You should hold an Eastern forehand grip with the left hand, but you have two options with your regular hitting hand. If you're fairly talented and comfortable on both sides, and you're pretty sure you'll stick with the two-handed stroke, continue to hold a regular Eastern forehand grip. Then you don't have to switch grips between strokes. But if you don't feel natural hitting from the left side, and you're undecided about two hands, you should hold an Eastern backhand, because the chances are good that you will eventually revert to a one-handed backhand, and you will thus already have the proper grip.

One early argument against using two hands was that it appeared to reduce the reach you have. It is true that you reduce your reach by half the width of your body if you're reaching for a low ball way out in front of you toward the net, but, ironically, the two-handed backhand has a longer radius on normal hits than a one-handed backhand. Try this experiment. Hold your racket for a one-handed backhand right at the point where you normally contact the ball. Measure the distance from the impact point to the nearest point on your body. Then, do the same thing with a two-handed backhand and you will see that the radius is a few inches longer.

Therefore, reach isn't the major issue, it's balance. A one-handed hitter can move through the ball quite easily without paying much attention to where each foot is. But a two-handed player is dependent upon his legs serving as stabilizers for the upper body to uncoil. That's why smart players try to make two-handers hit on the run. It's a difficult task — hitting on the run — but players are getting increasingly better at doing so.

BACKHAND DRILLS

1. You need to keep your body and racket arm synchronized for better rhythm, power, and a shorter swing. To see if you're doing this, and to practice the proper movements on the loop swing, try the racket-against-the-body drill described on page 71. Place the butt end of your racket on the shoulder of your hitting

arm and then go through the swing: turn back, drop down, go forward and up. Try the same thing with the racket on your front hip. Then use two rackets at once, one held in perfect hitting position and the other held against the front shoulder. As you take your swing, the two rackets will remain nearly the same distance apart and will make identical stroke patterns — if your body and hitting arm are properly synchronized. As a matter of fact, in a study we did on Andre Agassi, his center of gravity made a miniature loop swing which closely resembled the racket's flight pattern.

2. The left hand is basically submissive for most one-handed players. They tend to forget it's even there or what to do with it. But you can give it a split personality by telling yourself, "I'm going to learn a forehand with my left hand." First, have your left hand practice a forehand stroke by itself: take it back, down, forward, and up, remembering the rule on the forehand that "as the palm goes, so goes the racket." Then cradle the throat of the racket with your left hand as you begin your backswing and practice making that same motion. Let go with the left hand when it reaches the back thigh at the lowest point of your backswing. Making a perfect forehand stroke pattern with your left hand will help your right hand make a perfect backhand. This also forces you to pivot properly with your upper body.

3. If you can learn to swing with your body, you can have a weak arm and still hold your own on the backhand. But to hit the ball consistently on the center of your strings, and to hit with power, you need strong extensor muscles. These muscles lie along the top of your forearm and are crucial in maintaining a fixed wrist and a firm, extended racket arm throughout the swing.

Fortunately, you can develop these muscles without investing in a set of barbells. Just put a cover on your racket and practice taking your backhand swing. The wind resistance against the racket cover will give you good tension on the extensor muscles, and meanwhile you are practicing your stroke. Combine this with the "sit-and-hit" chair drill (see page 60) and you will strengthen all the muscles you need on the backhand. As your arm gets stronger, place one ball inside the racket cover, then two, then three, until you get up to six. Pretty soon you'll be able to hold that racket fixed the way it should be, without any flopping about by the wrist. By the way, some physicians have questioned my use of the term "extensor muscles." Whatever term you wish to use, go ahead, but we're talking about those muscles needed to extend your arm while holding and swinging a tennis racket.

Approach Shots, Volleys, Overheads, and Lobs

I F YOU WANT TO HIT GROUNDSTROKES from the baseline all day, that's fine. You'll get a tan, and you may even be fantastic — as long as your opponent agrees to play the same type of game. But you don't always have this choice in tournament play. You can't say, "Sorry, I don't play against anyone who attacks the net." Therefore, if you're serious about challenging good players, you must learn how to work your way up to the net and how to close off the point once you get there. You must learn how to anticipate the short ball, how to rush in and hit an approach shot, how to volley, how to lob, and how to hit an overhead.

Developing these strokes and an aggressive mental approach will enable you to thrive between the baseline and the net, instead of treating that area as no-man's-land. Plus, you'll realize how much more fun and challenging tennis can be when you venture out from the security of your baseline.

THE APPROACH SHOT

An approach shot is any shot utilized to gain or approach the net, either after the ball has bounced (an approach groundstroke) or while it's still in the air (an approach volley). Normally you will hit this shot near the service line, which is sort of your halfway house between the baseline and the net. Most approach shots are set up by an opponent's weak groundstrokes, but in beginning and intermediate tennis, many first serves and nearly all second serves present perfect approach-shot opportunities.

For some reason, the approach shot is commonly overlooked or downplayed, but I feel it's the third biggest shot in tennis. First comes the serve, which puts the ball in play, and then the service return, which determines where the point goes

At the baseline, the hitter sees an opportunity to get to the net. He chooses to hit the ball with a slight underspin to keep the ball low into his opponent's court (even though flat, hard drives actually stay lower than underspin if hit on the same trajectory). This will force his opponent to hit "up" and give him a higher volley. A fast start on the approach shot is also important.

The player hits forward with the racket face turned slightly upward and is swinging in a small "banana-like" pattern. He finishes with his racket head high, which places it in a perfect position to volley. It's important to run through the shot so that the racket head remains smooth. Stopping, while hitting the balls, forces the racket head down and places the hitter too far back from the net.

from there. But then comes the approach shot, the "bread-and-butter" play in tournament tennis and a psychological influence on nearly every point. In today's faster play, this shot now acquires an even greater importance.

In good tennis, the reason you want to work so hard on forehands and backhands — and keeping the ball deep — is that you never want to be the first person to hit a short ball. A short ball enables your opponent to come in, hit an approach shot, and take the net, while you are left with three difficult options: lob over his head, hit a passing shot down the line or cross-court, or try to give him a new navel. Whatever you choose to do, the pressure is now on you to execute. In fact, whoever owns the net will control the point nearly every time in pro tennis — something we witnessed in the 1997 U.S. Open when Australia's Patrick Rafter relentlessly attacked the net behind his approach shot and came away with the championship. Only a handful of players in history have been able to push their opponents around from the baseline, where you can only run a person three steps either way, but up near the net you can angle the ball sharply away from the fastest opponent around.

Unfortunately, many players don't realize the strategic benefits of gaining the net. If they do, and they want to be aggressive, they generally don't have the weapons to get them to the net — meaning strong, fast legs and an approach shot. And if they somehow reach the net, they usually lack the weapon they need to win the point or defend themselves — a volley. Thus I find that most people tend to react defensively rather than offensively when the ball is hit; the closer they get to the net, the greater their anxiety levels. The ball is coming faster and they have less time to react. As a result, if they run in to hit a short ball, they then either try to retreat to their baseline stronghold or they plunge ahead, saying, "Here goes nothing," which is generally true since they don't know how to volley.

Instead of getting caught in this mental trap, make yourself realize that when you get the first short ball you have been given a gigantic opportunity, and that the closer you get to the net, the happier you should be. Most points are so short that you can't afford to let your opponent get off the hook by hitting short balls while you camp at the baseline. Unless you're convinced that you can outlast your opponent from the baseline, you have to learn to attack the net at every opportunity. If he hits patty-cake second serves, never stay back — intimidate him by always moving in, hitting your approach shot, and then taking the net.

Finding Your "Short Ball Range"

Before you can start charging the net, you must learn your "short ball range"— that area on the court where you can hit an approach shot to your opponent and reach a position halfway between the service line and the net as, or before, the ball is on your opponent's racket. You can find this radius by having a friend yell, "Now," as he contacts your practice approach shot, at which point you should be in the desired position just described.

Once you know your short ball range, walk around it and get a feel for it. During a match, don't rush in to hit your approach shot unless you see that the ball is going to land in this radius. Otherwise you'll end up attacking balls that are actu-

Rich hits his approach shot with the back foot moving in front of the front foot. He then hits the same shot with the back foot coming behind the front foot. Many players feel this is a better-balanced movement, but it does create a slightly slower move to the net.

ally too deep, and you will still be running to your position near the net as your opponent hits his return. You'll spend the day trying to hit shots off your toes or saluting those that go whistling by as you run forward.

The Stroke

When you see a short ball coming, work to get a quick jump forward and to have good body balance while on the run. As you approach the ball, turn sideways to the net, but don't "break stride" or stop in order to hit it. Your feet are never in the same position on the approach shot, so don't worry about a standard hitting position — it's the rhythm that you seek.

Keep the racket head high, at about eye level, with your arm and wrist fixed. Take only a short backswing and hit through the ball with a slight high-to-low-to-high motion and a slight racket bevel in order to produce underspin. The low trajectory makes the ball stay low when it hits and forces your opponent to bend down for his return. Keep the racket strings on target throughout your stroke and just make a little shoulder turn with a down-and-up loop. Your body moving forward will supply all the power you need.

Underspin can be achieved by hitting slightly downward with the racket beveled a few degrees while swinging from a high-to-low-to-high pattern that re-

The approach shot is not an easy stroke to master. There's a definite "touch" involved that requires long hours of intensive practice. But if you can learn to hit that baby deep and low — preferably to your opponent's backhand — you are going to be deadly at the net. The following are some drills that will sharpen your approach shot and help you evaluate your stroke:

1. If you think you already "own" this shot, quit talking big and see how you fare against targets. Set up tennis cans in those four-foot-by-four-foot corners inside your opponent's baseline and sidelines. Then stand at your baseline and have a friend or a ball machine land balls around the service line, so that you can run in and try to stroke the ball into a corner. It's a humiliating feeling to see how far your shots land from the cans, and to realize you can't guide the ball the way you think. But it's a great drill to make you conscious of keeping the ball deep. You can also set up cans in all four corners and then rally with a friend. On every short ball, attack and hit an approach shot and see who's the first to knock over a can.

2. Using that four-foot radius will help you know if you are playing with your wrist. People who use the wrist on this shot will hit an occasional good shot, but when they miss, the variations are great. People who play with a fixed wrist are not as wild.

3. If you want to practice your approach shot under match-like conditions, challenge the person at the club who tries to overpower his first serve (although it rarely goes in) and then hits a meek second serve. This is where you always want to attack and hit your approach shot. But don't give your intentions away. You can't go up to the person and say, "Let's play a match — I want to practice attacking you." Be nice and the person will think, "Gee, they're finally recognizing my talent around here."

4. Most players feel that if they can't look at their target, they can't hit it, and thus they fail to concentrate on simply watching the ball come into their racket. So try this little drill to prove that if you have average peripheral vision, you don't need to look directly at your opponent's baseline corners as you swing. Righthanders, hold a ball in your hand at the point where you normally contact your approach shot, and with your eyes focused on the ball, point a finger to either corner. Then look up and see if your finger is pointed accurately. If it is, you know you can relax and keep your eye on the ball, not your target.

Two players hit their backhand approach shot from the same position and at the same time. Jay's back foot moved in front of his front foot in a running manner and takes him substantially ahead of Beau.

sembles the shape of a banana, or bow. One can have an excessive high-to-low movement, but the racket face must be open proportionately to guarantee that the ball clears the net and lands deep inside your opponent's court. The steeper the downward hitting angle, the more open the racket head must be, and this requires greater precision.

Just on all your other strokes (except the serve and the overhead), don't horse around with your wrist. Leave it fixed throughout your swing and let your body and racket arm do the work. You can't let the wrist go soft, or roll over, or lay back if you hope to have the racket meet the ball squarely. Try to have the arm only slightly bent as you approach the ball so that it can make the play as a fixed unit. By fixing the racket head, you can make some fairly large movements with your body without affecting the flight of the ball. But a slight wrist turn makes a giant exaggeration. One reason Jimmy Connors has always had such great consistency on his approach shots and volleys is that he locks his wrist and his racket head and then makes the play with his body. The racket doesn't turn in his hands, which ensures consistency as the racket head comes through the ball. But the average player fixes

his body and then turns the wrist under to supply underspin. Your body has some large muscle groups and they don't adversely affect the racket face as does your wrist.

Footwork

Although most people are taught to stop as they hit their approach shot, I feel this destroys the rhythm that you seek and your ability to volley effectively at the net. In fact, I've seldom seen a pro stop and hit this shot unless he is a typical clay court player. But if you contact that ball out in front — where you are supposed to — then you can run right through as you hit and move into position for your volley. (Another reason I don't want you to stop as you hit is the matter of deceleration-acceleration. When you suddenly stop running, your upper body continues to move forward and down, while your racket arm goes up to keep your balance. The result is generally an approach shot that is pulled down into the net.)

Two stories come to mind immediately. The first involved Arthur Ashe and Stan Smith while we were shooting an instructional video at my tennis college in the early 1980s. I suggested that we play devil's advocate and identify any pro player who preferred to stop on the approach shot and volley. None of us could

come up with a name. The second story involved another video session in 1996 with Jack Kramer and Pancho Segura. Both of these great players said that they normally had better net position than many of today's players because they "ran through" their approach shots rather than stopping to hit.

After hitting your approach shot, keep moving forward to the side of the center stripe to which you hit the ball, halfway between the service line and the net, and three feet from the stripe. You want to be in the center of your opponent's possibilities, so the only time you should stand on the center stripe is when you've hit the ball straight down the middle.

When you reach your desired position, stop momentarily with a little check-step — hopefully when the ball is on your opponent's racket strings. Then you can move quickly in any direction without stumbling over your feet. This is where anticipation is critical. Try telling yourself, "Drive or lob, drive or lob," as you study your opponent's swing and the direction of the ball as it leaves his racket. If it's drive — a passing shot — you want to get two steps forward on the diagonal toward the ball; avoid running parallel to the net. If it's a lob, turn and try to get three quick steps back. If you can learn to make these movements instinctively, without standing there flat-footed trying to confirm your decision, you may play at Wimbledon yet.

Here's another view of the approach shot, this time by a player hitting a two-hander but aggressively moving forward into the ball and continuing to the net without pausing. Notice how he keeps his eyes focused on the ball and his racket up on the follow-through.

Keep It Deep

Your first goal is always depth. Ideally, try to land the ball within four feet of your opponent's baseline so that you force him back and give yourself more time to crowd the net and to react to his next shot. Conversely, if you hit your approach shot short, with a high bounce, you decrease your reaction time on the next shot and place yourself on defense, even though you are closer to the net.

Jack Kramer wasn't that fast, but his approach shot was so deep and he was such an absolute fiend for hitting target areas that he would get position on you and there wasn't much you could do about it. After hitting his approach shot he would get those extra two or three steps toward the net and shorten the angle so much that it was virtually impossible to pass him, especially from a position about five feet behind the baseline. Former playing great Lew Hoad remembered how Kramer "always hit his approach shot so deep — always in a little two- or three-foot area, either in the backhand corner, in the middle, or in the other corner."

I visited with Hoad at the World Championship Tennis finals in 1975, and we got to talking about how many of the current players didn't seem to have a respect for keeping the ball deep, such as on their groundstrokes, approach shots, and second serves. "The emphasis seems to be on just getting to the net, rather than on getting to the net behind the really good approach shot," I said, and Lew agreed. "I

Flat Volley

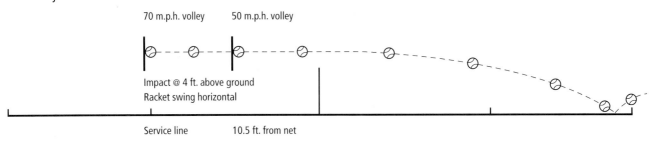

70 m.p.h. volley   50 m.p.h. volley

Impact @ 4 ft. above ground
Racket swing horizontal

Service line   10.5 ft. from net

This chart shows how hard one can volley flat and on a horizontal, while still keeping the ball in play. This is important, since the average volleyer is afraid he will hit the ball long and thus volleys down and softly. This is also an answer to people who say you must underspin the volley to take speed off the ball.

can't for the life of me see how they can consistently hit the ball short and get away with it," he said. "When I was playing, you had to really work on your approach shot, because any time you could go to the net, you had to go." We also noted that even though Rod Laver's game was going down, he was the only player in the eight-man finals who had any consistent depth on his approach shots. And Hoad felt it came basically from playing the guys in the older era.

It is my opinion that modern players have improved on the forehand groundstrokes of past players, but have become worse on approach shots. One reason is that the mentality of many modern players is to try to hit winners off their approach shot. However, statistics show that the pros rarely put the ball away and they subsequently have lousy position at the net because they have too little time to get there. I'm seeing more errors and poor placement at the expense of more speed. Citing Patrick Rafter once again, the U.S. Open champ sent a real message to other players that running through the ball, hitting the intended target area, and gaining good net position is more important than ball speed on the approach shot.

Placement and Target Areas

The major target goal for your approach shot is to aim at the spot where your opponent is most likely to hit a high and long ball. A high return produces easy volleys and a long return means that you haven't allowed him to hit short-angled passing shots.

"How do I know which shot tends to go higher and longer from my opponent?" you wonder. The answer is, scout your opponent and check it out for yourself. If you pay strict attention, you will begin to see patterns of play and you can normally count on those patterns to continue when you play that person. "Who has time to go out and scout future opponents?" My answer is always the same: "Winners."

If you're playing a one-handed backhand hitter, the normal approach shot is aimed to his backhand side, as this particular backhand tends to be returned slightly higher. But with so many improved two-handed backhand players today, you must scout this particular opponent to determine which side produces the highest and longest ball.

Now you're probably thinking, "Wait a minute, Vic. I'm just happy if I keep the ball in the court and you're talking about target areas. The only way I can hit that backhand or forehand corner is by accident." This may be true, I know, but everybody should at least practice hitting to target areas because this brings about faster improvement and realization of just how much you need to work on a particular stroke.

There are two reasons why you normally want to underspin your approach shot and aim it for your opponent's backhand:

1. Whenever you go to the net you want to force your opponent to return the ball high, where you can volley much better. An underspin approach shot (due to low trajectory) bounces low to your opponent, and very few club players will make the effort to get down low for the ball and to lift up with a vertical racket head. Instead, they remain stiff-kneed and simply drop the racket head, scoop the shot, and raise it high — which is exactly what you want.

2. Since most one-handed players hit backhands with underspin, and balls hit with underspin tend to sail, these players cannot hurt you nearly as much as those who can hit with topspin. When you come to the net against an opponent's topspin shot, the ball often comes over the net and down at your feet, which forces you to bend for the tough shot and sometimes plays havoc with your eyes. That's why you want to keep the ball low even against a player who pulls across on his backhand, because he can take a high ball and drive it on a flat line, just over the net — a difficult shot to volley. Keep in mind that many of today's players feel that it's better to slug the approach shot and force errors from their opponent. For most players in the world, I do not agree with this theory. Underspin floats a little and allows the hitter to get farther into the net. A hard-hit topspin bounces high and the approach shot hitter is usually not in position for the volley. I favor a slower,

PRACTICE TIP: A DRILL FOR CHANGING GRIPS

Hold an Eastern forehand grip while standing in a ready position. Suddenly move one foot sideways or forward while changing from a forehand grip to a backhand grip. The goal is to see if you can make your feet move faster than your hands. In all the years I've taught, I haven't seen a single player who can beat his hands with his feet. That means you can change grips before you complete a single step. And if you can't get a single step at the net, you will have to go to chess . . . or the baseline.

Jay attacks the volley, continuing to move forward as he hits so that he's closer to the net and will have a chance to volley again with far greater angles. However, he is also vulnerable to a lob if he doesn't put this ball away.

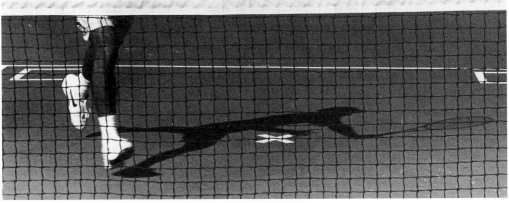

lower, better-placed underspin approach shot and better court position any day over hard drives that produce more errors by the approach shot hitter, and poor net position.

When approaching against two-handed backhand players, the key is to force them to hit from a low position while on the move. That is the dream approach shot against two-handed hitters.

Here are some factors which make most forehands lethal against net-rushers: (1) they can be hit later, (2) low balls can be hit with topspin quite easily, (3) the shot is a little more difficult to read, and (4) players are normally more confident on the forehand.

The Short-Angled Approach Shot

This may surprise you, but an extremely short-angled approach shot to the backhand side is almost as effective as the deep approach shot. When an opponent is running in, and at a diagonal, for the short-angle shot, he is normally reaching out from a low position and must elevate the ball quite high and with very little speed. This is an extremely successful attacking strategy against a great baseline player who hates to come to the net and fight it out at close quarters. But the player who intends to hit the short-angle approach shot must also attack the net and catch the ball high in the middle of the court while the opponent is still recovering. Arthur Ashe used this shot to upset Jimmy Connors at Wimbledon in 1975, and it's the same shot I would advise anyone to use against Steffi Graf and Martina Hingis. However, most players are afraid to try it, choosing instead to continue to lose from the baseline to these fine players. Or they play the conventional method of always attacking on a deep approach shot, which also doesn't seem to work against Graf and Hingis.

Positioning

A common mistake is to believe that no matter where you hit your approach shot, you should stay right in the middle of the court, close to the security of the center stripe. ("That line is the middle — I will stand on the line.") Yet in reality you are not in the middle but to one side, unless you have hit the ball straight down the middle. If you stand on the center stripe for a shot to your opponent's forehand and backhand side, then you leave yourself vulnerable to passing shots down both sides. Instead, you must determine the angle that your opponent has in which to hit and then stand halfway between.

For example, if you can hit to your opponent's backhand, and take your position three feet to the right of the center stripe, there's hardly a player in the world who can pass you on the left if you have good reactions and a decent volley. He must be able to hit with excessive topspin on his backhand in order to hit the ball hard enough, on a short cross-court diagonal, to keep it away from your volley at the net. Very few players even on the pro tour can do that. Thus, realistically your opponent can now only go to your right or over your head; you have eliminated 33 percent of his opportunities.

When people first try to position themselves correctly, they feel naked leaving all that space on one side, such as when they hit the ball to their opponent's backhand. They don't believe me when I tell them they want to tempt their opponent with that "wide-open" area on their own backhand side because it's virtually an impossible shot for the average player to pull off. They say, "Yeah, but what about the guy who hits it in here?" and they point to that little area on the court, inside the 65'9" diagonal, that very few people in the history of the game have been able to hit under pressure. I always tell them, "He isn't living, so you're in pretty good shape. Nobody ever 'owns' that shot."

Stop worrying about the extraordinary shot, and be much more concerned about what realistically is possible, given the physical laws and the court dimensions which govern this game.

Put me to the test if you still feel that it's nothing to hit those cross-court shots that dip over the net and away from your opponent. Divide the opposite service box roughly in half with some rope so that you can visualize the 65'9" diagonal (see page 14), then stand on the baseline at your backhand corner, bounce the ball, and just try to bring it down inside the diagonal. Keep score as in a game and see if you can beat my concept. Then put an opponent halfway between the net and the service line, three feet to your side of the center stripe, and try to hit the ball past him, while bringing it down inside the court. Unless you can hit with excessive topspin, you will either have to aim the ball too close to your opponent, or you will have to soften your hit, in which case your opponent can easily step across for his volley.

Anticipation

Okay, let's say your only strategy for ten years has been to to "hit and stay back," but it hasn't made you too famous. So you're going to start working on your approach shot, and rushing the net a little more often than every other April. Great, except for one warning: you will need more than a good stroke. In order to hit a consistently deep approach shot, you need anticipation and a fast first step forward so that you can reach the ball before it starts to drop after bouncing. This requires that you learn to think and react offensively, not defensively.

If you and your opponent are typical intermediates, and you have a baseline rally going, you're waiting for the first short ball, right? Then you can rush in and show off your new approach shot. But when will you get this short ball? Statistically, on the very next shot. If your opponent could keep it deep, he wouldn't be playing you — he would be out on the tournament circuit. He might hit an occasional deep shot by accident, but very few people can hit two deep balls in a row by design. So every time your opponent prepares to hit, keep telling yourself, "The next ball is going to be short." Stay on your toes, ready to move forward. Be surprised if the ball lands deep — never be surprised that it falls short — and this will change your whole game.

Alas, nearly everyone stands flat-footed at the baseline, waiting to see where the ball goes, then they cry, "Oh no, it's short!" and they go running in and reach the ball on the third bounce. They get disgusted that they didn't react fast enough, yet on the very next shot they remain glued to the baseline, and once again they're shocked by the short ball. All day long they hit and back up, unable to realize they're not playing Jimmy Connors. To get your feet moving, make yourself break toward the ball before it reaches your opponent's service line and you'll be on your way to good tennis.

If you can concentrate, think about always moving forward, and get your feet moving quickly, you won't need Rollerblades in order to reach a good hitting position for your approach shot. Then, if you can hit the ball deep to your opponent, and run to your appropriate waiting position, you will be in the same position as the pros: your opponent will be on the defensive and you will be poised near the net. You'll have achieved your first goal — to gain control of the net. But to hold the fortress, you next need to know how to volley and to defend against the lob.

THE VOLLEY

The volley is any ball you hit in the air before it touches the ground. Although you can volley from near the baseline, you generally will volley in the vicinity of the net, a fact which stirs a basic emotion in many players: fear. Beginners and women who play in competitive mixed doubles are always telling me, "I don't want to play the net. I get up there and I'm scared to death." This is understandable, since anxiety seems to increase proportionately the closer you get to your opponent — because he can easily provide you with a "fuzz sandwich." When you're up at the net, especially in doubles, everything is happening fast and you can sometimes be frightened into inaction. We once had a woman at the tennis college who froze in

(below left and center) Mary demonstrates the number one error on the volley, and that's leaving the elbow against the body and laying the racket head back. This requires extreme precision when impacting the ball. To cure "racket-head layback," Mary simply raises her elbow, which brings the racket head back to a vertical position. She then swings from the shoulder rather than the elbow.

(below right) Here Mary demonstrates the Jack Kramer–type volley by simply putting the palm out to meet the ball and creating a slight, but quick, hand movement toward the target. This is the favored volley position.

The volleyer positions himself in the center of the court when his opponent is also hitting from the center of the court. The volleyer moves in the same direction as the hitter moves toward the sidelines.

her ready position, watching the ball come right at her. "This ball is going to hit me," she grimaced, moments before it bounced off her forehand. A friend asked her, "Why don't you move back?" And she said, "When I do, I just get hit one step farther back."

Learning how to volley will help you overcome fears about playing the net in doubles and following your approach shot to the net in singles — not to mention making you a vastly improved player. But then another problem arises. People very often will hit an approach shot and make a great flurry to reach their preferred position halfway between the service line and the net. But when they land on this spot, they say, "Made it!" and they aren't about to budge for anything. They think they now control the point, when they actually are in danger of losing because they're not ready for their opponent's return shot. You frequently hear these people say, "Terrific shot, Bertha," as the ball goes zipping by.

Instead of becoming hypnotized in your ready position after hitting an approach shot, you must go to the net with the understanding that you are going to win or lose the point on the very next shot. You're not in the middle but at the end of a sequence. In most cases your opponent will make an error on your approach

shot, hit an outright winner, or return the ball weakly, thus giving you a relatively easy volley or overhead with which to end the point.

The Grip

I prefer to have pros and beginners alike use their regular Eastern forehand or Eastern backhand grip when they volley. Despite what you may have been told, our experiments show there is sufficient time to switch grips if you will simply practice switching grips as you take your first step. Also, the rate of speed of the ball hit by many professionals is a rate you're not apt to confront for several years.

I know that many pro players and teachers argue in favor of the Continental (halfway between the Eastern forehand and backhand grips) so that you can use a one-grip game. But remember, the Continental forces you to be much more coordinated and talented, especially on the forehand volley. Even top pros have admitted it is more difficult to handle the high forehand volley with the Continental because the bottom of the racket is beveled forward and they can't control it. When they try to get their racket out in front to volley into their opponent's backhand corner, the racket points on a diagonal away from that corner and they can't make the play unless they compensate by swinging late or if they are double-jointed. You try it, holding a Continental grip. The Eastern forehand grip allows a player to hit with the palm of her hand. That's much more natural than hitting a down-the-line shot with the thumb of the hitting hand serving as a guide while holding a Continental grip.

The Forehand Volley

Make sure you get into a ready position following your approach shot, or anytime you find yourself at the net. This helps ensure that you will volley properly. Then keep telling yourself, "Drive or lob, drive or lob," as you watch your opponent take his (or her) swing as you anticipate the shot. Just before he contacts the ball, bring your heels off the ground so that you can prestretch your leg muscles and push off your toes as you move forward to volley, or as you turn and retreat for a lob.

If your opponent hits a drive, break diagonally forward — toward the net post — to meet the ball. Remember, the closer you get to the net, the easier you can close off the point. If you run parallel to the net, balls which are sharply angled will simply get farther away from you.

On all your volleys, try to visualize a short, punching motion rather than an actual stroke, because the greater the length of your swing, the greater your talent must be. Your concern is with accuracy and placement rather than speed on the ball, so don't take your racket any farther back than the shoulder housing the hitting arm. Instead of a backswing, think of your hitting palm reaching out to intercept the ball, as if you were catching a baseball. Physicists Dr. Howard Brody and Dr. Patrick Keating, along with sports researchers Drs. Andrei Vorobiev and Gideon Ariel and myself, are pretty much in agreement that the volleyer will normally get close to 50 percent of the incoming speed of the opponent's shot simply by blocking the ball. So an aggressive short punch on the volley is sufficient.

Your goal is to contact the ball when it is even with your front shoulder and at eye level, so bend your knees to get down on a low ball. Volleying off your front shoulder gives you a clean view of the ball and the racket. If you try to contact the ball too far out in front, you have to contort your forearm and wrist to make the hit and you can't judge the ball coming into the racket. Also, the farther out in front you try to hit the ball, the more you must face the net with your body — and the more you face the net, the more your racket tends to pull down rather than carrying out. Players who hit too far out in front usually have a volley that is "pushed" rather than "punched."

At contact, your front shoulder should be toward the net and your racket head pointed upward at a 45-degree angle. Although there is little follow-through on the volley, never let the racket suddenly stop, pull across, or drop; stroke through the ball and carry the racket out toward your target so that you keep the ball deep. Try to imagine that you are swinging across a high table top, with the racket head always up and the face vertical as you hit through the ball.

Some pros actually teach their students to lay the racket head back on the volley, in order to snap the wrist into the ball at contact and produce more power. But once again, I argue that laying the racket back at any point on the volley is the kiss of death. Instead of fixing your racket with a locked-wrist position and letting your arm and body segments supply the power, playing with the wrist requires you to judge — under pressure — how and when to snap the wrist so that you can contact the ball properly. I'll admit, the wrist is indeed active on the volley when one wants to effect a slight forward movement of the racket, but not with the racket laid back. Jack Kramer made this volley style famous. By putting the palm out to meet the ball, one has perfect vision at all times and can activate a forward movement of the palm by activating a slight wrist movement. As I emphasized earlier in the book, when the racket is laid back, even though one's body has stepped forward into the ball, the racket must now move on an arc and it's normally too tough to time accurately.

Just as on the forehand stroke, you can prevent wrist layback by leading slightly with your hitting elbow on the backswing while leaving your wrist fixed. Visualize your arm extending parallel along a line; when you draw the racket back, your elbow should pass the line before your wrist or racket. Then, as you go out to volley, keep your hitting palm and the face of your racket directly in line with the oncoming ball so that your opponent sees only your racket strings, and never the butt of the handle. Always keep your hitting elbow out away from your body. Drills where you have a ball or your elbow pinned against your body as a way to prevent wrist layback will only increase this problem — for when your elbow comes in, physiology forces the wrist to lay back.

The Backhand Volley

The stroking principles are basically the same here as on the forehand volley. One difference is that when you step forward to meet the ball, think of your knuckles reaching out to intercept the ball, and not your palm. Also, the non-hitting arm can work in your behalf by cradling the throat of the racket on the backswing. But keep this hand and the elbow high and out away from your body so that the racket face is always on line with the oncoming ball, and not laid back.

The instant the ball leaves your opponent's racket, simultaneously turn the shoulder of your hitting arm toward the net and switch your grip from the Eastern forehand to the Eastern backhand. Then move diagonally forward, contacting the ball six to ten inches in front of your body and at eye level. Your body weight transfers from the back to the front foot as you make contact, and the racket head remains up and finishes high on the follow-through. You generate your power on this stroke by the forward uncoiling movements of your body and by keeping your hitting arm extended, not by bending your elbow and throwing the racket head at the ball.

Two-handed backhand and forehand volleyers will meet the ball on the front side of their body, as in the forehand and backhand groundstrokes, but the ball is normally met a little higher than on groundstrokes. The goal is to have the racket, the hitter's eyes, and the ball on the same level when contact is made. That means low volleys could be tough. Remember, the ball doesn't know you have a one-handed or a two-handed volley. It only knows that the racket has to be pointed in the right direction at the impact point.

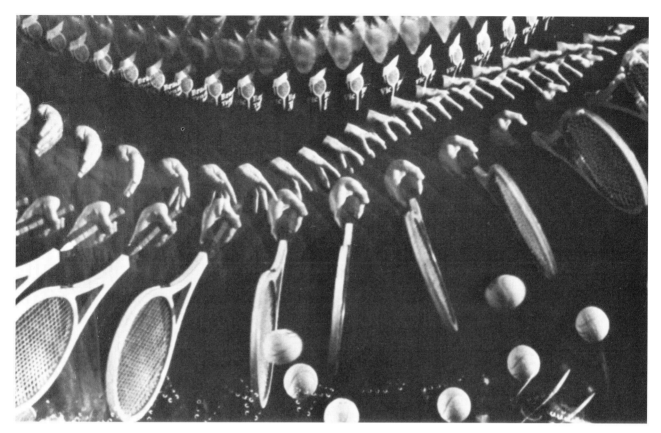

Anticipation

The main reason that most people don't have a good volley is that they don't move their bodies. Self-hypnosis at the net and the fear of making the wrong decision are as destructive as a lack of form. You can have lousy form but if you can get on top of the net you can volley with your earlobe and still make the play. Conversely, even with great form, if you wait for the ball to come to you instead of attacking you will always be on the defensive, forced to execute difficult volleys.

The reason pros can volley so well is that they start moving as or before the ball is hit, whereas the average player waits until the ball reaches the net. When the pro comes to the net and is about to be passed on either side, he runs one way or the other; he's not afraid to guess wrong. He knows he has to react instantly and that at least he has a 50-50 chance of outguessing his opponent. But the intermediate wants to confirm every decision. You can see him freeze on the center stripe thinking, "Is he going to pass me on the left or on the right? Son-of-a-gun. It was to my backhand," and he makes no move at all. He's got a 100 out of 100 chance of losing — but he's not going to look dumb by running the wrong way.

That's why I like the advice former pro Sandy Mayer said he received from his father: "I don't care if you guess wrong at the net, but you have to go, one way or the other. I never want to catch you standing on the middle line." If more people would learn to do this early in their tennis "careers"— reward themselves

In this sequence, Beau moves through his backhand volley and keeps his racket high. Two-handed volleyers need only keep the racket in the same position as the one-hander.

for making a move, even it it's wrong — then they would be on their way to a sound game. Yet kids, especially, are so fearful of reprimands from themselves or authority figures for going the wrong way that they begin to build in a subconscious braking system.

Footwork

When you reach a ready position near the net, understand that this is only where you want to land — not where you're going to volley — so don't let your heels touch the ground as you wait to see the direction of your opponent's return. Think instead about how fast you're going to have to exit to make your next play. You will be a good volleyer if you can gain one step forward by reacting quickly. In fact, you will render your opponent practically ineffective on the cross-court passing shot. The great volleyers get two steps toward the ball and their racket practically crosses the net when they follow through.

Another reason you don't want to get caught back is that the closer you can get to the net, the higher you will be able to volley. If you hesitate, the ball will drop lower than the tape of the net and you won't be able to make an offensive play. You will have to hit the ball defensively, concentrating on just getting it back into play and deep.

Closing Out the Point

Very often, when you hear the pros say that a particular player can't close out the point, they mean that he doesn't crowd the net by getting those two steps forward; thus, instead of being an immediate winner, he very often loses the point or is forced on the defensive.

For example, the charge against Cliff Richey — at one time the number one ranked player in the country — was that he didn't have enough shots. But Cliff had every shot in the book, plus he could hit the ball deep and keep it in play. What it really boiled down to was that although Cliff actually volleyed well, he couldn't get close enough to the net to really gain the advantage. When I was accompanying the Davis Cup team in 1967, Pancho Gonzales kept telling Cliff, "Learn to close off the point." Gorgo just couldn't understand how a guy could fight so hard out there but then, when he finally got a chance to win the point, he could only produce more opportunities to fight harder by just keeping the ball in play on his volley.

Placement

When you are volleying at the net, where should you aim if you have the time? Top players try to get as close to the net as possible so that they can hit the ball on a short diagonal, rather than deep and down the middle, because it forces their opponent to run farther. Plus, if their opponent does return it, his body weight carries him well off the court and out of position for another shot.

However, if you are not positive that you are going to end the point with a short-angle volley, then just strive for depth. Trying to force short-angle shots will very often cause you to miss. So be aggressive, but don't be impatient when you go to the net. Hitting your first volley deep will still keep your opponent in trouble and will provide more opportunities to move forward on your next volley to close out the point. Your ability to hit with depth will also give you the confidence to relax and not to panic on your first volley. But if you volley poorly, you tend to regard your first volley as an all-or-nothing shot.

On volleys where you are away from the net, such as near the service line, your only goal should be to keep the ball deep to your opponent's weakest side and in play. Don't gamble on hitting the angles. The farther you can push your opponent back, the longer his return shot is in the air and the more time you have to close in on the net for your next shot.

General Tips on the Volley

1. Treat easy shots with the same respect as difficult ones. Very often you will get an easy ball off your opponent's drive but you relax and fail to get your two steps forward. Suddenly the ball loses speed and drops below the level of the net and now you are on defense, having to raise the ball back up again. Furthermore, the softer the ball is coming, the harder it is to volley from a low position. You

have a tendency to let the wrist and the racket go limp with the shot, which causes you to dump the ball into the net.

2. When you run for the ball, keep your hitting arm and racket face up. When you stretch to make a hit, no matter how late you might be, keep the face of your racket high — never let it drop. Even on a desperate lunge, if you keep your racket head high you still have a chance to catch the ball on the strings and return it over the net. Try always to finish high. I have always appreciated Jimmy Connors's high two-handed backhand volley because his racket always finishes at the same height at which he contacts the ball.

3. Always be thinking, "Drive or lob, drive or lob," as you study your opponent's intentions at the baseline. Don't be afraid to guess wrong. Your guesses will become educated guesses as you learn to anticipate.

4. Even though you can't see the ball hit the strings, try to keep your eyes on the ball right into the racket, even on short-range volley exchanges, because this increases your chances to keep your racket head steady and make the good play. I have a pro doubles film in which there are four shots in less than two seconds, and Ken Rosewall has his eyes fixed on the spot where the ball meets the strings for both of his shots.

5. Learn to volley from a deep position, not just up at the net, because very often that's where you are caught if you don't move quickly between the baseline and the net. But remember, the farther back from the net you volley, the more talented you must be. You have to learn to hit out — to almost lift that ball from the service line. If you volley down even slightly, the ball will go into the net. Remember, when standing behind the service line and hitting a ball from a four-foot height, you can hit a ball 70 miles per hour on a horizontal plane and the ball will still land inside your opponent's baseline.

6. A good reminder on volleys at head level or above: people rarely hit them deep enough. Players are so afraid of hitting this shot over the baseline that they snap down severely with their racket, and the ball very often ends up in the net. A corollary to this precaution: the closer you get to the net, the more you have a tendency to relax and swing down. So always keep the racket head up and going out, unless you're right on top of the net.

7. One reason you may not volley well is that you never practice coming to the net and volleying. But you can't practice effectively or work on your weaknesses if you don't have a realistic idea about what you can actually do with the shot. After a match you may talk about how you were going to the net and volleying like a champ, but most people tend to remember the one or two volleys that they hit well and to forget the ten that they missed. This is why you must have a friend record where your volley is landing during a match, and how effective it really is. You need to learn how well you volley from the service line, from halfway between the service line and the net, and when up at the net. Then you can go out and work on a specific weakness.

8. An excellent drill to help make you react and move quickly at the net is to play without a racket while a friend throws or hits the ball from the baseline. You just try to catch it. This forces you to concentrate on the ball, to hustle into

Vince approaches the ball for a half-volley and begins to prepare his feet to run through the shot. Notice how he has slightly closed the face of his racket to compensate for the steep incident angle of the ball coming into his racket.

position, and to stretch out for the ball because you don't have that extra racket length to play with. But when you've put a racket back in your hand, don't forget to do what you've practiced.

THE HALF-VOLLEY

The half-volley is a difficult, important — yet unglamorous — shot that must be hit down around your sneakers, just as the ball bounces off the court. It's almost impossible to attack with a half-volley, nor do you arouse much envy by telling friends you have the best half-volley in your club. The tendency is to want to kick at a ball that low or to say, "Play two — I don't hit anything below my knees."

Some coaches, in fact, won't even teach the half-volley. They feel that their students shouldn't let themselves get caught in that area around the service line, that they should either be back far enough to take the ball on a normal bounce or else reach the ball when it's still in the air. But this approach ignores two important realities: (1) intermediates are caught all the time in that midcourt area, either by "hanging around" waiting to see what their opponent is going to do or by failing to know their "short ball range" on the approach shot; (2) the better you play, the more you need a half-volley to remain competitive. If your opponent has worked on his service return, he will land the ball at your feet all day long when you rush the net. You'll need to get that shot back over the net — and deep — if you want to win your serve.

• The Stroke

Forehand and backhand half-volleys require a short backswing, good knee bend, and a low-to-high lifting motion with a racket head that is vertical at impact to hit deep half-volleys. The racket head must be slightly facing down to hit low half-volleys in fast-action doubles play. In both cases, this enables you to get the ball up over the net and bring it back down safely into your opponent's court.

You can't expect to hit a decent half-volley by staying high with your body and simply lowering your racket head with the face beveled back to "scoop" the ball up over the net, as most people try to do. Instead, you must freeze your wrist position, lower your hitting arm, and then use your thighs and the lift of your body to supply the power. The slightest bevel in your racket can drastically affect the ball's flight pattern. But if you know the racket head is fixed, and not beveled, then you only have to decide how much to lift your thighs.

Don't get lazy with your knees. They must lower your body almost to the court so that you can bring the racket face right down to the level of the ball, and then lift the entire body up as the ball is hit. That's why the great old-timers had grass-stained knees on their white pants. Pete Sampras is an excellent half-volleyer, and he's also very rich. In the late 1990s, Jimmy Connors is still beating the senior field with some fine half-volley play.

Contact should be made immediately after the ball has bounced. Think of hitting the ball and lifting it up over the net, while keeping your eyes down on the point of impact. Don't try to take an early peek at how you did. Keep your head fixed so that it maintains its relationship with the racket, and have them lift together. If you let your head lift up early you will tend to scoop the ball.

If possible, the half-volley should be executed with little or no pause in forward motion so that you won't lose time moving to that side of the center stripe to which you hit the ball, and as close to the net as possible. Don't get trapped on the half-volley by letting the ball land closer to your back foot than to the foot closer to the net; this will force you to stop and make the hit. Remember, too, that the backhand half-volley must be contacted farther out in front of the body than the forehand. If you're late on the backhand here, you can rarely make a successful return.

The key is to meet the ball as it's rising on a sharp upward angle. If you try to scoop the ball, it will only turn into a lob and you will find yourself stuck in the middle of the court while your opponent is hitting an overhead.

Placement

In singles, just strive to keep the half-volley deep. This will give you time to get good position near the net. Your opponent is generally backcourt on this shot, but if the ball only goes to the service line, he can trot in and give you a new look.

In doubles, you must keep your half-volley as close to the net as possible, so that one of your opponents can't deck a high volley. The pros will try to hit a "soft" shot that goes over the net and dies, forcing their opponents to volley up. But be careful not to also soften the wrist as you make this play or you will dump the ball into the net. Keep a firm wrist, bend the knees, and then rise quickly out of this low crouch with your racket face tilted slightly down. This enables you to counter-act the steeply rising ball and produce a shot that stays close to the net and makes it difficult for your opponents to hit a winning return volley from a high position.

THE LOB

The lob is the only stroke in tennis that can pull you out of a hole and give you a giant win, even though you have nothing else. People make fun of those players who like to throw up a lob every two or three shots, but they seem to for-get that good lobbers have more trophies than any other person in the club. Even the legendary Pancho Gonzales, who had great pride in his serve and his attacking skills, would still go out and practice his lob, and he had one of the best lobs I've ever seen. People tend to think of it as a weakness in tournament tennis, but it's not — it's a gigantic strength.

Try to realize how devastating the well-timed, well-executed lob can be: (1) it can be used like the baseball pitcher's change-up to break up your opponent's rhythm and the pace of a rally; (2) it can be used to buy time to allow you to get back in position after scrambling off-court to make a play; (3) as a tactical weapon it drives your opponent away from the net and allows you to move in and take the offensive; (4) it will tire your opponent by forcing him to retreat from the net and to stretch up to hit overheads or run to the baseline.

So learn to lob effectively and see how dramatically it improves your game. As the late Raphael Osuna used to tell Raul Ramirez, Mexico's Davis Cup hero: "Remember the lob. The lob, the lob, the lob."

The Stroke

Both forehand and backhand lobs require the same Eastern grips used on your groundstrokes.

The elevation of your lob depends upon three factors: (1) the degree to which your racket face is beveled or turned upward to the sky, (2) the angle of the for-ward low-to-high striking motion, and (3) the speed of the stroke. Beginners should first learn to hit lobs high into the air with the racket face turned upward to the sky, while lifting with a low-to-high forward motion. As proficiency is gained, develop about a 55-degree stroking angle and add a slight bevel of the racket to help lift the ball. This will produce the greatest depth from baseline to baseline with the least amount of energy. On the follow-through, make sure you complete your stroke and finish with the racket head high.

The best way to learn to lob is to get out and practice, without the pressure of a match but under realistic conditions. Have a friend hit balls so that you can run laterally along the baseline and even off the court to make the play. If you only practice against balls that come right down the middle you can get into a pretty good groove and begin to think, "Gee, I'm lobbing pretty well." But then you get into a match and you start running laterally, with your energy going away from your shot, and your lobs come up short. (You can also practice on your own by just

Wayne demonstrates the same closed-face racket (tilted slightly downward) so that he doesn't raise the half-volley too high for his opponent to hit an easy winner.

bouncing the ball before you lob, but remember to run to the ball to simulate actual playing conditions.)

If you can only practice while rallying before a match, try to hit at least 20 lobs and work on having the ball land within five feet of your opponent's baseline. If the ball goes beyond the baseline, practice adjusting the upward angle of your swing and the bevel of your racket so that you can always swing with the same speed no matter what the pressure.

Placement

The most common mistake you can make is to make your lob shallow and thus give your opponent an easy overhead while you run for cover. One reason you might tend to lob short is that you look at your opponent out of the corner of your eye and unconsciously slow up on your swing. So learn to block out your opponent. Second, if you hit your first lob of the match too long, you generally overcompensate on the next one and hit it weakly to your opponent, who stands there at the net grinning. Thus you lose two straight points on the lob and you're afraid to lob again the rest of the match, which retires one of your greatest potential weapons.

To break these habits, while practicing before the match, always attempt to lob five to ten feet too long. Try to hit your first lob over the baseline. If you are long, try to hit your next one with exactly the same speed but with slightly more bevel in your racket so that your extra length will go into height and still give you the depth you want. Take a hint from the good players. When they lob long they think, "Good, good," because they know exactly how to gauge their correction. That's why you always want to try to lob before the match begins so that you can learn from your errors and have your "touch" adjusted by the time the match begins and you're playing under pressure.

Two refinements on the lob placement: (1) try to have your opponent look up into the sun, if there's sun, and (2) if you're near one of your baseline corners, try to lob on the diagonal to gain extra distance.

Concealing Your Lob

Most people don't even think about concealing their lob — they're just happy to get it up in the air and over the net. But with experience you should try to have your lob stroke resemble your forehand and backhand groundstrokes as much as possible in order to reduce your opponent's effectiveness at the net. When you conceal your intention to lob until the very last instant, your opponent can't anticipate what you're going to hit, and must hold ground until the last possible moment.

Pancho Segura, in the 1940s and 1950s, had the best concealed lob I've ever seen. He looked as if he were going to drive the ball, only to send up a lob. This forced his opponents to freeze at the net. They couldn't anticipate a forehand and step forward to volley, nor could they spot the lob coming and turn to chase it down.

Interestingly, Segura's student, Jimmy Connors, was probably more effective with the lob — and concealing the lob — than any other modern-day player I saw

Rich shows the role of the knees and the closed racket face on the forehand half-volley.

Mary demonstrates that the racket face must be opened (facing upward) to effect a deep lob.

in the 1970s and 1980s. Jimmy was not just a big blaster from the baseline; he loved to throw up that lob. The same was true with Pancho Gonzales. When I kept informal records on the pro tour, I found that he lobbed better than all the other players, even though he was considered a great net-rusher. He was really something.

To conceal your lob, remember to turn your front shoulder and have a loop swing identical with your forehand and backhand. This also means running to the ball with your racket head up and already back. Then work on racket bevel and upward swing. The lob is one shot on which you want to use the bevel of your racket, but obviously this takes a lot of practice and experience. One warning: don't sit back on your back heel as you go to lob because this is a dead giveaway to a smart opponent. Just step into the ball as if you are going to drive the ball, only you lob.

The Offensive Lob

The pros can anticipate so well, and retreat so quickly to chase down practically every good defensive lob, that they have brought a new shot into the game: the offensive lob hit with severe topspin. They ride the ball hard and it goes up like a lob, just high enough to be out of reach of their opponent at the net, but when it lands it kicks toward the back fence and is hit hard enough so that the opponent can't get back in time to make the play. Unfortunately, this is a low percentage shot. Even the pros find that it only works about one out of five or even one out of ten times, and that when they hit it too low they just get killed. Big money tournaments will force the top players to refine this shot into a more dependable weapon, but the average player should have it well down on his list of priorities. The biggest change I've seen in the past twenty years is that the same top players have literally perfected the shot as a weapon, but they choose more carefully when to use it. Though Michael Chang has been a master with the offensive lob in the 1990s, he was beaten on the key offensive lobs in the 1997 U.S. Open by Patrick Rafter.

Regaining the Offensive with Your Lob

If you lob successfully over your opponent's head and force him back to the baseline, then you should match him step for step and regain the net as he retreats for the ball. However, if you lob over your opponent's head but the ball comes down on a vertical plane and he doesn't really lose ground, then of course you have to stay back and wait for his overhead. Can your opponent hit an overhead from a deep position? Of course; a serve is hit from behind the baseline.

Jack Kramer tells the story of how Dennis Ralston's failure to take the net following his lob helped cost him a Davis Cup match against Australia in 1964. Ralston was leading Fred Stolle two sets to one and was one point away from breaking Stolle's serve in the fourth set. The match seemed virtually wrapped up. Stolle served and took the net, and Ralston hit a perfect lob that drove Stolle back to the baseline. But when Stolle turned around to hit, Ralston was still back. Kramer was doing the commentary for CBS and I remember him saying, "Oh, there's a serious tactical error by Ralston. He should have followed into the net." Given a reprieve, Stolle hit a deep return and started a rally, waiting until he got a chance to attack the net again. He went on to win the point and was now serving at deuce. On that very next point Ralston made the same mistake after lobbing and Stolle again won the point. He proceeded to hold serve and eventually he won the match. In the heat of battle, even a super player like Ralston can make a tactical error that costs him dearly.

Combatting the Lob

When I talk about how important it is to gain control of the net, people sometimes wonder, "Heck, if that's the case, why can't you just run up to the net and stand there every time?" Well, for one thing, you're not in good enough shape to do all that running. And second, you can't always play dummies. People can lob and drive you straight back to the baseline.

Remember, the thing that will make you famous at the net is your ability to get two steps forward or three steps back by anticipating the nature of your opponent's shot — ideally by reading his racket head. Just as getting close to the net will make you a more effective volleyer, your ability to retreat quickly will neutralize your opponent's lob. If you can turn and reach your service line before his lob reaches his own service line, you'll be sensational; even a good club player will never beat you with this shot because people simply do not lob that well, or that deep, consistently.

In reacting to a lob, however, many players make that same old mistake of becoming paralyzed at the net. They say, "Is it going to be a drive or a lob? Son-of-a-gun, it's a lob." Then they run back like crazy, but it's too late. People often tell me, "Hey, we have this lady at our club who never misses her lob — she can lay

Preparing to lob, Isis steps into the ball so that she doesn't give away her intentions, then turns her racket face slightly upward at impact to effect the lob. She completes her follow-through in the same manner so that she doesn't slow her swing down and hit short lobs.

that ball in a bucket." But the chances are excellent that she's not that great a lobber. It's just that her opponents never react fast enough when she lobs. They stand at the net, watching the ball and saying, "Nuts, she did it again." So if somebody is lobbing you all the time, start retreating the instant you smell a lob, and see how well that person lobs once you apply a little pressure.

If you can't follow the face of your opponent's racket to sense if he's going to drive or lob, try your luck at a lob-drive anticipation test. Pick out a person you've always wanted to beat and go out and watch him play. Take along a notebook and a pencil and try to guess whether he's going to drive or lob on each shot. Make your decision just before impact with the ball. If you guess right, give yourself a plus. If you're wrong, then a minus. At first you'll go about 50-50, with one right, one wrong, one right, etc. But before the match is over you should be guessing right almost every time. The reason for this is simple: people simply do not have the ability to hit the perfectly concealed shot. Some players practically call out, "I'm going to lob," and yet their opponents still don't move because they haven't learned to anticipate. Also, people have a tendency to play people — not the ball — and thus are distracted by body motions and fakes. So, first try to learn to follow the face of the racket because that's what dictates whether your opponent is going to drive or lob. If you can't follow the racket face, look for giveaway body signs such as a lower backswing on the lob or a falling back on the rear foot.

Anticipating the lob will be wasted if you don't also get back from the net and set up as quickly as possible for your return shot. I like people to turn and run like a baseball outfielder, looking over their shoulder at the ball, but running in the direction that they've learned to run in all sports — forward (though toward the

back fence). You can backpedal if you know you can move just as quickly while maintaining a good rhythm, but few players can do so. Put yourself to the test by having a friend time you as you retreat from the net to the baseline using both methods.

When you chase down a lob and you're forced to hit on the run, always try to make the ball go deep so that you keep your opponent from taking the net. A great tip I got from Jack Kramer, who got it from his coach as a kid, was this: when you're running back for a lob and making an over-the-shoulder return, always try to knock the ball over your opponent's baseline. You think you've compensated for how much energy you have going in the opposite direction, but you seldom have.

On a high lob, you should never let the ball bounce unless it has been hit almost straight up and your opponent has had time to scramble back in position. Then you should let it bounce and give yourself a clean shot, rather than a difficult overhead. But if the ball has any arc to it on the downflight and is driving you back, contact it in the air as soon as you can. The farther back you get, the more you lose good court position while your opponent regains it. Plus, you are unable to exploit your opponent's power if you let the ball bounce; when it lands, it slows down and loses force.

Another common question I receive is, "How can I keep my opponent from lobbing all the time?" This is actually a specialized problem because most players simply can't lob well enough ever to pose this threat, at least not consistently. However, for those players who do run across this problem, the best antidote is to try to make your shots stay low (by hitting with underspin) and keep your opponent running, especially for short-angle balls. People who lob regularly love it

Sebastian prepares to take a short backswing to hit an overhead.

Notice that he uses a bent elbow to "point" to the ball as it falls, instead of pointing with his finger. This action will help him coil his body and produces more power and rhythm in the swing.

when you hit a nice deep ball that bounces high. They simply stand about five feet behind the baseline and lob the ball easily. But if you can underspin your approach shots and volleys, the ball will stay low and your opponent will have a tougher play on his part. It's also much harder to lob while on the run. It's important to know that balls traveling with no spin will normally stay lower than balls hit with underspin. The ball traveling with underspin will, upon contacting the court, convert to topspin and normally bounce slightly higher than the ball traveling on the same plane with no spin. Thus, when we speak of underspin, we mustn't forget that balls hit flat (with no spin) are just as effective for keeping the ball low.

THE OVERHEAD

The overhead smash is a treat for some players. They love the feeling of power and the chance to slam the ball as hard as they want while their opponent cowers on the other side of the net. Yet a missed overhead triggers more response than any other shot in tennis, even more than a double fault or a missed volley. On the overhead there's the sheer humiliation of knocking such an innocent-looking shot into the net or out of play, and the shot preys on your mind for several points afterward. That's why whenever I was down match point — which happened often when I was learning the game — I always tried to lob. Most players are weak, or certainly inconsistent, on their overheads, and they tend to choke more on match point. They're thinking, "Jeez, this is it! If I hit this overhead I'll win the match." Then they proceed to dump the shot because they fail to hit out naturally. When you lob to your opponent under pressure you have double duty going for you: his tendency to choke on the shot, and his subsequent anger if the shot is missed. Your opponent kicks himself for blowing an easy one —"Nuts, I had him where I wanted and I missed it"— while you get a reprieve. In high school I once played a hot-headed kid from Michigan and I was losing 6–0, 5–0, and 40–30 when I threw up a lob. He missed it and he got so mad that I went on to win the match, 0–6, 7–5, 6–0.

Thus it can be a great feeling when your overhead changes from a handicap to a weapon. But this will only come through practice and experience — and learning to treat the shot much as you would a serve.

The Stroke

Holding the same Continental grip that you use on the serve, take long steps to get to the striking area, then short quick steps to position yourself for the hit. If you are retreating for a lob, either try to turn and run back naturally or backpedal very fast.

Use virtually the same stroking motion as you do on the serve, with one exception: shorten the backswing, and thus conserve energy and time, by simply taking the racket head back at eye level, without letting the racket drop. Then turn forward and pretend you're throwing a baseball into the outfield. Here's why. On lobs falling at a 45-degree angle, the overhead hitter must swing up at approximately eight degrees with a vertically planed racket face to counter the dropping angle of the ball. An overhead hit in this manner from a position near the service line will travel about 43 feet and land just past your opponent's service line. That means you can really slug it and not have to fear the ball going long. Jack Kramer could do this better than most professionals in tennis history. In 1997, when I interviewed Bobby Riggs, he told me that he could never remember Kramer missing an overhead. And Bobby himself had publicly stated years earlier that he, Bobby, was the best lobber in the history of tennis.

You want a shorter backswing on the overhead because the ball is falling from a greater height and at a faster speed than your service toss. Don't wait for the ball to come to you. Position yourself quickly and swing upward and forward to meet the ball in line with your right shoulder. When you let the ball get straight out in front, you prevent yourself from turning your front shoulder into the shot. Just as on the serve, you want to hit with plenty of shoulder rotation and close to 450 degrees of racket rotation so that you maintain rhythm and generate maximum power and accuracy — without trying to slug the ball. Just keep your chin up as you swing upward and try to maintain a continuous motion.

A minor controversy here is whether you should track the lobbed ball with your left finger or with the bent left elbow. I prefer to have people point initially with their left elbow — which facilitates a greater shoulder turn and promotes a smooth, baseball pitcher's motion — and then follow out with the finger. This provides a kinetic energy chain moving in sync with the hitting arm.

Players who immediately point their finger at the ball limit their front shoulder turn and diminish the amount of rhythm on their swing substantially. They have a tendency to get too stiff. However, I know I'm badly outnumbered by other coaches on this little point of technique, so if it's too uncomfortable to point with your elbow and you can't even find the ball, then stick with the finger point. But don't be rigid — point it comfortably so you maintain a relaxed upper-body pivot.

Normally, you should hit overheads before the ball has bounced, in order to shorten the time your opponent has to get back in position and to increase your angle for hitting put-away shots. But lobs landing near the baseline or those hit extremely high and dropping on a vertical plane may be allowed to bounce.

Placement

When hitting overheads from a deep position, speed is not nearly as important as accuracy and depth, since you already have your opponent on the defensive. Just strive for depth and nobody will be able to hurt you. Neither do you want to attempt short angles, unless you are right on top of the net. To this day, Frankie Parker, in the 1940s and 1950s, was the only person I ever saw who could hit exceptionally short-angled balls on the overhead from a deep position. That's how rare it is. However, it must be stated that the new rackets introduced in the 1980s and 1990s have allowed top players to produce some amazing speeds on overheads hit from behind the baseline.

Downplaying the speed of your overhead does not mean you should ease off. Learn to hit all out — while maintaining your rhythm — instead of turning conservative. When you get into a choking, pressure situation it's much better to just be able to hit hard with your normal swing than to suddenly ease off. Early in the match don't be afraid to hit two or three or four balls out, trying to find your range, because once you find it you will be lethal. But if you turn conservative on this shot, a smart opponent will lob you to death because he knows you can't hurt him.

Although you want to adopt a service motion as you hit your overhead, stop thinking "serve distance" when you visualize your actual target areas. For example, when you serve you have 60 feet from the baseline to your opponent's service line. But when you hit an overhead from the baseline you gain another 18 feet to your opponent's baseline. Furthermore, when you hit overheads from between the baseline and the service line, you still have more distance to play with than when you serve. Unfortunately, many players feel they have decreased the distance available to them, and that they must hit down on the ball — with the result that they always walk up to the net to retrieve their shot. So when you hit overheads between the baseline and the service line, remember to swing up and out at the ball in order to keep it deep.

Never be discouraged if your overhead is going long. Depth is the name of the this game, once you get it under control. The main reason you may be hitting long is that you are letting the ball get too far behind you as it comes down. To adjust, keep hitting up through the ball, but strive to contact the ball farther out in front of your hitting shoulder. If length is your only problem, you have good form and you're on the way to playing good tennis.

6

The Serve

HATEVER YOU HAVE READ or have been told about the serve, keep in mind the fact that in my 50-plus years of coaching, I haven't come across a single player who could swing down on the serve and have the ball land in the appropriate service box. And that includes an experiment with former pro basketball center Artis Gilmore, who is 7'2" tall. This means that you must learn to swing "up and out" with a degree of topspin, never down. Try to visualize yourself as a midget hitting up on the ball, rather than a giant hitting down, if you hope to serve the ball with speed and placement. When Drs. Gideon Ariel and Andrei Vorobiev and I studied the serve using three-dimensional equipment, even the tallest player recruited muscles that generated an upward swing to the ball. We did not find a single player who could recruit the muscles to "swing down" at the ball and serve it within the boundaries.

A second important overall concept is to learn to serve with topspin on the ball so that you can avoid the syndrome club players struggle with around the world. They try to slug the first serve, hard and flat, and while it might strike fear in some opponents, it rarely goes in. Then on the second serve they have the right idea but the wrong execution. Instead of fighting physical laws, the player goes, "Dear God, please let this one go in so we can play the point," and he hits a helium ball that gravity brings down into play. Unfortunately, a smart opponent simply comes in and gives him an early lunch, so he loses either way.

What everybody needs to realize is that the first serve should have the same basic physical properties as the second. They are not two distinct swings. You have to bend the ball over the net to get it in play and there are only two ways to do this: (1) with topspin rotation, which forces the ball to bend with speed, or (2) with gravity, which produces the trusty patty-cake shot.

Mary demonstrates the "palm down" theory in stage one of the arm's movement when throwing a baseball. This will facilitate 450 degrees of racket rotation when serving.

Another major underlying premise is to think of the serve from the standpoint of throwing a baseball instead of regarding it as a "down, up, down, up, down" motion. Get the feeling of both shoulders working together by rotating your upper body back on a horizontal plane so you will generate more energy when you uncoil your body. The principle here is the same as in baseball: if you try to throw a ball without using shoulder rotation you have only the power of your arm, and the ball won't travel very fast for most players. However, I have seen some pretty hard hitters use mainly arm motion, but they expend more energy and also place their shoulders and elbows in a vulnerable position for injuries.

A fourth crucial concept is that you don't have to go through a series of gyrations or a muscular kind of effort to hit the ball hard. The great servers conserve energy and generate all the power they need by synchronizing arm and body movements in a relaxed, flowing motion with well-timed forearm action at impact. In contrast to what we have thought for years, our research shows some wrist displacement before impact, but little or none at impact. The key movement is forearm speed and pronation to position the racket properly against the ball, a technique we'll discuss later in this chapter.

What always impressed me about Pancho Gonzales's serve was not his speed, but the fact that fundamentally he had a flawless stroke and normally hit with 60 to 70 percent accuracy on his first serve. He didn't have one hitch or one wasted

Mary begins to let the forearm drop as the elbow begins its forward movement. Her elbow is pointed forward and she can see her palm on the side of her head. If she were holding a racket, she would be scratching the back of someone standing next to her, but not her own back. Then, to get the palm out, or the racket face behind the ball, Mary must pronate her forearm. This is approximately the same motion as snapping an old-fashioned thermometer. The force of the pronation carries Mary's arm to the right side of her body and has caused a 180-degree directional turn with her palm from the ear to the finish.

motion; he never made any muscles work against him. He hit the ball harder than anyone, yet his motion was so fluid that he never had upper arm and shoulder problems. At 18-all in the third set, back in the days before the tie-breaker, he would still be hitting rhythmically and throwing in bombs.

Even in the 1960s, when he was winning matches at Wimbledon at the age of forty-one, Gonzales was still the greatest server in the game because he generated his power with rhythm and the proper use of each body link, rather than brute strength. At the old Madison Square Garden, wrestling mats were hooked up in the corridors downstairs and you could find Pancho warming up there before a match, working on his serving motion. He would throw the ball up and just swing nice and easy, trying to make sure there were no hitches in his swing. Sometimes he wouldn't even use a ball; he would almost close his eyes and go through the serving motion, trying to sense the rhythm of his swing rather than the isolated movements of his body.

Out on the court, whatever he did while serving or preparing to serve was calculated to keep himself relaxed. He never bounced the ball hard on the court. He never gave his motion excess gyrations. When he walked to the line he would try to shrug his shoulders and shake his arms loose. He looked so calm you would think, "Why doesn't he get excited?" The first time one of my students, Jeff Austin, faced Gorgo's serve, his motion was so easy that Jeff thought Gorgo was going to take it easy on him 'cause he was just a kid. But when Gorgo uncorked the ball right down the middle, Jeff wasn't ready and it scared the heck out of him. I have no doubt Gonzales would have served in the 140 m.p.h. zone with today's rackets. But a bigger issue is that he would have done it with very little force on his shoulder and elbow. In contrast, power servers like Greg Rusedski (143 m.p.h. in the 1997 U.S. Open) and Pete Sampras hit with a style that places their shoulder and elbow in great jeopardy.

So remember Gonzales the next time you go to serve — not to try to duplicate his speed, but to copy his loose, flowing motion. You needn't go through a lot of grunting and groaning and weird, twisting gyrations in order to hit a good hard serve. You can generate terrific power with an easy, rhythmical swing — if you know what you're doing. And that's what we're going to work on in this chapter.

J.J. coils his body first before releasing the ball.

The palm of his racket hand is down on the backswing.

THE GRIP

Many beginners prefer to use the regular (Eastern) forehand grip to hit a basic "flat" serve, but the sad truth is that a player holding this grip to serve will always be limited in the amount of power and spin he can achieve. In fact, I have never seen a famous player serve with an Eastern forehand grip. After explaining this problem to beginners, I never try to force a grip change if the player is having fun with the grip he's holding. The problem surfaces when a player refuses to use an advanced grip, but continually registers disappointment with his own serve.

Good serving dictates that players should use the Continental grip, halfway between the Eastern forehand and Eastern backhand, in order to facilitate greater ball speed and rotation with less stress on the shoulder, forearm, and wrist.

Some pros feel that everybody should start with a Continental, since this is the ultimate goal anyway. I like people to start out right, but I also want to motivate them to stay in the game. The Continental is just too doggone uncomfortable for many beginners because it places the face of the racket in an awkward position that forces you to pronate your forearm. Beginners often say they can't even get the ball in play and you hear them complaining, "This is a stupid game — we can't even play a point when I serve." So instead of driving these people into another sport by insisting on the Continental, I let them use the forehand grip — but always with the understanding that if they start playing well they must change to the Continental if they want to remain competitive on their serve. Most people who hold a forehand

J.J.'s body begins to uncoil, throwing the racket away from his body, as opposed to scratching his back.

His forearm has pronated to the right, as in the baseball pitch.

J.J.'s final move is to finish on the left side of his body to release the tension on the muscles.

Abi , a 16-year-old southern California champion, already has a 110-m.p.h. serve. At the beginning of each serve, her goal is to exhale to relax her muscles and then go for it.

grip only get about 90 degrees of racket rotation while the player using the Continental grip gets 450 degrees of racket rotation, which produces far greater ball speed.

Whatever your level of play now, try the Continental. But if you can't handle it don't feel guilty. Just shift to the forehand grip and try to gradually move your palm toward the Continental as your forearm becomes stronger and you will eventually develop a good serving motion.

THE SWING: AN OVERVIEW

When you begin your service motion, you need to coordinate three simultaneous movements — the ball toss and the actions of your body and racket. For many people this is the single most difficult aspect of tennis technique. But then, the serve is the single most important stroke.

I've seen a great variety of ball tosses over the decades, but the primary objective is to toss the ball to the right spot and height with the least amount of muscle recruitment. The toss most often taught is to cradle the ball with the finger tips while the palm is pointed upward. However, in our studies, we were surprised to find that such a toss on an advanced serve generates more muscle contractions. It's interesting to note that a baseball player actually turns the palm of his glove hand down when throwing the baseball because this places less stress on the non-throwing hand. Jack Kramer, in the 1940s, was the first player I saw who would treat the tossing hand in a manner similar to the glove hand of a baseball player. He would begin his toss with the left hand palm facing down and then gradually turn the palm upward near the end of the toss. Pete Sampras in the 1980s would start by holding the ball with the plane of the palm vertical — as though he were holding a glass of water. John McEnroe held the ball the same way.

Whatever style you prefer, the ball should be tossed to the peak of your racket's reach (some 20 to 27 inches out of your outstretched hand), at least one arm's length in front of your body and almost an arm's length to the right of your head. Beginners are taught to release the ball straight up, but as I'll point out, this inhibits a smooth coiling and uncoiling of the body and also places the shoulder in a vulnerable position for injury. Try instead to rotate your left shoulder back toward the fence, in sync with the racket arm, until your opponent can almost see the back side of your front shoulder. At this point your ball-toss arm is approximately parallel to the baseline. Now raise this arm upward and out toward your opponent as you release the ball. This motion enables you to maintain a simultaneous rotation with both shoulders. (A wonderful drill for tossing the ball on an advanced serve is to stand an arm's length from the fence while facing it. Simulate a serve, and toss the ball forward and parallel to the fence. This will keep the ball on the right side of your head and help you learn not to toss the ball back over your head.)

Meanwhile, the racket arm goes back toward the back fence until it reaches a horizontal position with the palm facing down. Then begin rotating both shoulders

Abi hits a flat serve, contacting the ball to the right side of her head as her forearm pronates automatically. Her racket finishes on the left side to relax the musculature.

PRACTICE TIP: A DRILL FOR THE TOSS

If you have a consistent toss, you should be able to point to the spot where the ball reaches its correct point for an imaginary serve. Bobby Riggs, in the 1940s, would even practice serving blindfolded in order to groove his toss, and he won a lot of bets as a result. But when I ask people at the tennis college, "Where do you throw the ball?" they say, "Somewhere out there." Well, "out there" isn't good enough if you are really serious about consistency. So try this drill to help you find the specific spot where you want to throw your toss on each serve.

Get a friend to stand on the other end of the court as you begin to serve. Have three or four balls with you. Now keep your chin up as you hit and do not look at your friend — just concentrate on where the toss is going, and where you contact it. Purposely throw the first ball straight above your head, but still hit up on the ball. Have your friend yell where the ball lands —"It's 40 feet out," or whatever. Then throw the second ball a little farther out in front until your friend says, "It's in by a foot." Then mark that imaginary spot where you contacted the ball, and start practicing to have your toss end there every time. Don't hit the ball unless you throw it to that spot. If you have a proper swing, that's your spot for the rest of your life (though this spot will change slightly as you learn to hit with more speed).

forward and allow the hitting arm to feel as though it's making a movement similar to a lasso. Notice that as you accelerate your racket, it never "scratches" your back. This loop by the racket — when uninterrupted — is one of the primary sources of power in your serve.

Then stretch up to hit the ball with an upward and forward striking motion while the forearm and wrist pronate (turn on a horizontal axis) to position the racket face behind the ball. "Pronation" sounds confusing, but it's very similar to snapping an old-fashioned thermometer. The feeling you should get is hitting up at the ball or hitting out, but never down. Try to contact the ball approximately two feet or more in front of your body, and to the right of your hitting shoulder, so that your weight — and swing — come forward naturally. Let your follow-through carry you into the court, even if you're planning to stay near the baseline.

Keep your chin up throughout the swing to help keep your body from sagging and pulling the ball down into the net, and focus on the ball until it has left the strings. Our research has found that keeping your head still at the impact point also serves as a notice to stop your upper body abruptly, forcing the racket to speed up. Dr. Howard Brody and I were doing some racket-string tests while shooting our "Science and Myths of Tennis" video. Howard spent some time calculating the effect of suddenly stopping one's upper body and allowing the racket to accelerate, similar to a hand stopping when making a whip snap. He determined that, if the stopping of the upper body comes rapidly and at an appropriate time, the racket-head speed can be increased by a factor of 1.7 times.

At impact, your racket should be extended to the peak of your reach and the face pointed toward the target. But when you hit with a Continental grip, the racket actually carries out to the right of your target line, and then in an arc down the left side of your body. This is a major point because if you try to make the racket go forward and straight down to your left side, you will have to interrupt the flow and acceleration of your racket by sending a message from your brain to tell your muscles to put on the brakes. Thus, you will lose a great amount of racket-head and ball speed on your serve.

SPECIFIC ELEMENTS

Ready Position

Before the great two-handed backhand service returns came into prominence, strategy generally dictated that players stand close to the centerline when serving from the right side in order to capitalize on hitting the ball to an opponent's backhand over the lower portion of the net. That has all changed now in advanced tennis. Today, there are many players who have a stronger backhand than forehand, and thus you must decide which is your opponent's stronger and weaker side and then stand accordingly. For example, if a righthander's forehand is the weaker side, position yourself a few feet to the right of the center stripe to make it easier to serve to the forehand side. Stand closer to the center stripe if your opponent's backhand is weaker. (The same rule applies when serving from the left court.)

As you prepare to serve into the deuce court, stand with your left shoulder pointed out toward the left net post (if you are righthanded), with your feet comfortably spread, hands and racket held at waist level. Make sure you don't have one tense muscle. Have your arms literally go spaghetti. Exhale (biofeedback studies have shown that exhaling decreases the amount of muscular activity while inhaling increases it) and wherever your shoulders fall, leave them there. Tell yourself you're going to have the smoothest swing in the world. Remember, there's very little relationship between the power of your serve and all the pre-serve antics some people like to go through. Jimmy Connors used to bounce the ball six or seven times as he prepared to serve but had very little power. Now he does less and he gets far more speed.

Adopt a Baseball-Throwing Motion

Ideally, the tennis serve utilizes the basic principles of a baseball pitcher's motion. That's why I've said for many years that in terms of tennis, the PE instructor or softball coach who teaches all students how to throw a ball properly is worth his or her weight in gold. It used to be that boys were forced to learn how to throw a ball properly or sit on the sidelines. Girls were overlooked, unless they had an enlightened gym teacher or an equal-opportunity parent to give them instruction, and as a result, when they tried tennis as adults they often had a lot of trouble coordinating the proper service motion. Now that women's athletics are as popular and competitive as men's, PE instructors and coaches everywhere should be doing their best to eliminate that common jibe "You throw like a girl." In the early 1980s, Dr. Gideon Ariel and I tested the throwing arms of students at a local high school. It turned out that, up to 120 pounds, the girls in our study could throw the ball at the same speed as the boys. After 120 pounds, the boys began to benefit from more muscle mass.

A good pitcher gets 270 degrees, or more, of shoulder rotation on his delivery

by pivoting with both shoulders on a horizontal level. He starts off by turning his back to the batter, and then he uncoils his body in the following sequence as he pitches the ball: his front leg comes forward, followed by his hips, shoulders, elbow, forearm, and hand. This unbroken sequence of body movements (also known as the kinetic chain) is what supplies his rhythm and power, and this upper body rotation is exactly what you want on the serve. Again, debate continues on which body link contributes the most power, but as you will see, it depends upon the style of "pitch" being used.

From a starting position, take your hitting hand back at about waist level as you turn away from your opponent with a horizontal pivot. But unlike the pitcher, keep both feet in contact with the court with a slight shift of your weight to the back foot when coiling your body. As you begin to uncoil your hitting shoulder and hips in toward the toss, let your elbow break, turn your forearm inward with your palm down so that your racket could be placed above your head as though you were looking in a mirror. This motion can easily be simulated by holding a ball with your palm facing downward, but the name of the ball visible between your thumb and index finger. As soon as you begin to turn your hand inward and the

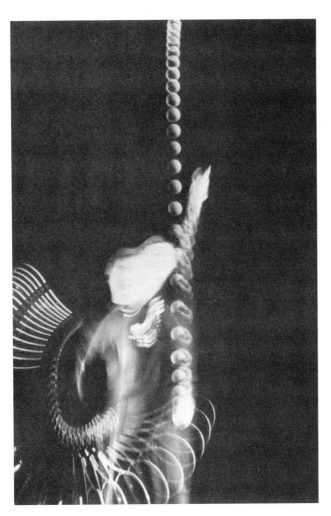

In this photograph of the typical beginner's toss, notice how the arm follows the ball up on just about a straight line. Learning to throw the ball straight up is extremely difficult, even for advanced players who try to demonstrate the toss to beginners.

On the advanced service toss, which requires a ball thrown farther toward the net and increased shoulder rotation, notice how the arm of the throwing hand is up near the head before the hand actually releases the ball, thus shortening the length of the toss and making it more consistent. Observe how the ball arcs out in front of the body so that the hitter can swing up and out and then follow through with a natural and forward movement. Also note that his chin remains up throughout the swing.

name of the ball is pointed toward your head, turn your elbow toward the net with a relaxed arm and your racket will automatically turn into a lasso while rotating a total of 360 degrees. No intentional effort should be made to form a loop with your hitting arm. Let it flow naturally, so that your hip rotation and the shoulder roll is followed by the elbow, followed by the forearm and wrist. Hip, shoulder, elbow, forearm, wrist . . . and then the back foot moving forward into the court, the same as a pitcher's. Rosie Casals, in the late 1960s, had this motion and that's why — at 5'2" — she could stand up there and serve as hard as most men. The Netherlands' Brenda Schultz has been clocked at 119 m.p.h., which is faster than many male pros on the court.

Serving with this type of motion sounds pretty easy to people until they get out on the court and give it a try. Then they have to overcome either their lack of a natural throwing motion or what they've previously been told or have learned about the serve.

For one thing, you can't use a beginner's toss and expect to develop a continuous motion. By failing to rotate away from the net with your front shoulder, you limit the amount of body uncoiling, which makes it more difficult to generate arm, hand, and racket speed.

Second, many people have been told to start with both arms held high, and then to "go down with both arms . . . up with both arms . . . then get that racket down and scratch your back," at which point they can expect to turn in and unleash this gigantic serve. But when they swing this way, they're doomed. First of all, they've destroyed the kinetic energy chain, leaving only the power in their arm to salvage any speed on the ball. And second, by forcing their arm down behind their back to form a loop, their arm normally stops and the racket either stops completely or slows down to little or no speed.

A similar problem occurs when you drop your hitting elbow as you draw the racket back or while forming the loop. I call this the "chain-puller's syndrome" or the "train-conductor's swing"— pull on the whistle, "toot, toot!" This action destroys the continuous swing that you seek.

The dropped elbow and the down-up-down motion can be traced back in large part to the artist who designed one of the original serving trophies. The model was Les Stoeffen, Sr., who teamed with Don Budge to win the Wimbledon doubles in 1934, and who had absolutely classic form and amazing speed. Unfortunately, the sculptor didn't know the first thing about tennis and he didn't like the way Stoeffen held his elbow high and his shoulder up on the backswing. So, for artistic reasons, he arbitrarily put Stoeffen's elbow down. It's a beautiful pose, but as a model sitting in trophy cases everywhere, it has done more to ruin good serves over the years than any other thing. If Les Stoeffen had actually served that way he wouldn't have beaten Clyde Klutz.

The Toss

Since the beginner's toss inhibits a smooth, rolling motion by the shoulders, I like to have people learn the advanced toss as soon as possible — and preferably without ever trying the beginner's toss. Why start with a technique that is so limiting to a good consistent serve, when the advanced toss is really no more difficult to master? The advanced toss delivers the ball much farther into the court than the beginner's toss and enables your shoulders to work together, thereby generating considerably more power. The key difference is that beginners are taught to throw the ball straight up from their outstretched arm, while advanced players turn their front shoulder and draw the ball back before releasing it up and out.

However you approach the toss, think about standardizing a smooth arm lift and just opening the fingers to release the ball. Let your arm do the work, and not your wrist or your palm. The arm won't produce drastic variations in the toss, but a little flick of the wrist can throw the radius off drastically. Nor do you want to have a death clutch on the ball at any point. Just hold it lightly and keep your tossing arm moving up in a flowing motion until the ball is released.

Trying to coordinate a consistent toss with the stroke is the toughest part of the game for many people. In fact, we've had people at the tennis college who are so nervous or confused that they can't even release the ball from their fingers as they bring the racket back. So I tread quietly here because I've learned that once people get the fear of an inadequate ball toss, they have to work extremely hard to overcome it. I also find that it helps students to look at a ruler and measure twice 25 inches; they quickly see that it isn't a very high toss to the peak of their racket.

Nevertheless, the fact remains: you will never develop a consistent serve until you learn to throw your toss in the same place every time. It takes a perfect toss to effect a perfect swing. You can swing beautifully, but if your toss goes in a different place every time, you will have to adjust your swing accordingly to get the racket to hit the ball. Yet people will throw the ball behind their head, then blithely say, "No problem, I'll just make this little adjustment." They have a lot of interesting twists to their stroke but they don't win too many matches because variety kills them. You want to make the same old boring toss to the same spot on every serve so that you can hit the same old boring winner. Ideally, this spot should be to the right of your head, about a racket's length from your outstretched free hand, and as far out in front of your body as possible, without disturbing the rhythm of your service motion.

When you adjust your swing to accommodate a bad toss — instead of developing a perfect toss to accommodate the swing — you defeat yourself in three ways:

1. Swinging at a toss that is behind your head or straight out in front of your body will stop your natural shoulder action and prevent a proper follow-through by forcing you to pull your hitting elbow in, arch your back, or make a severe wrist adjustment.

2. Your hitting arm takes a terrific beating and you can develop tennis elbow and shoulder damage. If you throw the ball behind your body, your arm must take nearly all the strain without any help from a rotating shoulder.

3. Swinging at a ball that's in a different place every time requires a different motor program and a different set of muscles, when the goal is to groove one's swing and master a toss to accommodate that swing.

Therefore, if you are serving in a match and you don't like your toss, catch the ball and try again. Your opponent cannot force you to swing at a bad toss. There isn't a rule that allows your opponent to say, "I'm giving you three tries and then it's a fault." The only rule is that play must be continuous. So if you are playing in a tournament and you spend 15 minutes trying to make the right toss, your opponent can call over an official who has the power to tell you, "Play the next ball or it's a fault."

Another myth that helps destroy good serves everywhere is the statement, "Give yourself plenty of time on the toss." This leads people to throw the ball so high that it takes two days to come down; if they play in a high wind they may never see the ball again. But remember, all you need to do is throw the ball 20 to 27 inches out of your outstretched hand (depending on the length of the racket

you are using) — to the peak of where you can reach with your racket as you contact the ball. This will give you plenty of time to complete a continuous serving
motion. In the 1970s, John Newcombe, one of the best servers in history, hit the
ball precisely when it stopped moving upward; when his toss reached its peak, his
racket was there to meet it. Roscoe Tanner also tossed the ball to about 27 inches,
and he had one of the fastest, most accurate serves in the game — even when he
was on the senior tour.

Why do you want to hit the ball at its peak? What's wrong with tossing the
ball high so that you can marshal your body for a gigantic hitting effort?

When you hit the ball at its peak you dictate a continuous swing. Each little
section of your serve should be part of a kinetic chain that builds up energy and
reaches maximum speed where it is really meaningful: at impact. Think of your
swing as sounding like a smooth-running motor that starts slowly and then quickly
increases speed without any hesitation. Then think of a whirring motor trying to
stay in sync with the average player's herky-jerky motion. The key ingredient here,
however, is that in a baseball-type service motion, the tossing hand has moved
backward, upward, and forward with the hitting hand so that the toss is actually
delayed. If you throw a ball to the peak of your reach, but the toss is released early,
out in front of the body, your hitting arm has too far to travel and must rush to
have the racket meet the toss at its apex.

Seen from behind, here are the contact points for three basic serves. The ball will be contacted with the racket head just outside the hand for a slice serve (left). The racket will be straight above the hand for a flat serve and between the hitter's head and hitting hand for the 45-degree angled topspin serve. Your goal is to eventually hit all three serves with a toss that appears to be the same for each.

When you throw the ball too high you must wait for it to drop, which means that somewhere along the swing you must build in braking motions. You may drop your hitting elbow going back or you may pause with the racket behind your back until you know it's time to go up after the ball. But when your swing stops or slows down in any manner, you must go like crazy and expend more energy just to regain the speed you have built up. You could even start your motion with the racket behind your back and serve just as well, if not better. I've had people stand flat-footed at the baseline, facing their target, and hit harder than they ever have in their life, just by swinging with a forearm and wrist and a continuous rolling motion of their shoulders — and using no footwork whatsoever.

Theoretically, if you are serving with a continuous motion and you throw the ball higher than the peak of your outstretched racket, you should miss the ball. But most people won't do this. Instead of learning to lower their toss, they continue to stop or slow down their swing. Thus I prefer to have people throw their toss too low rather than too high, because a low toss forces them to maintain a quick, easy shoulder roll. Remember: force equals mass times acceleration. Anytime the racket stops, you're at zero force.

Tossing the ball out in front of your body but slightly outside your hitting shoulder at impact is crucial in getting the most out of your serve. By keeping the ball out in front you achieve three things: (1) you contact the ball where the racket is traveling the fastest, (2) you enhance the ball-trajectory angle, because geometrically, the farther inside the court you are, the less chance you have of hitting the tape of the net, and (3) your front shoulder turns naturally and your racket eventually comes down to the left side of your body, so that you are ready to move into position for your opponent's return. It's interesting to me that Boris Becker and

Pete Sampras both stop their rackets on the right side of the body. This places great stress on the shoulder and both players have experienced some problems.

Try to go too far forward on your toss; get the feeling that you're going to fall on your face. By stretching out over the baseline you enable your forearm and wrist to snap into the ball ahead of your body, and not straight above your head, where all power is lost. Here's a simple test. Without using a ball, hit an imaginary serve and listen carefully to the sound. The loudest "swish" should be way out in front of your body. That's where the racket is traveling the fastest and where you should be hitting the ball.

Initially, don't allow the fear of foot-faulting (touching the playing surface before contact with the ball) to destroy the rhythm you want to develop on your serve. You need to develop respect for the foot-fault rule, but first get your rhythm down. I see beginners all the time who are afraid to even step over the line after they've served. They throw the ball straight up and they do nothing with their shoulders. You can see them thinking, "Don't go across the line," and their whole movement comes to a sudden halt. Their serve is lousy but you hear them saying, "Well, I never foot-fault."

You will eventually learn that the front foot needs to be planted to get the most power. I often get letters telling me that I should teach players to jump in the air and then hit the ball. Yet research clearly indicates that a player who jumps to hit before his forearm has achieved maximum speed actually loses power. In one study, we had some top pros jump off trampolines to hit their serve. In almost every case, the players lost approximately 50 percent of their normal power. Although many top servers jump too early, the most efficient players are reaching up and out into the court and are actually being pulled off the ground by their momentum — after the forearm has achieved maximum speed, and that doesn't detract from ball speed.

In our three-dimensional calculations, the legs turned out to be great starters for body uncoiling, but by themselves only produced a few miles per hour on the serve. The reason is that lifting isn't very fast and, in many cases, only produces about six m.p.h. of ball speed. Most people can't even lift their center of gravity 12 inches off the ground, which tells us how fast the legs can really lift upward. But again, the legs are very important as stabilizers to activate the appropriate uncoiling of the body segments. There are players who have their butt practically on the ground from such severe knee bends on the serve, but our studies showed that this only sells tickets.

The Racket Arm and Loop

Take your racket back at the same time you start to make your toss, even though it feels like you're not going to have enough time for the racket to complete its loop behind your back and still contact the ball at the peak of its toss. That's why you've always heard, "Throw the ball high and give yourself plenty of time." But I've filmed serves at 10,000 frames a second and the racket can make its loop and go up to strike the ball before the ball has even dropped an inch.

To facilitate the loop, keep your palm down as you draw the racket back, and keep your elbow up once you begin the forward motion. When your hitting shoulder starts rotating forward, have your arm break at the elbow — sufficiently to squeeze a finger — so that the racket falls naturally to your side. Don't force the racket down or dwell upon what you are trying to do because this will ruin the looseness you seek. Then turn in and stretch up to strike the ball, with the elbow and wrist snapping in a whiplash type of motion.

A good drill for practicing the motion I seek is to stick a ball in a fence the exact height of your shoulders. Stand away with your back to the fence and begin your service swing by taking your racket back toward the fence. When your racket reaches the ball in the fence, rotate your shoulders forward and let your arm relax. Your rotating shoulder action will automatically form the loop you seek, if your hitting arm is completely relaxed.

Ideally, if you start your swing slowly with a loose, spaghetti-like motion, your racket should be reaching maximum speed as it approaches the ball. Have somebody watch to see if your racket comes into focus as it makes the loop. If it does, then you know you've slowed up and are losing your kinetic energy; but if your racket is a blur, then you know you are generating real speed.

You want the racket traveling fast while your muscles take it easy. The job of your biceps, for example, is to flex your arm inward. If you tighten it, straining for more power, you simply oppose your own serve.

Your Head

Think about hitting up at the ball with the chin up, because everybody has a tendency to pull down on the serve. For one thing, few people respect how high the net actually is, and for another, when the chin drops, your stomach muscles tend to relax, thus pulling your racket head down. Keeping your head up also prevents you from opening your body too soon and thus losing racket acceleration, and it helps keep your eyes focused on the ball. I once climbed up into the rafters to photograph John Newcombe's service motion, and as he made his toss and contacted the ball, his eyes were looking straight up at me, not out at the target.

Impact and Follow-Through

When you go up to contact the ball, try to think of hitting to the sky, or the roof. Hitting the ball at the proper place in the racket swing arc will automatically bring the ball down. If you hold a Continental grip, your racket face will actually go from left to right (inside-out) at contact, while the forearm makes a 180-degree turn.

Experiment with the ball toss and note how your hitting forearm breaks naturally much farther out in front of your body than you might have imagined. Try to contact the ball approximately two feet or more out in front so that your right foot (if you are righthanded) will come over the baseline to support your body weight as it moves forward and to help keep good balance. Some top players even contact the ball as much as four to five feet in front of them. Physicist Dr. Pat Keating did a study which shows that if you can learn to get way out in front on the toss, you give yourself a chance to have your racket pointed slightly down as it impacts the ball. Dr. Howard Brody has published a specific chart showing exactly the angle at which the racket face must meet the ball at certain heights and speeds to hit the ball into the proper box. In most cases, it's not more than five to eight degrees for a 100 m.p.h. serve. However, I remind you that the muscles weren't recruited to

A front view shows that the flat serve is hit with the racket above the hand.

For a topspin serve, the racket head will be between the hitter's head and his hitting hand when meeting the ball with a lifting motion.

swing down. It's just that the arm swing generates an arc and the racket eventually begins it downswing even though muscles were recruited to swing up at the ball.

Good servers don't stop with the fall-in step. They take two more steps forward and then bring both feet together with a stutter-step, or check-step, while maintaining some slower forward motion. At this point the serve should be on their opponent's racket and they are in position to break in any direction with equal ease to handle the return. John Newcombe moved in farther off his serve than any player I have ever seen. His long strides often took him to within a foot of the service line on his third step, or about six feet ahead of most other players, pros included. In the 1980s, Stefan Edberg showed me some great moves going to the net, including the time I watched a player make a lousy, soft return of Edberg's serve and Stefan's racket actually crossed the net when he hit his first volley. Edberg basically became a U.S. Open champion as a result of his perfect balance and quick moves to the net. His serve didn't have as much speed as many players' but this allowed him to get farther into court and closer to the net for his volley. Many of today's net-rushers are hitting the serve with such great speed that they are also getting more returns at their feet. As a result, I'm sure that players will eventually measure the exact speed of their serve in relation to their foot speed so that they can arrive at the best position for a decent volley.

Reiterating what I discussed earlier, contacting the ball in front of your body on the serve provides three advantages: (1) you can be shorter and hit the ball harder with greater safety, (2) your center of gravity is ahead of your front foot, which enables a faster first step, and (3) you can take longer strides — and thus get closer to the net on your third step — because you're already on the move.

UNDERSTANDING BALL ROTATION ON THE SERVE

The four variations of the serve all have spin, so what we're really talking about is the angle at which the racket strikes the ball, and the degree of ball rotation. First is the "flat" serve, which has the racket contacting the back side of the ball and continuing forward and slightly to the right of the target line. Second is the "top-spin" serve, ideally contacted at about a 45-degree angle, halfway between a full vertical and a horizontal plane. Third is the "slice" serve, which is produced by a racket moving horizontally left to right and brushing the back side of the ball; it's a myth that you actually come around the outside of the ball. And fourth is the "American Twist," which is contacted with a severe upward lift that produces almost vertical rotation on the ball. I hate to teach this serve, however, because it places too much strain on your back and the hitting elbow. The American Twist can make you a hero in Pismo Beach, but you may eventually have to learn to play with your other arm. Over the years, I have warned coaches at seminars that they will find themselves in court one day if they haven't properly advised students of the physiological dangers of a "kick" serve. That day arrived for me a few years ago when I started having students sign a form that released me from legal responsibilities because I had advised them of the dangers but they still wanted to learn the "kick" serve.

The Flat Serve

In reality, the "flat" serve is a misnomer, since nobody can produce a ball that is hit without rotation. But the flat serve is hit with the least amount. Beginners who don't hit hard can make the racket follow straight behind the ball after impact, but for most players the racket strikes the ball going slightly from left to right, imparting a small amount of spin. When this serve is hit with an Eastern forehand grip, you can't make a natural snap of the forearm and hand. If you do go from left to right while pronating the forearm, the ball will hit the right fence for a righthanded server.

The Typical Topspin Serve

Eventually you will want to use the Continental grip so that you can hit your serves with considerable topspin, and thereby slug the ball as hard as you want, while bringing it down in your opponent's service box.

The principle of applying topspin to the serve is basically the same as on the forehand and backhand groundstrokes. You have to swing from low to high and brush the back side of the ball at about a 45-degree angle, with the racket moving from left to right for righthanders. This is why you must use the Continental grip. It places the racket in the right position at impact following a pronation of the forearm and hand.

Contrary to popular opinion, the racket does not go over the ball at contact but hits the back side. Even top professionals advance the theory that on the advanced serve you want to get the racket to come over the top right side of the ball to impart topspin. The problem with this concept is that you guarantee a double fault. You're not even tall enough to see over the net and yet some pros would now have you put a roof over the ball, forgetting that you can't hit down on the ball and get it in play unless you're as tall as the average pro basketball forward. I'll admit that coming over the ball is the feeling you seek. But I teach this only as a sensation to help you produce the correct swing, with the clear understanding that this is not what actually happens. You must hit "up and out," visualizing a dot on the back of the ball rotating from the lower left to the upper right — or from about 8 o'clock to 2 o'clock on an imaginary clock.

If you have been serving with an Eastern forehand grip and you switch to the Continental, don't feel like a klutz if you suddenly can't get your serve in play. With an Eastern grip there was no pronation of the forearm and now the Continental demands a new motor program. What counts is to concentrate on keeping the face of the racket brushing up and across the ball and carrying out to the right.

The Slice Serve

Like a curveball in baseball, a pure slice serve can be a valuable weapon, if you can make the racket strike the center of the back side of the ball while the racket moves across on a horizontal plane. Serving from the deuce (right) court, a

righthanded player can break off a ball that drives his opponent off the court and forces a weak, out-of-position return. Since the slice serve has a lower trajectory than topspin, it bounces lower and can be particularly effective against a tall player who hates to bend, or anybody who has slow lateral movement. Jack Kramer, who developed the most notorious slice of any player I've ever seen, could move you to the side fence on a 60-foot-wide court and take you right out of the point even if you managed to get the ball back. Arthur Ashe, in the 1970s, could do the same thing.

Still, tempting as the slice serve might appear, it raises dangerous problems for most righthanded players. For example, if you are a righthander serving to a righthander, you must slice the ball to your opponent's forehand, which is normally his stronger side, since it facilitates a topspin return that bounces at your feet. Thus you should never use the slice unless you are (1) positive your opponent has a weaker forehand than backhand, (2) positive you will ace your opponent, or (3) positive that you will pull him so far out of play — when serving from the deuce court — that he'll hit a weak return and give you an open court for your own return. If you're not positive you can achieve this with your slice serve, then concentrate on serving with more topspin to your opponent's backhand corner or directly into the body. The same principles apply in doubles.

Most people tend to hit a mixture of topspin and slice. When they brush up at the ball, they leave the horizontal plane but they fail to achieve the 45-degree angle needed for proper topspin. Thus, they may spread an opponent fairly wide but the ball has a more horizontal bounce when it hits, which gives their opponent an easier return to handle with their forehand. Similarly, most righthanders have trouble serving the ball to the backhand corner from the deuce court because they

have some slice to their serve. What they need is a more vertical upward swing so they can break the ball toward their opponent's backhand.

People are always asking me, "Why does a lefthander have a natural slice serve?" They think there's something physiological in the forearm and wrist of the lefthander that allows him to throw in a bigger slice. But that isn't the case. It's simply that the lefthander grows up playing primarily against righthanders, and he discovers at an early age that if he can slice his serve, he can spread his righthanded opponent wide to the backhand side and open up the court for an easy volley. So he starts working earlier on slicing the ball, whereas the righthander is penalized for slicing the ball to another righthander, unless he can break the ball off horizontally.

One advantage of a good slice serve for the righthander comes when he plays an opponent who has a strong forehand and a much weaker backhand. Most people in this situation make the error of trying desperately to serve to that weak backhand side, but their opponent keeps running around and hitting his powerful forehand. Instead, to get the ball to this person's backhand — serving from the deuce court — here's your strategy:

First stretch him wide to his forehand with a slice serve. That sounds suicidal, but remember that very few players in the history of tennis have been able to hit outright winners from the baseline, especially when they're pulled off court. If your opponent gets the ball back, return it sharply to his backhand and he'll normally be too far out of position to recover with a forehand. This strategy can backfire, of course, if you hit a weak slice serve that fails to move your opponent far enough off the court. Then he can knock off a big forehand and still protect his weak backhand.

In 1997, I produced a video with Jack Kramer and Pancho Segura entitled "70 Minutes with Big Jake and Pancho," in which they simply talk about the game. At one point they told how they would play Steffi Graf and Andre Agassi. In both cases, one of their suggestions was to slice the serve on the righthand side and force them to pass you while running for a backhand. Agassi, with his two-handed backhand, would have difficulty hitting a clean passing shot on the run. Steffi hits a one-handed backhand with underspin, which is also difficult to hit cross-court while on the run.

The American Twist Serve

A lot of men have become enamored of this serve, for it can be lethal in intermediate tennis with its high-bouncing kick. But go to a pro tennis tournament and see for yourself just how few players actually use this serve. They know that a big kick doesn't bother most good players. These players just laugh, step into the ball, and knock your brains out because your twist serve has lost too much speed.

The main reason I'm against this stroke, however, is that it can lead to tennis elbow or shoulder problems. Generally, the ball is thrown directly over your head or some degree behind you, meaning your body must bend backward in order to fix the racket on a horizontal plane before it starts its forward and vertical lifting motion. This in turn "freezes" your shoulder rotation and forces you to hit the ball with a sophisticated forearm, wrist, and elbow snap. By suddenly stopping your upper body movements much sooner than normal as you turn in to hit the ball, you have to rely on the strength of your arm to supply all your power. Placing these excessive pressures upon your shoulder and an elbow that is already severely twisted can cause a great deal of damage. Tony Roche used the American Twist effectively, and was one of the world's top players for a number of years — until finally he had no usable elbow and had to withdraw from the game.

STRATEGY AND THE SERVE

Target Areas

Due to improvements in the two-handed backhand service return, serving strategy has changed a bit at the pro level. Here, the basic goal is now to hit either corner with as much speed as possible. Base-liners hope that the subsequent service return will be poor enough for them to knock off a winner on the next shot. The net-rushers are hoping that their fast serve will produce weak returns for easy volleys.

At the club and amateur level, when playing 5.0 players and above, you had better be able to hit to the side which produces the highest and longest ball. A high return yields easy volleys and a long return makes short passing shots impossible.

For beginners and 3.0 players, the old strategy I have emphasized for years still holds. Once you can get your serve over the net and in play, start concentrating on at least aiming for your opponent's backhand corner. There are three basic reasons for this:

1. Most people at this level of play have less accuracy and power — not to mention a basic lack of confidence — hitting from their backhand side.

2. If your opponent is a one-handed backhand player, he will have to react faster on the backhand than on the forehand in order to meet the ball out in front of his body. Lateness is more damaging on the one-handed backhand, and most people fail to react fast enough.

3. From the records I kept in pro tennis, the chances are 85 out of 100 that your opponent's one-handed backhand will produce a higher ball, because players who are late can only underspin. Thus, if you are attacking the net, a high service return gives you a much easier volley. But if you hit to your opponent's forehand and he produces topspin, the ball may go over and down at your feet and you will be forced to hit from a lifting position, thereby losing your tactical advantage. Maybe you're thinking, "Yeah, Vic, but I like to serve to the forehand to keep my opponent honest." My argument is, "Why let him off the hook? If you are beating his brains out by attacking the backhand, don't give him a chance to get his confidence back by letting him hit his forehand."

The basic principle should be: always serve to the side which will produce the highest, longest, and weakest ball in return. Thus, the only times you should try to hit to the forehand are when you're positive you're going to ace your opponent because he's cheating too far to his backhand side, when you're positive his forehand is weaker than his backhand, or when you're positive you're going to pull him so far off the court that you will have an easy put-away volley if he returns your serve.

I talked earlier about how Pancho Gonzales could hit with speed and could also place the ball beautifully and move you far out of court. But what the players of his era remember most is the fact that he got a greater percentage of first serves in play than anybody. That was the real pressure he put on you. He was one of the few guys you had to play hard on the first serve every time because it usually went in, whereas against most players you had a tendency to relax on first serves. In fact, he produced a lot of service-return errors simply because his opponents were so tight and nervous, knowing what was coming.

Yet back in the early 1950s, when Gonzales was winning every tournament on the pro circuit, the other pros managed to convince themselves that they could handle his case if he didn't have the big serve. So they came up with what they thought would neutralize Gorgo's greatest weapon: a one-ball-serve tournament. They figured that with only one serve, Gorgo would have to ease off and hit like the rest of them, and then if they could keep the ball in play they could beat him. Jack March bought the idea and organized the tournament in Cleveland. The other pros were so happy they could hardly wait — they were going to knock off the King.

Well, Gonzales never had such an easy time winning a tournament. He was so sound on his service stroke that he was even more effective than everyone else with just one ball. Before the tournament was even dreamed up, he was already in the habit — mentally — of serving only one ball; when he walked up to serve, he never thought about serving two balls. But the rest of the guys were going, "Dear

This woman is practicing having her service toss travel out in front of her body, off her hitting shoulder, so that she's already on the way to the net as she follows through. Her goal is to reach the final box on her third step (the check step), at which point her opponent should be returning the ball so she can break in the appropriate direction.

God, I've only got one!" and then hitting the most pitiful serves in the world. They single-faulted the tournament away. Ironically, the one-ball-serve concept has begun to surface in recent years as a cure for the inability of players to return the big serve, which makes tennis less appealing on television.

Taking the Net

If you're a typical beginner or intermediate player, you should simply serve and stay back, then wait until you get a short ball before you try to take the net. Most tournament players, however, don't even wait around for a short ball — they serve and attack automatically so that they can volley their opponent's return. They say, "If I don't go, my opponent is coming to the net against me." But the pros are different from you and me. They know that when they go to the net on their serve they are going behind a weapon. Plus they are playing seven days a week and are in good shape. So before you try to emulate them, you need three things:

1. A good first serve. You can't attack behind a helium ball. That's like throwing a hand grenade and running underneath it.

2. A strong volley. This enables you to defend yourself in that no-man's-land between the baseline and the net.

3. A sound heart. If you're not in shape and you try to attack the net on every serve, your friends will be carrying you out prone after five or six games.

If you have the ingredients to play a serve-and-attack game, then your footwork after the follow-through is crucial. Remember the three key steps after you fall in, ending with the little stutter-step, while still moving slowly forward as you

bring both feet together momentarily in order to prepare for your opponent's return shot. Some people get so pumped up when they serve —"Attack, attack, you little devil!"— that they go barreling in without stopping. Then their opponent hits an angled passing shot and all they can do is salute the ball as it goes by: "Terrific shot, Bertha."

Okay, so you serve and move in three steps, moving forward at a speed which will allow you to break in any direction. Then what do you do? It's simple: you either move forward on the diagonal to hit an approach volley, or you retreat for a lob. If your opponent drives the ball, break instantly in that direction, on a diagonal; don't hesitate or you'll get trapped down around your feet by half-volleys. Your goal is to get ahead of the service line to make your second play. If you advance that deep, the chances are enormous that you will hit your second shot while it is in the air, before it bounces (an approach volley). This means you won't get funny hops and you can contact the ball above the level of the net.

When you get to the ball, try to punch the volley to your opponent's weak side (which is that side which produces the highest and longest ball) and move up to take the net, halfway between the service line and the net, to the side of the center stripe to which you hit the ball. Remembering what I discussed in the previous chapter: if you hit a deep volley your opponent is in serious trouble. He will have only four different options: lob, hit a passing shot straight down the line, hit a short-angled topspin shot to keep it away from your lunge at the net, or hit right at your navel. All of these strokes are tough for most players to execute, with or without pressure. When a baseliner is hitting from far behind the baseline due to your deep volley from midcourt, it's almost impossible to pass you.

Practicing his serve, Eric brings his throwing arm back to guarantee a desired body turn, while keeping the racket head down. The ball is tossed on the right side, which will allow him to move farther forward on the hit while protecting his options to hit a slice or flat serve. His elbow begins to move forward before going upward to meet the ball. This allows the kinetic chain to stay intact. Going up, the racket head is on edge, which preserves the ability to pronate the forearm for more speed.

Whether you're a beginner or an experienced player whose philosophy has always been to serve and stay back, don't be frightened off by the footwork and exertion required to play like the pros. Rushing the net at every opportunity is critical if you want to raise the level of your game, maximize the physical conditioning that tennis offers, and add a new dimension of excitement. You've elected to go for the home run ball because statistics show that you will normally win or lose the point on the very next shot.

Therefore, when practicing — and even during a low-pressure match — try to fall in as you serve and move into your stutter-step position. Then as your serve improves, your footwork will already be ingrained and you won't have to break the habit of automatically staying back.

The Second Serve

Nearly everybody asks me, "How do I keep from choking on my second serve?" They talk as if they own a good second serve, if only pressure wouldn't interfere. But I've found over the years that most people choke simply because they don't have the stroke. Even without stress they can't get their second serve in play. Furthermore, their first serve isn't very good, so why should their second one be any better?

Another reason most people don't have a good second serve is that they haven't related the first one to the second as specific strokes for specific purposes.

Usually they simply think in terms of speed differentiation —"The first one didn't go in, so now I have to ease off on the second"— when actually it's a ball rotation differentiation.

For example, I think the serve should always be an all-out but properly controlled effort on both attempts. This is why I like to have people learn to hit with a Continental grip so that they can serve with speed and control under pressure: all they need to know is at what upward angle they should brush the ball to impart topspin.

Let's say your first serve has gone long. If you hit with a Continental, you know that you can actually swing faster, except that you want the face of your racket and the stroking pattern to be more vertical so that you can produce greater topspin. This causes the ball to react with a greater arc and brings it down more quickly into play.

That's why you always want to hit your first serve deep. If it goes long, you know precisely the amount of error you made, and you have the confidence to swing just as hard on the second serve as long as you increase the amount of topspin on the ball. (If you hit at the same speed, increasing the number of ball revolutions per second increases the spin and thus slows the ball down because you get less ball depression.)

Here's how most people go wrong. If they hit the "flat" serve with a forehand grip, and their first serve goes long, their only alternative is to reduce the speed of their swing. But it's very difficult to gauge speed reduction, especially when you have a choking feeling. It's far safer, I feel, to be able to hit out and hit hard, by just using a system which makes the ball spin faster. Better to throw the ball out in front and hit with excessive topspin — knowing that you can never hit too hard — than to throw the ball straight up and think to yourself, "I hope to heck this goes in."

People should change the arc of the ball not by slowing down their swing but by increasing the vertical lift of the racket. Having to swing softly or daintily under pressure, when you really want to hit all-out, is one of the worst feelings in the world. That's why many of the men who play club mixed doubles, as well as pros who play against celebrities, serve so poorly in these circumstances. They don't want to kill anybody, so they try to hit patty-cake serves and end up double-faulting all the time because they reduce the speed of their body and arm motion rather than just increasing the spin on the ball, and that takes a very different motor program.

A second common problem occurs with those who hit a topspin serve on their first attempt. If the ball goes long, most people have a tremendous fear of also knocking the second serve long. But instead of swinging faster and on a more vertical plane, they turn the palm out and hit their second serve flat. Yet even though they swing slowly, the ball still goes out because the flat serve can't bring the ball down in time.

Summing up, the best players in the world often hit over 100 m.p.h., but the percentages tell an important story. It's not uncommon to watch many of the best players hit fewer than 30 percent of their first serves in the box. It's a wonderful day when they are hitting 60 percent. Thus, the typical scenario is a big bomb on the first serve and an 80 to 90 m.p.h. second serve with topspin to force the ball downward. There seems to be no difference with club players, except that their bomb is far less than 100 m.p.h. and their second serve moves at the pace of a helium balloon. And it's the second serve that normally puts the average player in a hole as the opponent attacks the slow-moving ball and hits a winner.

My bottom-line advice? Work hard on your second serve. When Andre Agassi learned that, statistically, he had the best second serve on the tour, his first serve immediately improved. He knew he didn't have to rely on the first serve anymore, or have to put so much faith in the first attempt. Stefan Edberg, who also had a great second serve, shared the same relaxed confidence hitting his first serve.

TIPS AND CHECKPOINTS

1. When you walk to the line for your first serve, think about serving only one ball. Don't let the second ball be a crutch.

2. Don't worry about the result of your serve: be concerned only with the process of hitting a good serve.

3. Remember, you are not looking down on your opponent's court — you are looking through the little holes in the net. Thus if you try to hit down on the ball it may go under the net. Think "up and out," not down.

4. Take your time. The serve is 100 percent your own stroke and creation. No one can run in and grab your toss.

5. Try to be calm and let everything glide. When you think about your serve up at the line, be more concerned about overall rhythm than about isolated movements of your body. (Remember that sports psychologists have determined that people choke because they're outcome oriented rather than "process" oriented.)

6. Learn to start your swing slowly and speed up steadily so that your motion is continuous. Don't start off with a gigantic effort and finish with a cream-puff delivery.

7. The serve is one stroke where you don't want to worry about bending the knees. You don't want anything that promotes a "down-up, down-up" type of motion. Think "around and up," and pivot on a horizontal plane. Strive for a nice easy shoulder roll and work to eliminate the hitches and jerky movements that rob you of rhythm and a natural throwing motion. An Aussie once showed me that you can face the net and still hit the ball 100 m.p.h. if you rotate your body and snap your hitting forearm and hand properly; you don't even need footwork.

8. Whether you are attacking the net or not, toss the ball out in front of your body to the right of your head, not straight ahead. And don't fall for the myth that you have to throw the toss high and let it drop so that your racket has time to catch up. Release the ball to the peak of your outstretched racket and the proper swing will make perfect contact if you use the delayed tossing method.

9. Keep your chin up and eyes on the ball — don't be opponent-oriented.

10. Hit "up and out" and let the snap of your forearm and wrist plus ball rotation bring the ball down.

11. Don't serve and back up. Tell yourself that you want to be stretched out over the baseline before you hit the ball, so your weight comes forward and you maintain a natural flowing motion.

12. As your serve improves, practice taking three steps forward and bring your feet together momentarily on the third step (while leaning forward), ready to move in any direction for your opponent's return.

13. Establish a psychological pattern that, if you make an error on the serve, it will be long, and never into the net. When you keep your opponent deep you prevent him from taking the net and you give yourself more time to react to his return.

14. If you make service errors, feel good about going long. Long serves are more easily corrected than those which hit the net, plus you get used to hitting deep.

15. If your serve is going long (and your forearm and wrist are breaking properly), your only error is that you are not throwing the ball far enough in front. You can also make the serve fall shorter by brushing up against the ball with a vertical racket head.

16. If your serve is falling too short or going in the net, you have two possible errors to consider: either you are swinging down on the ball rather than up and forward, or you are throwing the ball too far in front, which is rare.

17. Serve into your opponent's backhand corner the majority of times against beginners and low intermediates. Most backhand returns are weaker and normally at a higher elevation, making it easier for you to hit volleys and groundstrokes. If your opponent seems to have good strokes on both sides, aim at the side which produces the highest and longest ball.

18. If you've been telling yourself, "I'd be terrific if I just had a second serve," you may be blaming the wrong stroke. Does this mean that you already have a great first serve? If so, then you hardly ever need a second serve.

19. Before you can serve and attack, make sure you have a weapon. Some people beat their serve to the net and they can't understand why they lose. If you get hit in the back of the head with your own serve, you have to stay back.

20. Practice. Get out during the week and try to serve as many balls as possible. Don't settle for 10 to 15 practice serves before your weekly match. When you practice, set up target areas, and always try to hit deep. Even if you're wild, be tickled to death if every ball winds up on the other side of the net.

7

The Service Return

N GOLF, the long driver can belt the ball all day and if he keeps it in play, there's nothing his opponents can do, short of talking on his backswing. But in tennis, your service return gives you a nice tactical and psychological weapon. If you can take your opponent's best serves and get them back in play, you may demoralize that person in a couple of games, especially if his serve is his pride and joy. He'll try to save face by straining to hit the ball harder and harder, but this generally leads to a loss of rhythm and a succession of double faults — providing you can keep the pressure on by returning the serves that manage to go in.

The service return, in fact, is the second most important shot in the game. If the serve goes in, the return determines where the point goes from there, in every match in the history of the game. Therefore, when you receive serve you should think of it being your only shot. Your second, third, and fourth shots become important only if you make an effective return of serve.

Yet how many times have you practiced service returns? Or even given them much thought? Most people regard the service return as simply a forehand or backhand, and not a stroke all in itself, as it must be against good players. So they hit a lot of forehands and backhands when they rally before a match, thinking they're also practicing their service returns. But when they meet an opponent who can serve the ball reasonably hard with accuracy, they don't know how to get their racket on the ball in time, let alone get it back in play, and thus they're forced to always win their serve just to stay even in the match.

The serve would be much less important than it is if people worked to develop better service returns. Then the game would come down to who had the better groundstrokes. Once you learn to return serves consistently, you force the server to beat you with other strokes; you don't allow him (or her) to win by being

Jennings, a nationally ranked player, hits a fine service return while never dropping his racket head.

a one-shot artist. Good service returns can provide another benefit psychologically. Since you likely spend most of your time working on groundstrokes from the baseline, your tension is reduced dramatically if you can get the serve back. You're now ready to play your "comfortable" strokes and you've placed all the pressure on your opponent to make the first mistake.

Jimmy Connors and Andre Agassi have shown how the service return can actually become a devastating offensive weapon against even the fastest servers in the game. Although Connors had one of the weakest serves on the professional circuit in the 1980s, he also had the best service return. And in 1989, after improving his serve, he found himself in the semi-finals of the U.S. Open on his fortieth birthday. Meanwhile, Jack Kramer told me that Agassi, when he plays his very best tennis, is more punishing on the service return than any other player he has seen. "He's the only player I know who could have forced me to stay back on my serve and wait for my chance to go to the net." Jack's point is that when the receiver can read the serve and get into position to crush the return, the server's speed becomes a weakness if he now tries to move in. The return is coming back so much faster, and sooner, that he has to make shots from a deeper position on his second hit.

Still, while it's nice to ultimately think offensively on the service return, my goal is to first have you learn to return the ball consistently —"Get it back and dig," said Kramer — before you worry about more sophisticated aspects such as placement and varying the pace of the ball.

Returning serve, Jay is positioning himself halfway within the range he feels his opponent can serve to either side of the court.

The first two shots in every rally ever played are the serve and the service return. Here, one player practices following his serve to the net as his friend works on service returns by trying to drive the ball cross-court.

PRELIMINARIES

The Grip

Hold your regular Eastern forehand or Eastern backhand grip. Against a hard server, where you need to gain every split second possible in order to reach the ball in time, hold a forehand grip in advance so that you only have to switch if it comes to your backhand. Most people fail to hold either grip as they wait and thus must switch no matter where the ball goes. If your opponent is always serving to your backhand, then hold a backhand grip in anticipation. But be careful with this plan if you're playing an alert pro. Most players take a little longer switching from the backhand grip to the forehand grip and the smart server will notice your backhand grip and throw the ball into your body. Grip changes in this position are more difficult.

Wherever I give clinics around the world, a giant debate always seems to surface with hard-liners who feel you should always hold a Continental grip on service returns. Their argument is that there's insufficient time to switch grips when a blazing serve is hit, but I've found that to be quite inaccurate. I watched Boris Becker change grips against Goran Ivanisevic's 130 m.p.h. serve and nail placements. I also watched Kramer hardly miss a service return against Gonzales's great serve.

An important point is to hold the racket firmly, but not too tightly. In our

studies of top professional players, as soon as the hypertrophy (or swelling of the muscular) appeared when tightening the grip, the racket's acceleration rate decreased.

Where to Stand

In principle, you should stand halfway between the distance the server can stretch you on the forehand and the backhand. Most top players, for example, will straddle the singles sideline. But in typical club tennis, you can generally stand several steps closer to the center stripe because most people can't break the ball wide and draw you off the court. If you don't have a backhand then I know you like to stand way over by the center stripe, as if to say, "Bertha, anything to my backhand is out." Unfortunately, you can't get away with this against good players. They will slice the ball wide to your forehand and you'll have to call a taxi to get your racket to the ball in time. So stand in the proper position and force yourself to start working on a backhand.

One question most frequently asked of me on the Internet is whether one should run around a weak side to hit off the stronger side whenever possible. My answer is emphatically, "Yes." In the 1940s, when Pancho Segura learned to run around his backhand and hit his devastating two-handed forehand, he immediately won the NCAA singles championship and went on to have a great pro career.

If your opponent is getting his first serve in play, you can usually determine your position fairly early in the match. But ideally you should chart him before-hand (see Chapter 8) so that you already know how far he can stretch an opponent to either side. Remember, breaking his serve in the first game is as meaningful — and perhaps even more valuable psychologically — as breaking it in the fifth.

Ready Position

There is no universal ready position — only that position which will get you to the ball the fastest. However, you should start from a high body position so that your first move is forward, and not up. When your body is up and you start to run, the heels of your feet sink and the muscles are stretched early, which allows for a faster start. If you're low, you have to rise high so that you can stretch on the downflight. Watch the pros carefully and you'll see how they rise up on their toes just as the server is about to strike the ball.

When practicing your service return, try to find an opponent who can hit a "kick" (American Twist) serve so that you can become familiar at detection and execution. That big back arch is a good clue that a big spin serve is coming and it could likely kick to your left. Fine form, but the serve is a fault due to his foot fault.

Standing a little more upright becomes even more important on second serves. Top players will normally put a little more topspin on the ball to play it safe, and topspin jumps a little higher after the bounce.

Still, I see people all the time who are obsessed with the low crouch. They are trying to imitate the pros they see in tournaments, but they make one crucial mistake: they look away to watch the server, and they fail to see the receiver stand straight up. Remembering only the low crouch, the spectator goes out to play and now he gets down with his nose almost touching the court because he wants to play like the pros. But for you to be successful returning serves from that position, your opponent must serve the ball under the net.

THE STROKE

When you play against a patty-cake server, you will have time to hit your regular forehand and backhand groundstrokes. In which case, concentrate on returning the ball deep in your opponent's territory so that he is forced to hit defensively. As a matter of fact, if you like going to the net, you should never allow a weak serve to be hit without your hitting an attacking shot and going into the net.

It used to be that against fast serves, most forehand returns were hit with a blocking motion — similar to the volley — which usually produces a relatively flat shot. However, that has changed. Today's top players rip the service return just as hard as their groundstrokes from the baseline. There's an explanation for that. Rackets in the 1930s through the early 1960s could easily weigh 14 or 15 ounces, and it was too difficult to get the racket back for a full swing, so we saw a lot of blocked shots. But modern 10- to 12-ounce stiff rackets allow players to take a much shorter swing and crack the ball with great precision. A second major change is the development of the two-handed backhand. Armed with the light rackets, players are able to take a shorter swing and hit with confidence on the backhand side. As a result, many players have weaker forehand service returns than they do on the backhand, which would have been a rarity two decades ago.

So now we're talking about a service return that is hit almost identically to a normal baseline forehand and backhand shot. However, when the server is cracking the big bomb, the forward and upward swing will be closer to 20 degrees rather than the 30-degree swing discussed in the forehand and backhand chapters.

The underspin service return still has a place in the game, but it's almost always hit on the backhand side. In the 1970s, Vitas Gerulaitis tried to perfect a forehand underspin service return, but finally gave up on it. Just when most tennis fans thought the chipped backhand return was fading into oblivion, up stepped Patrick Rafter in the 1997 U.S. Open to hit dozens of chipped backhands, which he often followed to the net, even against Pete Sampras in the semi-finals. And he won the singles championship!

The underspin shot resembles a banana shape (high to low to high) with the racket only slightly beveled. If you bevel the racket too much, you will need to have a steeper downflight of the racket to compensate for the "opened" racket face. The image I've long tried to leave with my students is that of Jimmy Connors's racket finishing on the same level as the spot where he contacted the ball. And no one can dispute that Jimmy's flat two-handed backhand service return is one of the best ever.

One-handed backhand players like to chip their backhand service return because it's easier to make a shot like this when they are a little late on shots. Also, a chipped backhand is hit from high to low and utilizes gravity. A topspin service return on the backhand side requires tremendous strength in the forearm muscles. Still, never forget that a weakly executed chip shot can easily become a beautiful "sitter" for an aggressive net-rusher.

On the forehand return, the most common problem against fast serves is that people try to do too much with their racket. They lay the racket back too far and try to take a full swing, only to get caught late every time. You don't need all that motion. With the new rackets, a very short backswing is all that's needed. When Andre Agassi first played at Wimbledon, he had one of the shortest swings in the game. Yet John McEnroe told him to shorten it even more for grass-court play, and Andre proceeded to win the tournament. Another striking example for me was watching Stefan Edberg hit with such a short backswing that the receiver (the server) only saw the face of the racket the entire time. There was no layback of the wrist and hand. If you find your forehand swing is too long, simply raise your elbow a little and that will prevent a racket layback.

A crucial goal on the service return is to get a fast first step. Once you determine whether the ball is coming to your forehand or backhand, don't hesitate to run in that direction, even though you don't know exactly where the ball will land. If you delay your decision, you could lose nearly a second and that often translates into nine feet of movement.

Since your swing is almost identical to your normal forehand and backhand swings, there's not much difference in your preparation. However, it's of major importance that you aggressively hit through the ball while moving forward, if possible. When you hit off your heels or back foot, you often will raise the ball up high for an easy shot by your opponent. Remember why you want to step forward. Research has shown us that stepping into the ball doesn't generate much racket-head speed, but it does facilitate the body-link uncoiling that generates racket-head speed.

FOOTWORK

Your speed afoot is not nearly as important as your ability to get a fast first step toward the ball. To do this you must concentrate on the serve, anticipate the direction of the ball, and then react as quickly as you can by telling yourself, "It's a forehand!" or "It's a backhand!" Make your first step go forward; don't automatically go back when the serve comes harder than expected. Do all your backing up before the serve has been hit by finding the place where you feel safe enough to move forward into every ball. Also, get up on your toes as the ball is served so that your weight is forward and you don't settle in on your heels.

A good drill next time you play is to try to move in against every serve, no matter how fast it comes, instead of automatically stepping back and waiting for the ball. You'll be amazed at how many balls you actually get back, and at how much quicker you learn to react and move to the ball. This forces you to concentrate on the serve and prevents you from settling in on your heels. Plus it makes you realize that all you really need is good concentration, a firm grip at impact, and a vertical racket head that makes a clean hit. Your opponent's shot will supply all the speed you need.

Don't be afraid to guess wrong about a fast serve. Break one way or the other because your guesses will later become educated, and at least you'll have a 50-50 chance. Most people simply stand in the middle and do nothing, hoping they can call the ball out.

In the early 1980s, I purchased an Eye Mark Recorder that measured pupil (eye) activity. I was so excited because we could now monitor the eye movement of those players with great anticipation and discover their secret. The camera has a small light that shines into the eye and reflects back on film from a camera fitted on a player's nose. One of the best anticipators told us he was looking at his opponent's hips for giveaway signals, when actually he was looking into the trees. We discussed this with him and it turned out that he was going with statistical cues rather than visual cues. His opponent would always hit the same shot under particular circumstances and he simply played the numbers game.

In another case, we found a woman who was always late and she told us that she could never tell where the ball was going. However, when the film came back from the lab, we learned that her eyes were tracking the ball perfectly but her brain wouldn't send a signal to the feet to move. It was almost like she was saying to herself, "Be careful, this could be a trick." The moral here is: trust your eyes and take off.

TACTICS

Before you worry about getting fancy with placements, work to get 10 out of 10 returns back in play. You'll force your opponent to play tennis, and you'll be surprised at how many easy "sitters" he misses. But he'll never get the chance to make that first mistake if you don't get the ball over the net. When we chart players in a 3.0 as well as a 6.0 tournament, they usually can't believe the number of service return errors.

Once your game improves to the point where placement becomes important at your level of competition, don't let yourself be fooled. For of all the shots in the game, you can involve yourself in strategy least on the service return. You can talk all you want about chipping the ball down at the server's shoelaces, or underspinning it down the line, but if your opponent hits a hard, deep serve then your only real play is to get it back and scramble. Still, when you do have a chance to "control" your service return, you should have two main objectives:

1. If the server is rushing the net, try to hit the ball at his feet so that he is forced to bend and scoop for his return shot. This reduces the angle at which he can hit and forces him to lift the ball, which of course gives you a much easier shot to return. And when your opponent raises the ball, you should already be moving forward to distract him as you prepare to hit a mid-court volley. Ken Rosewall, the great Australian player in the 1960s and 1970s, would hit a service return at his

Jay, a highly ranked junior player from India, attacks behind a high racket head to ensure a deep shot to his opponent's baseline, making it easier to attack. Notice his center of gravity is forward, allowing for a faster approach to the net.

opponent's feet and the player could hear Ken's feet churning as he headed for the net. Nothing is worse after serving than having to hit a low ball on your second shot while knowing that your opponent is attacking.

2. If your opponent remains at the baseline, return the ball deep so that he can't take the net. Then start looking for the first short ball to come from your opponent so that you can gain the net.

When you scout an opponent before a match, concentrate on whether he comes in behind every serve, and how far he gets. If he takes those three big steps and practically reaches the service line as his opponent is hitting the return, you have a right to feel a little nervous. You're going to have to lay your return in at his feet — either with severe topspin or by taking speed off the ball — or throw up some lobs to keep him off-balance and away from the net. You also want to learn whether he has a tendency — and the control — to throw the serve into a particular corner on certain points. Or perhaps he also likes to catch his opponent off-guard by hitting a "change-up" every so often. In addition, try to determine how well his serve holds up when he gets tired. If he starts to lose a little of his first-serve speed and accuracy as the match drags on, be patient and keep pressing him with your service return because he will have a much greater tendency to "choke" on his serve as he tires.

Remember, too, that the server, in intermediate tennis, is generally trying to serve to your backhand. This is normally your weaker side and the tendency is for you to lift the ball high. On the advanced level, in fact, you know that your opponent is going to aim for your backhand, and he knows that you know. Everybody knows. The question is: "Does your opponent have an accurate serve, and do you have a backhand?" It just boils down to who has the strokes under stress. You can be a brilliant strategist but first you need the fundamentals.

A final point: Just as your poor service return will put real pressure on your own serve, a strong serve will also make your service return more effective. Pancho Gonzales was a great example of how these two strokes can be closely related. When Gorgo was at his peak, the fact that he always won his serve gave him a great psychological advantage going into a match. He knew the best anybody could do against him was to tie, since he was going to win his serve every time. Thus, when he returned serve he knew he had his own serve as a stopper and he could just stand back there and flail out. If he won the first two points with good returns or he got the score to deuce, then he would fight for the game. But if he fell behind 30-love, he would virtually concede the game, catch his breath, and put all his effort into his next serve. When the opponent served again, Gorgo would go all-out early in the game, knowing that he just needed to break serve once each set to win the match. His attitude was: Why beat your brains out in big-time tennis when your chances of breaking your opponent's serve are relatively slight anyway? Better to grab more oxygen and concentrate on your own serve.

That's great advice . . . if you serve like Gonzales. Otherwise, I'm not encouraging you to let up on your service returns. The average player can be serving and leading 40-love but he tends to make so many errors that you still have a chance to win the game if you're fundamentally sound. When you serve yourself, in most cases, you are fighting just as hard to win as when you try to break your opponent's serve. In fact, if you are leading 40-love, it's wise not to relax but to continue playing your heart out.

CHECKPOINTS

1. Exhale and relax while waiting for the serve. Strain only during the hit. If your body tightens up, you won't move your legs.

2. Start from a high position, especially if you are tall, and work to get a fast first step. You can bend down before the serve, but make sure you come up in plenty of time to take your swing. (Research indicates that you can move faster laterally by using a higher center of gravity.) You don't stay low when you hit a service return.

3. Move forward and into the ball; think aggressively, not defensively.

4. When you're learning to return fast serves, remember: the better you get, the shorter your swing will be. Instead of getting caught in the middle of a big backswing, develop a compact little stroke that enables you to meet the ball out in front of your body with a perfectly positioned racket face. The server will supply all the power you need.

5. Don't let your racket head lay back. Keep the racket face nearly vertical and swing upward from 20 to 30 degrees.

6. On the forehand backswing, keep the elbow of your racket arm raised and slightly bent. On the backhand, keep the elbow of your non-hitting arm raised as it cradles the throat of the racket going back.

7. Try to watch the ball as long as possible, and then keep your head down and focused on the point of impact until you have followed through.

8. Maintain a firm but not a death grip at impact. This will help ensure a good return even if the ball hits off-center.

9. On one-handed backhands, don't let the racket head drop below the level of your wrist, and have the hitting arm and racket finish high on the follow-through.

10. Scramble, get the ball in play — and then work to get it deep.

11. How well you return serve at 30-all or deuce is what will make you famous. This is the pressure point, the one you need to win to force the server into a "choking" situation, the one he desperately wants in order to gain the advantage. So have a friend chart all of your service returns and see how you fare at different points during each game.

Singles Strategy

TENNIS STRATEGY presents an endless challenge to most players who get hooked on the game. Others feel that if they can learn a lot about strategy, this will somehow overcome their lack of strokes. They love strategy because they want to win without a forehand, backhand, serve, and volley. But let's face it, unless two players are evenly matched in stroke production and thus seeking the winning edge, overall strategy and point-to-point tactics are basically overrated for most people. If you can just get the ball back consistently — with good depth — you're going to be tough to beat without knowing the first thing about "hitting the lines," "opening up the court," and other fancy stratagems. Even at the pro level you must have the basic weapons to win, not a unique theory.

Instead of espousing new horizons in strategy, I'm much more concerned about delimiting the number of options that are available to people. Everybody worries about not having enough shots, but in reality there are only about five things you can do with the ball at the baseline: hit to your opponent's left, to his right, over his head, at his feet, or through his navel. You can have 100 different bizarre shots and tactics but they won't make you famous. The winner isn't the one with all the fancy shots, but the one who can keep giving his opponent one more chance to take gas.

Nevertheless, developing your strategy and putting it to intelligent use during a match will make the most of your strokes when you play in tournaments, challenge players on a club ladder, or just try to knock off your neighborhood rival. Strategy also means devising a realistic game plan, which forces you to evaluate your own game and to learn how to scout future opponents. This in turn leads to faster progress, more success, and more fun. Learning about strategy and match-

Veteran coach Mark Walpole shows five vulnerable positions of an opponent which should cause you to be ready to attack for a midcourt volley while catching your opponent out of position.

play tactics is also kind of comforting. It's nice to know that what you thought you should be doing on the court really isn't all that complicated.

We could really cut to the chase by quoting Jack Kramer, who said, "If your strength is greater than your opponent's strength, then stick with it. If it's not, you have to make your opponent hit shots he doesn't like to hit." Taking that approach, the major issue then is: Do you have any sizable strengths, and do you possess shots that your opponent doesn't like to hit?

"STRATEGY" FOR THE BEGINNER

Though I love to watch beginners play, it's tough to outline a strategy for those who hit the ball into the net every other shot. Strategy is basically an automatic response to a given set of conditions, and with beginners there are no "givens." The player hitting the ball doesn't know where it's going or why it's going there once it leaves his racket, and his opponent is just as mystified. So they simply try to hit the ball back and forth, giggle a lot, and have a lot of fun. That's the way it should be. If this is the way you play, you may not care the first thing about strategy. But if you're tired of losing to the same people all the time and you're trying to develop sounder strokes and the right habits, here are some overall thoughts that can make you more successful.

Your first goal is to get the ball back safely, anywhere in your opponent's court. Then, as your shots improve, visualize a five-foot semicircle around the center stripe — at your opponent's baseline — and try to hit every shot there when the two of you are playing from near the baseline. It's hard to keep landing the ball in or around this target area, but "down the middle and deep" gives you an easy system to remember and one that can be trusted against any type of opponent, and on any kind of playing surface. It can help make you a winner in four ways: (1) you keep your opponent hitting from behind the baseline; (2) the net is 4½ inches lower in the middle than at the singles sideline, meaning you have less chance for error; (3) you can concentrate more confidently on the stroke you are taking because you're not gambling by trying for the corners or the sidelines; and (4) by playing the ball straight down the middle, you reduce the length of the diagonal available to your opponent if he wants to hit a cross-court passing shot. Short-angle passing shots must be hit with topspin in order to produce the proper speed and accuracy.

The only trouble with hitting down the middle comes when your opponent has only one strong shot, either a forehand or a backhand, and he can step around and hit from his strength every time. But if you can keep the ball deep enough, nobody's going to hurt you. Besides, once you learn to keep the ball in play and deep, you can adjust your semicircle away from the center stripe toward your opponent's weak side, and just concentrate on hitting to that target. In modern professional tennis, even the best players don't do much with deep shots down the middle.

I talk a lot about hitting only the shots that you "own," and by that I mean hitting a specified target area under stress. By this definition, most players don't even "own" one shot, and thus strategy is almost a contaminant. If these people worry about strategy they now have two problems: (1) they begin to think too much, which normally inhibits the proper muscle movements, and (2) they begin to hit shots they don't own.

I'm always amused by the beginners who want to know, "When will I know I'm no longer a D player — that I'm now a C?" I tell them that their peers will let them know. "When you begin to win, they'll start calling you dirty names and avoiding you at the club and making excuses not to play you. Even without a 'ladder' you can consider yourself a C player when you start to lose some friends."

STRATEGY FOR THE REAL BUFF

No matter how successful you become in this game, hitting "down the middle and deep" should always remain a fundamental aspect of your strategy. Throw in an adequate serve, two good legs, and a high frustration-tolerance level and this "system" can take you right to the top, as we saw with Chris Evert, Arantxa Sanchez Vicario, and Mary Jo Fernandez. Unfortunately, few of us can hit with this kind of relentless precision and thus we must look for ways to gain an edge on our opponents with the weapons we have.

1. The basic starting point for all intermediate and advanced players should be: the advanced player will attack the net at every opportunity and the intermediate will wait for the first short ball before going in. This assumes, of course, that you know how to hit an approach shot and how to volley, and that you appreciate how important it is to gain control of the net.

Again, this is a highly debated issue. Jack Kramer was the best net-rusher I've ever seen and his theory was, "If players can beat me with clean passing shots for an hour and a half, they deserve to win." Remember, that passing lane against a good player who hits deep approach shots is only 1 to 3 degrees.

An argument against going to the net as often as possible, even with a good approach shot, is that some players simply aren't comfortable up there. A good example is Andre Agassi. I was in the Davis Cup media room in April 1997 when Andre told the world that he had no intention of going to the net. Of course, Andre was one of the few players who also had a giant weapon from the baseline. But what's just as important when considering Andre is that, if he isn't playing well from the baseline on a particular day, he's normally history as he has no backup strength. The tennis world has seen Andre do amazing things from the baseline and win the major events, only to suddenly lose in the first round one tournament after another. I applaud his fantastic baseline strengths, but my heart goes out to him when these strengths unravel and his game falls apart.

The biggest mistake made by intermediates who try to emulate the net-rushing pros is that they fail to anticipate the first short ball when playing at the baseline. They hit and back up, or hesitate too long, instead of thinking, "The next ball is going to be short," and getting that fast first step forward if it lands in their short ball range. In fact, against most intermediates you should play just inside the baseline and start running as soon as the ball is hit because statistically this shot will be short. The average player is average because he seldom hits the ball deep, except by accident.

I don't want you to think you can beat many players by always backing up and digging in at the baseline, unless you have sound groundstrokes and a long fuse. Good tennis is a game of closing out the point and not letting your opponent keep playing. This means you must fight to get to the net — preferably behind a deep shot that keeps your opponent pinned behind the baseline. If you can develop confidence in your approach shot and volley, and force yourself to concentrate on going forward rather than automatically staying back, your opponent will feel the pressure. Let him know that you are going to rush the net on the first short ball and you will affect his concentration and the rhythm of his swing as he tries to keep the ball deep.

I'm often asked, "What kind of person should go to the net more often?" In intermediate tennis, it's the person who has the short fuse, who is frustrated by baseline rallies and wants every point to be quickly settled. This type of player should be up on his toes, ready to pounce on the first short ball.

Then people ask, "Well, what if I have a short fuse but I don't volley well?" And I tell them, "Then you're going to lose. If you don't have the patience to stay back and try to win with groundstrokes, you have to learn how to hit an approach shot and to volley."

2. Strive for consistency by playing the percentages; it's variety that kills you. The trouble with the "Hit the lines" concept is that very few people can play with that kind of control, and they put too much pressure on themselves in a baseline rally. Kramer was the greatest strategist I've ever seen and he played everything for position and percentages —"deep and safe," he used to say. When he went for the "corners," he usually aimed about four feet inside the baseline and four feet inside the sideline. However, Jack hit his forehand approach shot with a little sidespin and his opponent often found himself hitting from behind, or outside, the alley.

The reason you want to simplify your strategy is the fact that there are very few places you — or your opponent — can actually hit the ball. The fancier you try to get, such as by moving your opponent from forehand to backhand to forehand, the more you risk hitting the ball out. Why gamble like this if you can already get the ball back consistently? Statistics show that someone is about to make an error. Better your opponent than you.

3. A corollary to this would be: never try to hit a shot you don't own. Temptation shots normally lead to a second-place finish in a field of two, whether you are in control of the point or on the defensive. If you are in trouble, always hit the shot which has a high probability of getting you back out of a hole. Don't look for a miracle shot to win the point. Surprise your opponent by just getting the ball back and he may end up dumping it into the net.

If you have the upper hand, keep hitting the shots that put you there. That's why I hate to see a player try to hit a drop shot under pressure. The pressure is on him to thread the needle and lay the ball just over the net, and if he misses or hits it too hard he gives his opponent a big boost.

I once sat with Kramer and Arthur Ashe to watch Gonzales play Laver in Los Angeles about 1965. Gonzales had the service ad in a key game but he tried to drop-shot Laver and Rod came up, got the ball back, and won the point. Kramer turned to Ashe and me and said, "Let that be a lesson to you. Never drop-shot on a big point. Why do you want to add pressure on yourself?"

About two years later, when I was with the Davis Cup team in Ecuador, Ashe was playing Pancho Guzman in the second singles match. They were in the fifth set, but Arthur had won the fourth, 6–0, and now led 2–1. He was just one point away from breaking Guzman's serve and Guzman was so choked up he could only hit a little baby serve. Arthur came in, but instead of hitting his approach shot, he tried a drop shot — a shot he didn't "own." The ball went into the net and suddenly Guzman had new life, while Arthur's confidence went skidding down. Guzman went on to win the game, the set, and the match — which enabled Ecuador to knock the United States out of Davis Cup competition by a 3–2 score.

4. When playing under pressure, don't let the situation dictate your shot. Hit the shot you know you should hit. When the average player is down set point and faced with an approach shot, he usually thinks, "I just want to play it safe and get out of this alive." So instead of aiming deep to his opponent's backhand and following his shot to the net, he simply tries to get the ball over the net and then retreats to the baseline. But a player like Laver would always say to himself, "Deep and go. If it's out, it's out."

Remember to hit cross-court when you get pushed out of court and your opponent remains at the baseline. One, you'll hit a longer ball, which will give you more time to get back into play. Two, if your opponent wants to hit to your backhand, he will have to hit your cross-court shot down the line, which is one of the most difficult shots in tennis. And three, your opponent will never be able to run you beyond the singles sideline.

This player practices with a pro, receiving severe cross-court shots and measuring her target. If she simply holds her racket head still, she must aim for the center of the baseline to have her shot go into the backhand corner (in order to counter the angle of deflection). If she has slow movement forward with her racket, she will aim halfway between the center mark and the backhand corner. And if she has a pretty aggressive movement with her racket on the volley, she will aim about three feet inside the corner.

Rod's old rival and friend Roy Emerson once told me, "That's why you were never comfortable playing the Rocket. When you got him down match point, that's when you started worrying. You would be thinking about winning the match but you knew he was just concentrating on hitting the shot that needed to be hit. He had the guts to make the play, where others would choke. And if he hit the big shot and won the point, you got mad because you had him on the hook and lost him. That's what made him so great."

Pete Sampras grew up in junior tennis with Laver as his idol. Years later, American Davis Cup captain Tom Gullikson observed about Sampras, "One of Pete's real strengths is that he hits out in the big moments."

5. The moment you are pressed on a ball or your opponent starts to move you around, elevate your next shot 10 or 12 feet over the net in order to buy time and to disrupt his momentum. People love to stand at the baseline controlling the pace of the match while you scramble all over the court trying to get the ball back. When you find yourself on the run like this, the normal tendency is to want to regain the upper hand by blasting the ball back, hoping for a miraculous placement or an error by your opponent. This usually leads you into more trouble. But if you can return the ball high and deep, you can change the rhythm of the game unbe-

lievably. Your opponent goes crazy waiting for the ball to land while you regain good position. Plus, the ball bounces higher so he can't crack his hips into the shot and you aren't supplying the power. I will never forget a match between Jim Pugh and Andre Agassi. Pugh was at his best in the first set, outslugging Andre from the baseline and taking a big lead. It looked as though he was on his way to a major upset. But then Andre changed his tactics and started hitting nothing but high top-spin shots — and Pugh went from totally controlling the play to looking confused. He ended up losing the match 7–5, 6–0. Andre said afterward, "I didn't know what to do — I was getting killed — so that was the last resort" (playing like a dinker).

6. Try to learn from the dinker. If you don't like to hit a ball that comes up around your chest — the kind often hit by dinkers — you are not alone. Why don't you offer your opponent the same kind of shot by elevating the ball so that it lands near the baseline and bounces high? This is especially true if you play against a person whom you've heard complain, "I don't like to play Bertha — she ruins my rhythm." Bertha, in other words, is giving this person a variety of heights and speeds, when what she wants are low, hard groundstrokes that always set up nice and fat in the same place. People like this have a short fuse and you want to give them plenty of high-bouncing balls so that they can never get in the groove. Instead of trying to blast them off the court with power, use a little finesse, like the clever pitcher who mixes up his pitches.

Throwing off timing is not the only reason you want to bounce the ball high to certain players. Twenty years ago I noted that the pros were starting to smarten up against the short guys in the game by emphasizing topspin ground-strokes. For example, after losing to Bjorn Borg in the WCT championships in Dallas in 1976, 5'6" Harold Solomon commented that he had to keep reaching up against Borg's high-bouncing shots. "The ball was over my head all the time," said Solomon. "So much topspin means you have to hit the ball very hard to make it go anywhere, and when it comes as high as Bjorn hits it, I can't get any body weight behind it. I am forced to just use my arms."

7. Try to play your opponent's strong shots and force him to beat you by hitting his weaker shots. If he can only hit his forehand with confidence, and he prefers to go down the line with this shot, then overplay the court on that side so that he must win the point by going cross-court. Let him know: "You can beat me, but you're going to have to use the weaker of your two shots to do it." Don't let him win with his strength. If he swings on a horizontal level, then overplay to the cross-court side because that's where he's going to pull his shots, unless he purposely swings late — and then you are forcing him to add another variable.

Also remember to move to the side of the court to which you hit the ball when you rush the net. Tempt your opponent to hit what looks like the easier shot — away from you — but which actually is very difficult to execute.

8. Hit cross-court on sharply angled shots that draw you off the court. Try to return the ball on a diagonal — with a lob or a drive — and don't be tempted to hit straight down the line. On the forehand, especially, the tendency in singles is to try to hit down the line to your opponent's backhand corner when he is on the baseline. But you are much safer and wiser to go cross-court for the following reasons:

- The net is lower in the middle than on the sides (though as Dr. Howard Brody points out, the angled ball hit from the baseline has a longer distance to travel and air resistance reduces the value of the lower net).
- If you hit the ball eight to ten feet over the net, you keep the ball in the air longer and you gain time to scramble back into play. You may also bother your opponent's rhythm.
- The singles court is 78 feet long down the line and 82½ feet on the diagonal, giving you extra length with which to hit.
- By hitting on the diagonal, you now tempt your opponent with the tougher of two returns — down the line to your backhand. Even if he hits a great forehand, he is threading the needle and he can only move you to the singles sidelines.

  For example, let's say you have been run off the court to hit a forehand and you return the ball to your opponent's forehand. If he now tries to hit into your "wide-open" backhand corner he opens himself up to the following problems:
- There's no margin for safety when you go down the line; the ball can only land in play on one side of the singles line.
- The ball is arriving at his racket on a diagonal and it tends to deflect off the racket at a slight angle when he tries to go straight down the line. This helps send it off-target and out of bounds if he doesn't compensate.
- Meanwhile, even though he is hitting to your backhand, the easiest shot in the game is to hit a straight ball cross-court, since most people have a natural tendency to pull across their bodies and hit the ball on the diagonal. You have to be a talented player to hit a straight ball straight, anywhere on the court. If you don't believe me, get a friend to rally with you in one of the 4½-foot doubles alleys and see how difficult it is to keep hitting the ball inside the alley.

Now, with these thoughts in mind, visualize yourself again running off the court to hit a forehand, only this time you try to go down the line to your opponent's backhand. Not only are you attempting the toughest shot, you are increasing the number of steps your opponent can run you with his own return. First, your momentum may carry you farther off the court when you try to hit down the line. (This also gives you less time to recover for your next shot.) And second, even though your opponent must hit a backhand, he can use his natural pull-across swing and hit it diagonally — to your backhand — which also pulls you off the court on the other side.

Therefore, unless your opponent has a weakness which dictates otherwise (such as a wimpy backhand and a powerhouse forehand), always go back on the diagonal when you are being run off the court and you'll be way ahead of the game. Also try to lob the ball high in order to gain more recovery time, unless your opponent can take a lob and really push you around with his overhead. Then you will have to drive the ball back, but only as a last resort. One year I was working with the wonderful Chinese player Hu Na, and I put a millisecond clock on the court. When Hu Na would drive a high, deep topspin cross-court, it resulted in her having three times more recovery time than if she hit a low drive cross-court.

9. Every hot-dog strategist likes to talk about "opening up the court" with a variety of fancy, high-risk shots that very few players in the world can hit with any consistency. You have to learn to recognize when you really have an open court, but the question is: can you still hit a winning shot? When you get an opponent off the court or in one corner, how often are you able to hit the ball into the other corner for a winner? If your opponent is at the baseline, how often can you really catch him off guard with a short-angle roll shot or a drop shot that barely clears the net, hits, and dies? Realistically speaking, the number of times you win a point outright by hitting into an open court is going to be a lot smaller than the number of times you win a point because your opponent makes an error.

For beginners, worrying about an "open court" is a joke. Their opponent has to be against the fence, and even then the likelihood of a placement is slim. But for more advanced players, my advice would be to keep a purpose in mind for every shot. You can't "open up" a court by always hitting the ball deep; you have to learn to hit a drop shot or the soft, short-angled shot that falls inside the service box and then bounces into the alley, forcing your opponent to race in just to get his racket on the ball. If he makes the play, you have to be prepared to put his shot away before he has an opportunity to recover.

10. Use the lob to tire your opponent. Pros have found that they can tire older opponents faster with the lob than with any other stroke. Not only do you exhaust opponents by driving them away from the net to chase the ball, but you make them stretch their stomachs out entirely when they go up to hit an overhead. That's why the younger pros would wait as long as possible before hitting their lob so that guys like Segura and Gonzales would crowd the net even more, and leave themselves more vulnerable to the lob. Often we hear announcers on television tell us to "keep the ball on the strings" as long as possible to allow the opponent to commit to a movement. Unfortunately, the ball doesn't know it's supposed to stick on the racket and it always leaves in about four milliseconds. But it is true that one can hit slightly later and buy a few more milliseconds.

11. The great offensive players normally have exceptional serves, volleys, approach shots, and overheads. If you do not have these qualifications, then a great defense is the best offense: develop your forehand and backhand so that you keep the ball in play — with depth — and provide your opponent with the opportunity to beat himself. Don't give him a helping hand by going for winners when you're out of position.

I see juniors all the time who think the name of the game is to hit the ball as hard as they can, even if they don't have control. They think they're too good to just try and keep it in play. But I'll never forget the time I brought two leading junior players from Argentina to train with me in Palos Verdes, where I was the pro at the Kramer Club. They were very fine players (not too long after that they had a win over Arthur Ashe and Clark Grabner) and I wanted Kramer to watch them play. Jack drove 65 miles to do me this favor, but when he arrived they tried to look good by just slugging the ball. They were young and they were going to im-

Although deep, this player steps into his lob and confuses the net player, who has anticipated a drive. He suddenly swings upward for a beautifully disguised lob— a valuable shot in singles and doubles alike.

press Jack with all their power. But Jack took just one look and got back in his car and left. "Why do I want to watch thse clowns?" he said. "They can't keep the ball in play."

Another time, Jack was the player who was trying to do too much to the ball. He was very young and was losing to Frank Kovacs in the 1940s when Bobby Riggs called him over to the side on a third set break and said, "You're trying to do too much. Just keep the ball in play and Frank will find a way to lose." Sure enough, Jack went on to beat Kovacs that day and never lost to him again.

PREPARING FOR A MATCH

Charting

If you are playing in club tournaments, or you're serious about moving up on your challenge ladder, don't wait until you rally before a match to start brewing up a game plan. Take the time to scout people you play regularly, or those you are likely to encounter in club tournaments, and pretty soon you will have a "file" on possible opponents that you can draw on before a match.

This is where charting is invaluable. Only by charting can you supply the two key "academic" ingredients necessary to build a winning tennis game: (l) knowing your own strengths and weaknesses, and (2) pinpointing your opponent's strengths and weaknesses. If you can learn to use the Match Recording Chart discussed here, you will be able to quantify match-play data that are far more trustworthy and revealing than your own memory or interpretation of a match. With this information you will know how to best deploy the strokes that you have, and how to attack your opponent's weaknesses.

Charting is like detailed scorekeeping. Whether you are charting a future opponent or having a friend chart you during a match, the idea is to record errors — where they occur and with what stroke — since they outnumber placements by a large margin. There are normally so many errors on the overhead, the serve, and the service return that you should keep separate box scores in order to have room on the paper.

Having a friend chart your match provides you with a much clearer idea of which shots actually worked and which ones let you down. This makes you far more objective about your own game, and enables you to go to work on specific weaknesses. For example, if you have a cluster of errors on your forehand approach shot, that's what you need to work on in practice. You may think you have a good serve because you seldom double-fault, but if you discover that only two out of ten first serves are going in, you are putting too much pressure on your second serve. In fact, you don't really have a serve — you have a prayer and a cream puff.

Charting should also clear up misconceptions about your groundstrokes. For instance, you see the following phenomenon happen all the time in club tennis. One player says after a match, "If I just had a backhand, I'd murder the guy, 'cause my forehand is terrific." Well, he doesn't have either stroke, but he gets his backhand over the net with a little dink shot that always goes in. He doesn't try anything fancy since he knows he doesn't have the stroke. But when the ball comes to his forehand, he thinks, "Great, this is my weapon," and he slugs the ball as hard as he can — but right into the net. Charting would show him on paper that his forehand, and not his backhand, was actually producing the most errors.

Charting your own match requires a friend or a spouse who knows how to chart, but there's no excuse for you not to chart future opponents at the club. Tournaments themselves can offer an excellent opportunity to observe other players while you kill time waiting for your own match.

When charting, also try to observe such things as: Is the person slow to get his racket back and slow to get into position? (If so, try to take the ball on the rise because you'll reduce your opponent's reaction time by 50 percent from normal. This means he will have to be even faster.) Where is the ball when he starts moving? Does he have trouble handling the lob? How quickly does he react and get back? Does he hit his groundstrokes with topspin or with underspin? Does he like to rush the net? (If so, how far does he get after his approach shot in order to volley?) Does he move in behind his serve? How hard does he hit his second serve? What shots does he rely on most? How does he seem to react to pressure? Does he seem to play harder and concentrate better when the score is 30-all than on the first point? What does he tend to do on important points? Does he seem to have a short fuse, or a lot of patience? Does he play better when he's ahead or when he's behind?

Answers to these questions will obviously help you formulate a realistic strategy for when you play a match — providing, of course, that you have the strokes to capitalize on your opponent's specific weaknesses. If you have some weapons, I've found that good charting stimulates logical tactics on the tennis court. Knowing your own strengths and weaknesses helps keep you from playing recklessly and encourages you to stick with the high-percentage shots — the ones that you "own." This is what produces victories.

It's worth repeating Kramer's theory that you should stick with your strength if it's better than your opponent's and, if not, then hit shots your opponent doesn't like to hit. This means you need to know your own strengths and weaknesses as well as those of your opponent. And keep in mind that it continues to surprise me how so many people often have an unrealistic viewpoint of their own game.

Devising a Game Plan

Strategy is defined as your overall game plan, while tactics are those tools which you use to implement this plan. For example, your particular tactic may be to keep the ball low, but your overall strategy is to try to tire your opponent by making him bend down more often. By devising a game plan with these specifics in mind, you can go out on the court with a mind that is free to hit. You can't try to devise your strategy as the match unfolds, experimenting with different tactics and strokes game by game, point by point. Anybody I've seen who has tried to play this way is usually a loser.

Even among the pros there is very little intellectualizing during a tennis match. They just want to be free to hit the ball under pressure. They know that tennis is basically a trained response to a given shot, and that it is played best when played instinctively, assuming your instincts trigger the proper strokes. As Laver once told me, "When I start to think too much on the tennis court, that's when I know I'm going to lose."

Jon Niednagel, the founder of Brain Typing, says that we will see the day when neuroscientists can record the movement of glucose, which tells us what part of the brain is being used, and watch it go to the left hemisphere when players begin to think too much. And, he concludes, it's the active left hemisphere that produces stiffer movements.

Unfortunately, most players do their thinking in the middle of the point because they don't have a game plan. When they run for the ball they're thinking, "Bertha is going to run that way, so I'll hit over here. No, she's running the other way — got her." But the ball rolls off their racket and down their thigh. Another problem is to start arguing tactics as the ball is coming. "I just hit to her forehand, so I'd better go to her backhand. Yeah, but she likes the backhand — maybe I should lob." Debating with yourself like this will simply destroy your ability to anticipate your opponent's shot and to get that fast first step, while inhibiting a rhythmical swing once you do make up your mind.

Before you can develop a realistic strategy, you must have an objective understanding of your own strengths and weaknesses. The reason most game plans fail is that they're based on some weapons that people don't even own. For example, you might say, "I'll take every second serve by my opponent and attack." Okay, that's good. But if you don't have an approach shot, you'll end up losing more points than if you simply stay back and rely on your groundstrokes.

Just the fact that you sit down and try to devise a strategy forces you to ask questions about your game that most people tend to avoid. They just play, play, play without ever stopping to analyze their game in an objective way. That's why I've found that stroke production seldom matches the strategic plan outlined by the average player, but that this discrepancy narrows considerably with winners because they are much more objective about themselves.

Even without playing a match you can get a very realistic idea of what shots you "own" and don't own. If you are always losing to people who attack the net on every short ball, go out on the court and place a friend in a volleying position — let's say halfway between the net and the service line, to your backhand side — then just bounce the ball and see if you can hit your backhand past your friend, either down the line, cross-court, or with a lob. If you're not interested in humility yet, take your friend off the court and try to hit your target areas without any visual pressure at all. You'll find that you still can't hit certain shots, with or without stress. This really brings you home fast.

If you then try to draw up a game plan that is based strictly on the shots that you "own," and takes into account your opponent's abilities, you will realize how few options you have under pressure. People tend to think they have 20 or 30 options available, but when they write down the strokes they can rely on under pressure, and their corresponding strategy, they discover there's not much to decide.

A good game plan will also include specific objectives that you want to pur-

When your opponent is hitting from her back foot and scooping the ball with an open racket face, be ready to run back for a lob. Trust me, she's not about to drive this particular shot.

sue, depending on your opponent's playing style and the shots you have that you feel can hurt him. In addition, there are certain rules of thumb that can be applicable no matter whom you play. Review the following checklist before every match (adding your own reminders, and deleting those which you feel don't apply to your own game) and try to work these points into your subconscious so that you can learn to react and move and stroke the ball under stress automatically:

1. Every shot is important because statistically it may be your last.

2. Try to avoid hitting the first short ball. If you keep your opponent behind the baseline, and away from the net, he'll need sound groundstrokes and patience to beat you.

3. Your first instinct at the baseline must be to move forward, not back, unless you have an agreement with your opponent that if he promises not to attack, you won't attack.

4. Beginners and intermediates seldom get beyond the serve or service return before hitting a weak shot, so be ready for the first short ball from your opponent, then move in to hit an approach shot.

5. Get yourself in the frame of mind that you came to play — not to put the ball away. Concentrate on reducing your errors and let your opponent go for broke. Against big hitters, if you can hang tough until they start to miss, they will very often fall apart.

6. Don't spend time worrying about being vulnerable to the extraordinary shot.

7. When your opponent runs you wide, off the court, "buy time" by returning his shot on the diagonal, with a high drive or a lob.

8. If your opponent gets you on the run, break up his rhythm by elevating your shots 10 to 12 feet over the net and slowing them down.

9. In a baseline rally, when you're undecided about where to aim, just remember "Down the middle and deep," and let your opponent do the gambling.

10. Keep your feet moving. Almost all of us have a tendency to "fall asleep at the wheel" as the match progresses.

11. If your first lob in the match is long, don't choke or overcompensate and hit the next one short. Swing just as hard but elevate the ball a little more.

12. Try to hit every serve deep. You can learn more from a serve that goes long than one that goes into the net, plus you keep more pressure on your opponent when the serve is good.

13. Don't be bashful about even writing yourself little notes to review when you switch sides during a match.

Warming Up before a Match

A close match can actually be decided during the warm-up rally, depending on how thorough your rally, what you detect in your opponent, and what you give away about yourself.

First of all, if you are an intermediate or advanced player, never start a match without attempting every shot you might want to use. People love to hit forehands and backhands from the baseline, but what are the first two strokes in every match? The serve and the service return. So hit at least 20 serves (which allows your opponent to practice his service return), 20 overheads, and 20 lobs, and practice your approach shots, half-volleys, and volleys, in addition to your regular groundstrokes. You want to be ready to play your best tennis from the first game on. Here again, most people rally briefly and then one of them steps up to the line, takes a couple of warm-up serves, and says, "First ball in." Well, F.B.I. doesn't go in big-time tennis. Once that match begins you have to have a serve. (Similarly, if your opponent doesn't try any warm-up overheads, then you should lob as soon as possible, before he's ready to crack a winner.)

Second, don't worry about impressing your opponent with your power. Concentrate instead on getting into position and hitting rhythmically. Kramer, for example, would take great pains to see that his strokes were perfect while warming up. He would take his racket back quickly, step forward early, swing easily, and return every shot. Pretty soon his opponents would realize that they were the only ones hitting the ball long or into the net. So they would start to hit harder in order to put a little pressure on Jack and get him to miss a couple of shots. But Jack would just knock the ball back and remain cool and calculating while his opponents were getting out of sync by trying to go beyond their ability level. Thus he gained an obvious psychological edge going into the match. (Another of Kramer's tricks to test for his opponent's weak side was to hit the first warm-up shot right down the middle. Whatever direction his opponent stepped in, that was his confidence stroke.)

Third, while warming up (and, naturally, during a match), don't be so worried about yourself and how you look that you fail to detect flaws in your opponent's stroke or footwork. Even if you've never seen him play before, you can pick up some revealing information. If he swings from low to high, on the horizontal, or with a lot of underspin, this will give you an idea of what type of shots to expect and whether or not he can hurt you with particular strokes. Watch to see if he moves better to the right or left, and how quickly he reacts and gets his racket back. If he keeps contacting the ball on the center of the strings, you are in trouble, but if he hits a lot of shots "off the frame" on the backhand, that's a good tip-off to a weak stroke. Try to sense if he is high-strung or relaxed. If he overreacts to everything and seems to like a fast tempo, then think about slowing everything down during the match by varying the pace of your shots.

Remember, the way a person swings on his first couple of shots in warm-ups is usually how he will swing in the match, under pressure. At the tennis college, we used to photograph our students hitting a forehand on the first morning, before they've had a chance to warm up. Then in the evening we gave out a large print to each person, just to have a little fun. But occasionally people got a little upset at how they looked and would complain, "Jeez, I didn't even have time to get warmed up." Yet I've discovered that although people will swing a little better as they loosen up, they often revert to their same old style once the pressure is on. Regression under stress is so strong and the initial response a person makes is so innate that on his very first swing of the day, he's really doing what is natural for him.

Playing a Match

The beautiful thing about tennis is that you can talk a great game in the locker room, and you can tell everybody how terrific you are — but, pal, eventually you have to play.

1. Occasionally, when you win the racket toss, let your opponent serve first if he or she hasn't warmed up sufficiently. You gain a nice psychological edge if you can break serve in the first game.

2. Remind yourself (before the first point is played) that if you allow yourself to think too much during the match, your game will suffer. As motor learning expert Dr. Richard Schmidt emphasizes, "Take care of details when you practice and make a conscious effort to improve your strokes, but when you go out to play an opponent, the effort has to be unconscious. Just hit the ball."

3. Be observant. How many times have you played an opponent who happens to be lefthanded, and for about five minutes you're thinking to yourself, "Boy, there's something really weird about this person"? When I was the pro at the Kramer Club, a fellow came up to me after losing two sets to Beverly Baker Fleitz, the ambidextrous former playing great who would switch her racket and hit forehands off both sides. "Vic," he said, "you won't believe this but I didn't get the ball to her backhand one time. It didn't matter where I hit the ball, she would step

Match Play Recording Chart

Stroke Symbol Legend

cc = cross-court
dl = down-the-line
w = wide
l = long
n = netted

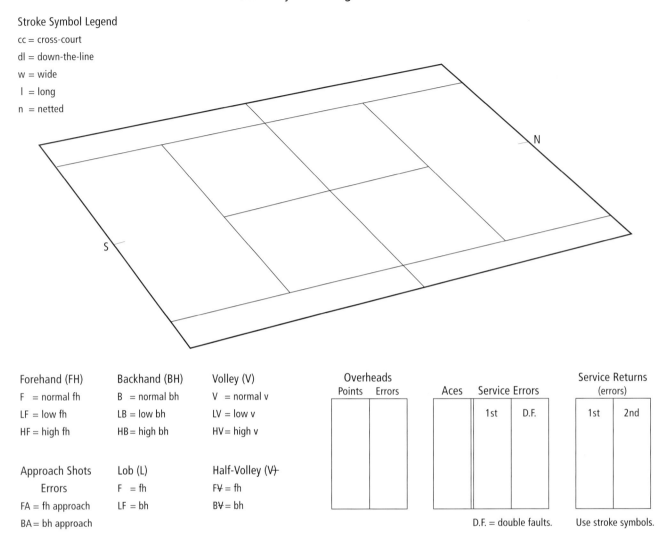

Forehand (FH)	Backhand (BH)	Volley (V)
F = normal fh	B = normal bh	V = normal v
LF = low fh	LB = low bh	LV = low v
HF = high fh	HB = high bh	HV = high v

Approach Shots Errors	Lob (L)	Half-Volley (V̶)
FA = fh approach	F = fh	FV̶ = fh
BA = bh approach	LF = bh	BV̶ = bh

Overheads

Points	Errors

Aces | Service Errors

Aces	1st	D.F.

D.F. = double faults.

Service Returns (errors)

1st	2nd

Use stroke symbols.

---

around and hit this big forehand." The poor guy never noticed that she had two forehands.

Keen observation will help you detect other patterns in your opponent's play. Most people stick with a style of play and seldom deviate. If they react a certain way under stress on a particular shot, they will usually respond the same way when that shot comes up again. You can learn this by charting, but also by observing your opponent while the match progresses. Rod Laver, for example, kept alive his Grand Slam hopes in the 1962 French Open by being willing to gamble on the basis of what he had learned earlier in the match. Laver was serving in the fourth set and was down match point to Marty Mulligan. But Rod had been noticing that Mulligan always tried to hit his backhand returns down the line. So Rod served to Mulligan's backhand and broke for the sideline, where, sure enough, he was able to cut off Mulligan's return with a winning volley. From there he rallied to win the match.

4. Learn to be adaptable. I've found that one of the similarities of tennis champions is their flexibility and their ability to adapt to new situations that arise during a match. Old-timers remember Pancho Gonzales as only a big hitter, but he was a master at keeping the ball in play. In fact, as the point increased in length, his chances of winning it increased tremendously. He hated to lose those long rallies. He had the big game and the slow game, and that's what made him great. But when a lot of players lose their rhythm playing the big strokes, they can't adjust, and their game falls apart.

Top players display their adaptability in other important ways. If their opponent is really getting down low on the ball and making the play, they'll start bouncing the ball high with topspin. If their opponent is killing them on the high ball, they'll start hitting with underspin so that the ball bounces low and forces their opponent to bend down. They have their game plan set up beforehand but if they start losing they already have an alternate plan which was worked out in their head before the match. Thus they can shift gears strategically without losing their rhythm or their ability to hit instinctively. Contrast this to the average player, who falls apart if his original plan doesn't work — provided he even has a plan.

Losing the first set is not a reason to automatically junk your game plan. If you are just playing poorly and you feel you need to try new tactics, that's one thing. But if you are playing well and your opponent has just been hitting the cover off the ball and playing over his head, then all you can do is hang in there, keep the ball in play, and hope your opponent will start playing like a human. Not unless you can analyze a match in this way, and keep yourself from panicking when you get behind, can you ever come back after losing the first set.

This is another reason why it's so important to chart and to know your opponent. Some weaknesses don't begin to appear until a player starts to get a little tired or is kept under persistent pressure. He may be an unbelievable hot dog in the first set but he still needs your assistance before he can close out the match.

The way I watch for a person who's choking during a match is to look at the distance between his hitting elbow and his body as he contacts the ball. I talked earlier about how most players have a tendency to allow the ball to get too close to their body — instead of striding out to meet it — because they feel safer, in a Freudian way. This closeness tends to increase as the stress gets greater and the person begins to lose his confidence. But when I see that person hitting out away from his body, then I know he's pretty confident about his stroke. This is especially true on the one-handed backhand, where you must contact the ball farther out in front of your body than on the forehand.

5. Concentrate on the ball and nothing else. Kramer knew that his success in tennis stemmed from his ability to focus all of his attention on the ball, and on his stroke in relation to the ball. When he got a service break or he fell behind in the match, he would just keep reminding himself, "Watch the ball, watch the ball," or whatever was necessary to keep his attention on the ball. In fact, he never felt comfortable about the outcome of the match until he touched the locker room door. Even after winning he would stare and be very intent during the trophy cer-

emonies, as if the match were still in progress. Not until he reached the locker room would you see him finally breathe a real sigh of relief, when he knew the match was over and he could feel good about winning.

Scientists studying performance anxiety certainly support Kramer's theory. They have isolated two events that cause people to choke in tennis (as well as any competitive sport): one is worrying about their personal level of play and the second is worrying about the outcome of the match. In other words, players who are outcome-oriented can fall apart quickly due to performance anxiety. The secret is to be process-oriented, that is, do what Kramer did by thinking only about what needs to be done to hit the ball properly.

6. Never give up. If you run and stretch out for a ball that is seemingly out of reach, you might flick it back and still win the point. If you lose the first five games of the set, your opponent must still get to six. In the third round of the 1996 French Open, for example, young Chanda Rubin saved seven match points and rallied from a 0–5, 0–40 third-set deficit to beat Jana Novotna.

I've never known a more determined player than Glenn Bassett, my doubles partner back in our younger years and a former nationally ranked player. He never had a big serve but he won with guts and intuitiveness and a "get back in there and fight and don't give up" spirit. No matter what the score, the game was never over and the match was never over until the final point had been won. When Glenn would be playing in a tournament, let's say against a guy named Jones, you would be on one court and you could hear the umpire on another court saying, "15-Jones . . . 30-Jones . . . 40-Jones . . ." and you'd figure that Glenn didn't have a chance. But before long you'd hear, "Game, Mr. Bassett." When he coached the UCLA tennis team for many years, Glenn instilled that same kind of fight in his players, which I really loved to see.

7. It may sound simplistic, but it's important to remind yourself: every game is important. Some tennis buffs like to theorize that the seventh or the ninth game of the set is the most important, but this leads people to think subconsciously that the first three or four games are worth less while later games are worth more and they tend to play with corresponding levels of intensity and concentration. The smart player simply concentrates on each shot.

Coping with Different Court Surfaces

I like my students to understand that an individual who has sound strokes is going to be good on any surface, whether it's cement, clay, grass, or artificial carpeting. Individual surfaces, however, will allow people to capitalize on particular strengths or penalize them for specific weaknesses.

For instance, a person with a big serve and hard but erratic groundstrokes should stick to a fast surface, such as grass or cement. It will reward his speed and help him end the point quickly before his groundstrokes betray him. Conversely, when this big hitter gets on slow surfaces against a person who can get the ball back, he's going to have to return a lot more balls to win each point — and the more times the ball goes over the net, the greater his chances of making an error. So the hard hitter should look for a surface that helps end the point quickly, while the steadier player should find a surface such as clay that demands greater stroke production.

In the 1990s, Goran Ivanisevic, a hard-serving net-rusher with groundstrokes that were suspect, at times would simply duck some major clay court tournaments. And Thomas Muster, a clay court specialist, would duck grass court tournaments like Wimbledon. Ultimately, both players realized the message they were sending to themselves and others and began playing, with some unsuspected success, on courts they normally loathed.

Another reason players with a serve-and-volley game favor a surface like cement is that it guarantees sound footing for when they follow their serve to the net. Very few players are able to serve and attack effectively on clay because their feet tend to slip and slide. Only the great servers will attack regularly on clay because they know their serve is so good they're going to produce weak returns. Some of the new synthetic surfaces are so slow that they, too, inhibit an attacking type of game by having the ball hit and "sit up." Thus the average server finds it wiser to stay back and try to win from the baseline.

One of the great virtues of topspin, of course, is that it remains effective on every type of surface. Even on composition clay, a topspin groundstroke that lands short will still kick deep and keep most players behind the baseline, whereas underspin — due to its initial trajectory — stays low and slows up a bit, and therefore is dangerous for the hitter when the shot is too short.

On grass, groundstrokes tend to skid low and stay low longer, making them difficult to handle for some players. But it's a myth that this inhibits or penalizes a topspin game. Physicists tell me that when you really want to topspin the ball, you want it to bounce low so that you can brush up against it with a big lift. And, they say, it's harder to topspin a high-bouncing ball. Therefore, grass surfaces favor topspin, especially on the forehand side where you have a split second longer to contact the ball properly. This also means that players who use a two-handed backhand gain an advantage on balls just below the waist because they are actually hitting with two forehands. However, if the ball is extremely low, the two-handed backhand is more difficult because of a restricted range of motion due to the second hand.

I once asked Kramer, "If you had to play Gonzales when you both were in your prime, and if you had the choice of one surface, what would you choose?" I thought that because Jack was the innovator of the big game, he would choose a fast surface. Yet his answer was, "The slowest surface in the world."

"That amazes me," I said. "Why do you say that?"

"Because I had better strokes," he replied. "Gorgo had a couple of weaknesses, and if we played on a slow surface, he would have to hit them sooner or later. I also had a little better concentration span, and Gorgo knew that. So when we would get into a position where those things were evident — even if we played a five-hour match and it was very close all the way — I would know I was going to win, and he would know I was going to win."

So it only goes to show that the great champions are confident that if they are put under pressure, and they can't pull off the big game, they can still win with their basic fundamentals on any court surface. One giant hitter and great player,

Pete Sampras, has never won a championship on the clay courts of the French Open through 1997. But he has the strokes and determination to pull it off before he retires.

Handling the Wind, Heat, and Sun

Smart players always check the wind before they play so that they seldom have to experiment during the match. Unfortunately, most people find out which way the wind is blowing on a key point when they try to throw up a lob. When they miss it they think, "Well, I'll make the right allowances on the next one." But that chance may come at set point against you.

If wind is generally prevalent where you play, take time before your next match to see how it affects lobs hit from both ends of the court. When you have a cross-wind, you want to know how far you should lob the ball to the right or the left of the alley so that the ball will come down into the court. Check one side, then check the other. When the wind is blowing in your face, experiment to see how hard you have to hit. Against a strong wind I always tried to lob to the back fence. When the wind was at my back, I tried to have my lob land at the net and it would come close to my opponent's baseline. Checking these things out before-hand will give you the confidence that you won't have to experiment at a critical moment in the match. A four-time Wimbledon champion, Louise Brough, would always check the wind by tossing up blades of grass, even when it seemed there was no wind. I worked out with Louise before her 1955 victory and I used to smile when I saw her check the wind, no matter where she was playing. Of course, she also won Wimbledon, while I was at home reading the results in the paper.

I've always been fascinated by how much a hat can bring down body temper-ature in hot, sunny weather. Rod Laver would even put a piece of cabbage inside his old Aussie hat, while other players will use a wet sponge to keep the head cool and to absorb perspiration. I think it's smart to learn to play with some kind of hat, as long as you can find a hat that fits, and providing you don't try to experiment with a new hat during a crucial match, because it can be distracting. People who try to play with sunglasses should also practice with sunglasses.

Dealing with the Player Who "Cheats"

The best way I know to head off disputes over line calls is not to have a "play it over — take two" system. Instead, players should know beforehand that if they don't see the ball land definitely out, it's automatically in.

Still, you will always come up against people who give you bad calls. Some players just have poor eyesight but most of them are cheating you, and when they do you have four courses of action. One, if you think he's your friend and he's cheating you — he's not your friend, so why keep playing him? Two, if he's your friend and you don't want to challenge his bad calls, then you have to forget them and tell yourself that you're playing for the fun of playing, or the exercise. Three, if your friend is convinced he's making accurate calls (and he even suggests that *your* eyesight might be failing), then you should try to have an impartial person watch a

If you pull up too early to see where your shot is going to travel, the result will be a lot of balls hit off the edge of your strings.

match to see how accurate the calls are. Four, if it's in a tournament, you can call for an umpire.

In the end, however the calls go, you have to keep from getting frustrated and letting it interfere with your concentration and your stroke production. In most matches, the bad calls on both sides tend to even out.

In 1995, I prepared a questionnaire for junior players and one question was, "What bothers you most about tournament play?" The number one answer was "cheaters." I always tell youngsters to watch for cheaters and remember that this type of opponent has to cheat to win. But the day will come in tournament play when there will be lines people on the court and that same person will have lost his or her biggest weapon —"cheating"— and will usually choke.

Miscellaneous Shots

Put-away, or "Kill, Shots"

I haven't dealt with these shots during the book because most players can't put a ball away in the manner they intend, and when they do, it's because somebody else has made an error by hitting them a short lob or a weak groundstroke.

Drop Shots

This is mostly a strategic shot for clay courts — and for pro players. I can't remember ever seeing a player who could hit an effective drop shot from the baseline. Even the pros who try to hit a drop shot from the backcourt rarely win the point. The ball either goes into the net or bounces up and allows the opponent to rush in and hit a winner. Thus, never hit a drop shot unless you're well inside the baseline, your opponent is out of court, and you know you're going to win the point or you want to tire your opponent.

How to Beat a "Wristy" Player

Periodically you are going to come across an opponent who plays with a lot of forearm and wrist action. Forearm and wrist-snappers are identified by an occasional wild shot that goes into the next county when their timing's off, and if you watch you'll generally see their racket face come behind their body on the backswing as they lay the wrist back; fixed-wrist players rarely go back this far. "Wristy" players also tend to follow through around their neck or their chest, and they're either too early or late contacting the ball.

Wrist-rollers (who like to think of themselves as "finesse" players) survive on touch, rhythm, and concentration. Thus they love it when you hit the ball at one consistent speed — the faster the better. When the ball always arrives with relatively the same pace, they can learn just when to roll the forearm and wrist. The trick, therefore, is to never give wrist-rollers the same pace twice in a row. Hit the ball fast, slow, medium, fast, medium, slow, fast . . . and watch their game unravel. That's why a wrist player will knock off a hard-hitter one day, then lose to the club dinker the next, because the dinker hits it slow and slower, and the wrist player can never learn exactly when to roll his wrist. His only defense is to berate the poor dinker and try to shame him into hitting the ball hard. "You're such a lousy player, you ruin my rhythm," is the general attack, but the dinker just keeps playing smart tennis.

You also want to mix up spins and speed to the player who hits with underspin, which normally occurs on the backhand. He, too, is dependent on more sophisticated calculations and you don't want him to get in a comfortable groove. You can usually detect an underspin player by the way his racket head stays high on the backswing, up at shoulder level, and then comes down to contact the ball.

How to Beat the Dinker

We all know that dinkers are despised around the world. I mean, they play the game like sissies, right? They try nothing new, they never drive a ball hard, and they go up to the net once every spring. But while you're making fun of them, they're winning another trophy. Dinkers are successful because they just keep the ball in play with a minimum of speed and fanfare, and a maximum of high bounces and patience . . . waiting for you to miss. In fact, instead of scorning dinkers, you should realize that they are simply capitalizing on basic physical principles and a keen understanding of psychology.

One reason dinkers produce so much aggravation is that they never give you a ball that lands in the middle of the court, between the net and the baseline. They always throw up helium balls (also known as "moonballs") that land deep and bounce high, forcing you to hit up around your armpits all day. You'd much rather play against Bertha, who hits the ball short and with just the right speed to bring it up around waist level so that you can crack your hips into the shot. Not only is it harder to hit off a high bounce, but you also get tired of slugging the ball from behind the baseline. You think you can push the dinker around the court by hitting the ball hard, but he has plenty of time to get ready.

Psychologically, dinkers have developed more patience and a higher frustration-tolerance threshold than most opponents. They keep stoking your boiling point by giving you one more chance to lose until finally you blow up. You decide to do something fancy to win the point and that's when you knock the ball in the net or send it out of play. The dinker just keeps smiling and getting the ball back until eventually your game breaks down entirely.

At the pro level, Spain's Arantxa Sanchez Vicario is my favorite example of a baseline specialist who prefers to rally and use whatever defensive tactic is necessary to win. One year, after defeating Jennifer Capriati in the Hilton Head tournament, 2–6, 7–5, 6–0, Vicario said, "I knew if I won the second set, the match was in my hands; mentally I'm much more strong." In the 1996 French Open, after being jeered by the crowd for her successful strategy of hitting high lobs to Katrina Habsudova, her quarterfinal opponent, Vicario told Robin Finn of the *New York Times*, "I don't care what the crowd says. You always try to do what the other player doesn't like to play. She hates high lobs — I win the point. I am not going to play the way she likes to play." In the semi-finals, Vicario defeated Jana Novotna, a serve-and-volley player who afterward aired a familiar complaint. "It's always difficult to play a player like Arantxa because she doesn't really hit hard; she doesn't give you pace or anything. She just runs around the court and waits for somebody else's mistake."

Well, that's Vicario's intent, of course. But despite having well-entrenched weapons, a baseline counterpuncher like Vicario — as well as the club dinker — is still vulnerable against the player who knows how to come to the net. There are methods you can use to spoil his fun — short of trapping him in a dark alley — but you have to be fundamentally sound.

First, you must make the dinker play your game. You can't try to outlast him by playing from the baseline, unless you enjoy losing. The dinker just loves a long point. If the ball goes over the net ten times, you're going, "I can't stand this guy," but the dinker's smiling and thinking, 'This could go to 100!" That's why I warn people: play a dinker for three hours and you're looking for oxygen while he's looking for another match.

Second, there's one place dinkers hate to be, and that's up near the net. They're the happiest people alive when they can stand back and play from the baseline. But when you bring them up, and the distance decreases between them and the net, they begin to worry. You can even see their faces contort the closer they get.

Third, the problem is to bring the dinker to the net with the kind of shot that puts him on the defensive — either a drop shot that barely clears the net, or a short-angle roll shot that forces him to bend down near a singles sideline. If you hit a short ball that goes too deep or just bounces up nice and high, then he doesn't even have to be a good net player to put you away with a placement.

Okay, let's say you learn to hit the short ball so that you can draw the dinker away from his pillbox. The first time you do this he may come in, hit a good approach shot, and then retreat to the baseline, as if to say, "You're not going to trick me." If you're a typical player you may think, "Ah, nuts, he doesn't fall for it," and you won't try another short ball all day. The smart player, however, will keep bringing the dinker to the net over and over again. The dinker will run up and run back, up and back, until about the sixth shot, when he starts turning blue. Then he'll say to himself, "I think I'll stay at the net and show him I'm a great volleyer."

Now the typical intermediate does another unwise thing. He (or she) tries to pass the dinker down the line, but the dinker stretches at the net and hits a lucky volley that wins the point. The intermediate shakes his head and thinks, "Gee, he can volley, too. It's amazing." And he stops bringing the dinker to the net. Instead, what you must do when dinkers come to the net — if your passing shots aren't working — is try to give them a new navel. Blast the ball right at them and call their bluff; don't let them get away with lucky chops or lunges. That's how the pros find out who can really volley, for when the ball comes right at your stomach, at about 80 or 90 miles an hour, you can only be lucky once; the rest of the time — if you can't volley — you'll be digging fuzz out of your navel and saying, "Nice shot . . . nice shot . . . nice shot."

Don't forget that when a dinker does move toward the net and is going after a low ball, she's already nervous. If you would like her to pass out from anxiety, try attacking the net when she is attempting to hit that low ball while running forward. She will spot you coming forward, all the while knowing that she must lift the ball — an absolute nightmare for a dinker.

Also remember, the authentic dinker is one who can only play from the baseline. I point this out because people sometimes complain, "I did what you said, Vic. I brought this dinker up short all day but he kept hitting the approach shot deep, he could volley, and he just killed me." Well, if a person can beat you long and beat you short, he's no dinker — he's Sampras in disguise. The only thing left is to get him in the bar.

To summarize, if you hope to beat a dinker you must learn to control the short ball so that he must leave his stronghold to hit approach shots and volleys. You must make him play your game. You can't "outsteady" him by letting him stay back. Yet I see people try to beat dinkers this way all the time.

The average player might spend months working on his game, obsessed with finally destroying the club's most notorious dinker on his own battleground. This person tells his friends, "I've been waiting to beat this guy for ten years. If he wants to dink, terrific. If he wants to play six hours, fantastic. I've been running five miles a day and hitting thousands of balls and I'm ready." Yet once the match begins, the challenger seldom lasts for much longer than six or seven games. He might have the dinker down 4–0, playing from the baseline, but the dinker knows he has the match in his hip pocket. He knows his opponent will never have the patience — or the shots — to outlast him, and that his opponent will be a loony bird before the match is over, simply because he doesn't have the experience or the temperament to hang in there that long. Sure enough, the challenger finally ends up smashing his racket against a net post and crying, "Take it! You can have the match if that's the way you want to play."

Ideally, therefore, what you're striving for in tennis to be able to dink from the baseline when you have to dink and to attack the net when you have the first opportunity. You want to be aggressive but you also want the dinker's patience. Most dinkers can't do both — attack as well as stay back — but their patty-cake system helps them beat about 95 percent of the tennis-playing population around the world, until they meet somebody who can match them from the baseline and can bring them up to the net.

Why not try to be that person?

Tennis and Your Psyche

ALTHOUGH TENNIS still comes down to a mastery of the fundamentals, these weapons can literally be tossed away if you're unable to control — if not master — the psychological stress brought on the sport's "one wins, one loses" syndrome. Tennis is a popular sport, people are having tons of fun playing, and advertisers are using the game to push health and well-being. But nobody can pretend that stress doesn't exist out on that court. In fact, if you just talk to some people before they play an important match they can barely remember their name. They have all the strokes at 1:30 — but the match doesn't start until 2:00. When their opponent says, "Ready to play?" they panic, and if they have to serve you hear them say shakily, "Dear God, let this go in."

The purpose of this chapter, therefore is to help you find ways to play with confidence and intensity — and a rhythmical swing — from the very first point in the match. I'll talk about how you can learn to rule out psychological contaminants; how to raise your frustration-tolerance level; how to close out a point when you have the strategic advantage; how to finish off an opponent when you have the lead; how to keep from caving in when you get behind; how to keep from "choking" on second serves, overheads, and other crucial points; and how to recognize and deal with the personality quirks of your opponent, deliberate or ingrained as they may be.

A key element to remember throughout this chapter is that the brain is the engine for everything you do. So your brain needs only to send the correct software package to your body to make the correct stroke, if you're in the right position to hit the ball. Therefore, your brain must be uncluttered and allowed to focus only on those things that will produce the right response from your body, arm, and racket. The ball doesn't care if you're having personal problems or are scared to death about something; it only knows that it will do whatever the racket asks it to do during a four millisecond contact. Anything you do or think that detracts the brain from its original intent will normally spell your downfall and will corrupt your software package like a virus, and causing your whole program to "crash."

What follows are suggestions to help you minimize those lousy messages to the brain which help ruin a shot and mess up your whole day. The person who can minimize those interferences to the brain represents my definition of "mentally tough."

REDUCING STRESS BEFORE A MATCH

I've found that most stress in tennis is really self-imposed, and not the result of antics by your opponent. This pressure can stem from a fear of losing, of being humiliated in front of club members, of looking out of style in your cut-off Levi's, of letting down your doubles partner. Some people even have hidden masochistic tendencies — they enjoy suffering. Thus it's much more important to understand and to learn to cope with your own psychological makeup (as well as your own strokes) which will help you stop worrying about your opponent.

It's difficult — and perhaps not even advisable, in a competitive sense — to go into an important match completely relaxed. Even when you know you have the edge on your opponent, the anticipation of victory and thoughts about a possible upset are going to make you nervous. But there are a number of steps you can take prior to the match to establish the correct amount of nervousness. Stress in itself is not bad, as long as you know how much you need to help you perform properly. The human needs a certain amount of stress to perform at high levels; the key is how you manage this stress.

1. Learn to think like a winner. This isn't possible if you are already setting up excuses for losing: the weather is bad, the court's not clean, you didn't get enough sleep last night, your knee is hurting, you forgot to wear your lucky sweater. Instead of dwelling on "ego outs," think positively and visualize your strengths.

2. A realistic approach to your problems is a great stress-reduction mechanism. In other words, if you had specific weaknesses a week earlier and you've gone out and practiced hard to improve them, you will come into the match with much more confidence. Most players, however, avoid their weaknesses in practice and thus have the same old problems and the same old frustrations week after week after week.

3. Be in sound physical shape. You give your opponent a great psychological lift when you look exhausted after the first set and he realizes that you're no longer trying to chase down every shot or that you have stopped coming to the net behind every serve.

4. Know your equipment is in excellent condition. Broken strings can be discouraging.

5. Don't sit in the sun for extensive periods before matches or you'll be tired before you walk on the court.

6. If you have a great deal of energy, "hanging around" the tournament watching other matches may make you even more nervous. Some players solve this problem by appearing for matches 10 to 15 minutes before their match is scheduled to begin.

7. Have an objective game plan. Unrealistic goals and excess ego involvement will only lead to intense frustration. Know your own ability level and tell yourself before you go out to play that the best you can do is to make a strong effort in every department — and have some fun while you're at it.

Knowing your own strengths and weaknesses will help keep you from being psyched out during warm-ups. If you're unsure of yourself to begin with, you can easily be intimidated by the opponent who wears color-coordinated clothes, has all the latest equipment, and who informs you that today he's going to concentrate on his topspin lob and his American Twist serve, while experimenting with his latest theory on power tennis. That gets you to thinking, "Why hasn't my pro been teaching me these things? How can I win with my $50 prestrung racket against this guy? What am I doing here?"

I mentioned earlier how most tennis players fail to notice anything important about their opponent before a match. That's why, even before two players have swung a racket, you can sometimes pick out the eventual winner and loser. The winner is concentrating on preparing himself for the match, while the loser is looking at the winner. He's all wrapped up in his opponent and is already going down psychologically. If the winner has a big black satchel, the loser is thinking, "I wonder what's in the satchel?" Then he spots his opponent's shoes. "Wow, I've never seen those before in my life — he must be fast!" If his opponent then makes a big flourish as he sprays his racket strings, the loser walks up the net and says, "If it's all right with you, I don't feel like playing today."

8. Be aware of those things you do which sabotage your game. In therapy, a psychiatrist can actually get patients, at times, to stop obsessing by simply saying, "Stop it!" Give that a try if you find yourself obsessing about negative things.

9. Keep in mind that the major networks are not going to call you for your scores. As a matter of fact, even your friends often forget your scores within a week.

10. I've had many people tell me that they're afraid to play a particular match because their opponent is so great. "Forget it," I gently tell them. "If they were great, they wouldn't be playing you; they would be out of town on the tour and not available to play." If you have similar self-doubts, remember: your opponent usually has the same fear about you.

11. Try to become "process-oriented" as opposed to "outcome-oriented." When you think about the process you must activate to hit the ball properly, the outcome is automatic. When you worry about the outcome, the process gets fuzzy.

12. Don't be afraid to lose. The great players I know aren't afraid to lose if they know they have given it their best shot. That's why they can handle losses week after week in a 64-player draw, where only one player ultimately wins. But they hate to lose if they didn't practice or failed to play intelligently.

13. Try changing your vocabulary to "I chose to get angry" rather than "They

made me angry". . . and "I chose to hit silly shots" rather than "They made me hit silly shots". . . and "I chose not to practice my overhead" rather than "I was too busy to practice my overhead." In other words, take responsibility for your wins and losses. Your coach, your parents, and your friends did not make you win, you did it all on the court by yourself. And if you played great you chose to play great. Don't forget: you're the only one who knows what's going on inside your mind. When you have a good win, don't be afraid to tell yourself that you did a super job. Others will forget to mention it.

MATCH-PLAY PSYCHOLOGY

Ruling Out External Stimuli

One of the similarities between tennis champions, I've discovered, is not that they can think of so many unique things to do on the court, but that they can stick with the simple fundamentals and rule out external stimuli while they play. Even though top business people are accustomed to working under intense pressure, they rarely can bring that same kind of concentration to tennis. When they play they are bothered by the wind, the sun, comments from spectators, people playing on the adjacent court, and so on. A top player, however, can shut off distractions as though he has a light switch in his brain.

Sure, Pancho Gonzales was one of the game's most notorious rednecks, but nearly everybody overlooks the fact that he had an amazing flexibility. He had a short fuse; if somebody started heckling him he would storm into the stands. But when he came back down, he would be absolutely calm — ready to play tennis again. He'd be thinking, "Watch the ball," while the average pro would be so livid he would just fall apart. Gorgo would just go right back to beating your brains out with a 130 m.p.h. serve. I don't advocate going into the stands as a way to let off steam, but Gonzales is an example of how all the great champions are able to refocus their attention on the next point immediately after blowing up, without letting the incident affect their play.

The problem is, how do you achieve that icy concentration where you can learn to rule out distractions such as the weather, bad line calls, thoughts about winning or losing, unnerving movements by your opponent — while focusing completely on the object that is most important to you: the ball? How do you detach yourself from any kind of personality involvement and become "process-oriented"?

First, do whatever you can to keep your attention glued on the shot you are making or anticipating. Pay attention to your breathing or some little checkpoint on your swing that keeps you thinking of the present condition, not the past or the future. If you dwell on a shot you've just hit into the net, or if you're thinking ahead a few shots — how you're going to set your opponent up for the "kill"— then you're not giving enough respect to the shot you're on. In addition, you're asking too much of your brain to solve so many issues. The brain has to deal with everything you surface, but it also has to send clear messages to your muscles. It can do a better job when it only has to send down one clear message at a time. As

I learned from Dr. Richard Haier, studies have shown that the smartest people, who solve extremely difficult problems, also use the least amount of glucose in the brain. Studying glucose metabolic rates is one way to determine exactly what area of the brain, and how much of the brain, is active when performing. Or, putting it another way, when it's said that we only use 30 percent of our brain, hopefully it's less when we're playing tennis. When there's too much brain activity, it appears we're less efficient.

Second, don't get caught in an internal debate, where voices inside you are arguing, "Concentrate, you dummy! Why can't you concentrate?" You can concentrate too much and forget about hitting the ball. It's fascinating to me that people have to fight off intruding thoughts at every level of the game. There's no real difference between a ten-year-old girl who's thinking, "I've got to win because my folks are in the stands," or a pro who comments after a victory, "I hadn't won a match for so long I was really nervous." But then with this mentality you know that while he was playing he was thinking that he hadn't won a match in a long time. This is one reason why, as a coach, I'm almost afraid to try to "psych up" a player to win a match. Some level of arousal is necessary to perform better, but basically I want him to be detached, unemotional, concentrating on his strokes. He should do his analyzing and worrying during practice sessions and reflective thinking hours, then rely on his game plan and his instincts once the match begins.

Third, don't lose your energy — or your concentration — getting mad. Concentrate on the shot you are making and don't brood about the easy overhead you just whiffed, or a bad line call. The bad calls, the lucky breaks, and the crummy shots tend to fall both ways in a close match.

Fourth, don't be discouraged by your opponent's unbelievable saves. In basketball, for instance, you can shoot your very best jump shot and if it goes through the basket nobody can do anything about it. But if you hit a fantastic shot in tennis, your opponent can still return it for a winner. This can have a disheartening effect if it happens throughout the match, since you tend to forget your own good shots while only remembering his remarkable saves. All you can really do is dwell on the present and keep making the play.

Fifth, as part of your post-match routine, try to recall the distractions that arose and at what point they began affecting your concentration. Remember, the experts have a great deal of trouble defining what concentration is, and they warn that sometimes just telling yourself to "relax" or "concentrate" will actually cause your brain activity to go up. So the key thing is to know that you're focusing only on those things that will help you have a good hit, and to find out what it is that relaxes you or keeps you from focusing on the hit. By going through a little checklist of extraneous distractions that appear to harm your play (for example, players talking on the adjoining court) or typical situations in a match that cause you to tense up, you can begin to gain greater mental toughness.

Learning to Close Out Your Opponent

Every pro will tell you from sad experience: never let up when you have an opponent in trouble. Don't relax, don't ease off because you feel sorry for him, don't give him a break on line calls. If he falls and you have a wide-open court, concentrate on hitting a winning shot, then see if he needs any help.

Tell me it's not true that when you let a person off the hook and he gets back in the game, he shows no mercy. If he goes on to beat you, he just says afterward, "You're getting better." He completely forgets your generosity. So finish the guy off when you have him on the ropes and let him go get a cold drink and a sandwich. Never feel guilty about winning, no matter what the score.

Kramer's feeling, and I agree, is that if your opponent is a friend, do him a favor by beating him fair and square, as fast as you can. When you give people games or you try to be nice to them, you haven't done anything for them. You've let them think that you've played your best and that they're better than they really are. An honest system in a match is to have opponents know that you are always going to play as hard as you can, and that whenever they do win, they'll know that they really earned it.

A rule of thumb closely related to all this is: if you are winning, never change your style of play to keep your opponent "honest." If you take a big lead by playing aggressively, don't suddenly turn cautious and conservative when you sense victory. If you're winning two out of three points attacking your opponent's backhand, you're crazy to go to his forehand just for the sake of variety. Why change a winning tactic? Your opponent may have lost all his confidence, but if he knocks off a big forehand winner he might revive and climb back into the match. Momentum is an elusive element and often impossible to retrieve once lost. (If you are losing, however, then you should change your strategy, and the point at which you change should be determined prior to the match.)

All this doesn't mean you have to acquire a "killer instinct," whereby you want to destroy your opponent, humiliate him, make him want to quit the game. I've never seen the pros go that way. They want to win, but they have great respect for one another. What it really means to them is, "Look, the rules of this game are one man wins and one loses, and I'd rather not lose."

Okay, let's say you buy my argument about showing no sympathy when you have break point on your opponent's serve, or set point, or match point. But when you go out to play you still have trouble holding on to a lead. What are you doing wrong?

I've found that many people, including young pros who are trying to break into the top level of play, very often have trouble playing well as they come closer to winning, that is, they become "outcome-oriented." They get emotionally involved and their thought processes increase. They have a tendency to let their mind wander to victory —"Jeez, I can win now if I can just hold my serve"— and very often that's when they begin to lose. Instead, they must remind themselves, "I've been winning by concentrating on each shot. If I maintain that system, that's the best I can do. All these other thoughts are contaminants."

To keep the anticipation of victory from ruining your concentration and making you even more nervous than when you are behind, try to ignore the set score. If you're ahead 5–3 and you're thinking about the next set, then you're failing to take care of each shot as it comes. This is why so many people lose their serve after breaking their opponent's serve. They make a fatal mistake by thinking, "Now I've got her," when they should be saying to themselves, "Chin up, watch the ball . . ." That's one reason why Kramer was so devastating: when he broke your serve at 5-all, you knew he was going to hold his own serve because he concentrated only upon his present stroke. And he had a passion for winning.

I think it's worth repeating here that top players aren't afraid to lose. What they hate most is not sticking with the "process" of hitting the ball properly and finding themselves switching to worrying about the outcome. So when you get the lead — and throughout the match, for that matter — let the other person do the extra thinking. Remember, whenever you have the server only one point away from a service break, he or she is worrying more about that than about a proper service motion. In fact, this is where most players tend to do their greatest amount of thinking. They know they're supposed to win their serve — the service break is like a recovered fumble in football — and yet they're suddenly down 30–40. These thoughts are negative, and you don't want to let your opponent get an emotional reprieve. So if his next serve lands in, just keep the pressure on by maintaining your winning system. Keep in mind that the ball doesn't care about the score; its only concern is how you strike it.

Whether you have the lead or you're behind, try to maintain a high frustration-tolerance threshold. Don't let overconfidence or your eagerness to win ruin your patience. If the ball goes over the net three or four times, don't think you suddenly have to do something big to win the point — you tend to die young when you try to get fancy.

Finally, learn to treat the first point of every game with the same respect as 30-all. This habit will help you play match points with the same confidence as other points, and help you approach every point with the intensity of match point.

Developing a Competitive Ethic

When people who have managed to avoid head-to-head athletic competition finally get into tennis, they can't believe how hard it is to play well under that kind of pressure. Many people, in fact, just refuse to play a match — they are lifelong rallyers — because they don't want to be forced into a win-lose situation. This is a sad kind of thing to me because they've missed the competition. There's much to be said about the invigorating power of good healthy competition. That's why I feel that people need to depersonalize the game, and their opponent, by focusing on self-improvement instead of worrying about their won-lost record. They should measure their success and reward themselves based upon their relationship to the ball during a match: the gains they made on a particular stroke, how well they kept the ball in play, their ability to anticipate and react to the first short ball, and so forth. If people could learn to do that early in life, "winning" would take care of itself, and we would have many more gracious winners and losers.

"Winning is everything" is such a narcissistic viewpoint. What we're saying is that the world is made for a select few. In a 64-man tournament, we commit 63 people to failure. This is truly a short-sighted approach. Sure it's a frustrating game when you lose; there are days when you want to kill your opponent — or yourself. But I say, forget about your losses. Laugh and hit. Chances are you'll have more fun, and you'll win more often in the long run.

For years I've watched people go through this metamorphosis: a youngster starts out in tennis, and you try to get him (or her) to have fun. As his strokes improve, he starts playing in tournaments and getting into tough competition. He gets to a point where maybe he's the city champ, but when he finds he can't win on the state level, or nationally, very often he drops the game. Not until later, when he's in his thirties or forties, will he start playing again — free of all those expectations that were made for him by his parents and his coach and himself when he was a teenager. What a tragic thing that once he got hooked on the game he couldn't play all the way through and just enjoy himself, no matter what level of success he attained.

So don't be consumed by a "win-or-else" philosophy. Half the people who play this game every day are losers, but that doesn't mean they can't have fun and feel good about striving for improvement. Yet so many people who lose consistently just get down on themselves and get so frustrated —"Jeez, I'm such a crummy player"— that they are never going to improve. Champions have flexibility: they can adapt to losing situations and learn from them. But I find that losers can't hack it — they lose and the whole world is on their shoulders. They live in the past instead of trying to work on their future by improving their strokes in the present. When a champion like Rod Laver would lose an important match, he wouldn't moan about his bad luck or go off sulking. He would just admit the truth: "I didn't play well, I didn't hit the right shots, I missed an easy volley at 3-all in the third. So I've got to get out and work on my strokes. If I hit the ball well, I'll win; if I don't hit it well, I'll lose. All it means is that I have to work a little harder." But he wouldn't let this spoil his enjoyment of outside interests.

Laver, the only two-time Grand Slam winner, was known for his unbelievable comebacks after being down match point. I don't think he "came back," I think his opponent facilitated his recovery by doing something different. Rod just kept hitting the same old boring winner.

PERSONALITY TYPES IN TENNIS

Most people take up tennis as a way to ease tension and to get a little exercise. But they soon discover that the pressure to win and to "look good" can bring to the surface deep emotions that they've been able to submerge in other aspects of adult life. For example, company presidents are able to rationalize daily setbacks by playing with words. They can state that they expected to get 28 percent of the market but "due to a sudden shift of the business climate" they only got 24 percent. Yet when they go out to play tennis it's a very definitive pressure: one wins and one loses; nobody ties, no matter what the climate.

Unlike other sports, where you are also competing against the golf course, the ski mountain, or the ocean, tennis comes down to just you and that person (or persons) across the net. Laying yourself open like this to direct competition is what trips off a lot of crazy behavior as people try desperately to protect their self-esteem. Many people even admit that they are startled at their behavior on the tennis court. They tell me, "Vic, I'm usually reserved but I'm out there calling this person an idiot and accusing him of cheating me."

The fact that tennis can trigger these raw emotions has given me a chance to isolate and observe many distinct personality types and behavior patterns over the years. If you can learn to recognize these traits in your friends and enemies (and perhaps yourself) you should be able to develop effective counterstrategies. You will also gain greater insights into people. Andrew Young, our former ambassador to the United Nations, told me that he learned a great deal about his fellow delegates by how they behaved on the tennis court. Those who cheated on the tennis court, for example, seemed to have the same propensity in the U.N.

The Unbelievable Dresser

He has everything — sweatbands, headband, "40-love" underwear, a golf glove for his hitting hand, a sun visor, and embroidered tennis rackets on the towel he carefully lays over the net. Everything is immaculate. But I seldom see people who are obsessed with wearing the latest clothes win too many matches. They place too much faith in a new pair of shorts. If they lean against the fence and get their sweater dirty, they're broken up for the day — it's worse than losing the match.

The only time these people gain a psychological edge is when they play somebody who is worried about his own self-image, who is easily intimidated if he feels he is not dressed right. I know I went through this as a teenager, early in my tournament career. My parents were kind and generous but simply couldn't afford the very best, so when I played in junior events against kids with fancy sweaters and starched tennis whites, I'd think, "Man, I can't wait to see this guy play." But the moment we started to rally, I'd realize I could beat him easily — if I didn't let myself be distracted by his clothes.

The Equipment Freak

Show me a club player with four matching rackets and a leather case and I'll usually show you a loser with an expensive hobby. This person has everything except the strokes, but instead of going to work on his weaknesses, he blames all of his trouble on his racket. He misses his shots, loses the match, and immediately runs over to the pro shop and buys a more expensive model.

The Sensualist

The sensual kind of player flits about the court with unbelievable movements, but his pièce de résistance is his service motion. He's picked out some exotic body image that he has tested for hours against a mirror, and all the lessons in the world won't get him to change. Instead, he gives you 30 or 40 weird gyrations until right before impact, at which point he stops and goes "doink!" and hits a marshmallow serve. This kind of "twist" serve is big on the celebrity circuit.

The Trophy Seekers

They're beautiful. Their needs are so great that they look all over the doggone country for tournaments where they might win a trophy, often claiming they are 3.0 players when they are really 4.0s. I even know people who literally stage their own tournaments and buy the trophies so that they can end up winning one for their living room mantel.

The Scorekeepers

They can remember every score and every highlight of every match they've ever played. If you make a great play, they always have a story to top it. "I remember in '58 I was playing Burt Brown and I had him down 4–2, 30-love, when I hit a shot even better than that . . ."

The Theorist

He's great at theorizing about the game but he fails to take into account one thing: he doesn't have the strokes to carry out his grandiose plans. "Down the middle and deep" doesn't have enough pizzazz for him, so he keeps coming up with a new "winning" strategy to replace the one which helped him lose, 6–0, 6–0. He often hangs out with the Equipment Freak, exchanging rackets and theories.

The Sadist

His only goal is to give people "the new look." Thus he loves doubles, where he can pick on people who are already fearful at the net. He tries to hit the ball as hard as he can right at them, getting sheer delight out of watching their frightened expressions. He starts a lot of fights in mixed doubles by never hesitating to go after the woman across the net — especially if it's his wife.

The Manipulator

He can't tolerate being in a position where he feels as though he's going to be manipulated, so he does everything he can to gain an immediate psychological edge. Opening a can of balls before the match, he'll tell his opponent, "I really shouldn't be playing you, I'm so much higher on the ladder." When play begins he goes for speed and power, trying to overwhelm his opponent. Yet his need to dominate seems to go beyond winning. He usually beats his opponent to the clubhouse, beats him giving the scores, and beats him in rehashing the match to friends.

In a sense, nearly everybody who plays club tennis is a manipulator. They're business executives, lawyers, doctors, housewives, or whatever, and they're used to manipulating. But now they run up against other people who manipulate, which leads to some interesting rivalries on the tennis court. This is also why club management is such a tough thing. If you have 450 members, you have 450 people who know, in their own minds, that they could be doing a better job of running the facility than the manager.

The Power-Motivated Type

Some people are so power-motivated that hitting their forehand with speed and feeling the sensation of their serve traveling 100 miles an hour are greater rewards than keeping the ball in play, or even winning. If they lose, they're happy as long as their opponent appreciates their power by saying, "Jeez, you hit the ball so hard I could hardly hang on to my racket."

The Recognition Seeker

Other players couldn't care less about winning, or even playing, as long as they are recognized at the club. If Jim Volley comes to the club wearing his tennis sweater and carrying his rackets, and everybody says, "Hi, Jim," and he gives them all a friendly wave, they just made his day and he hasn't hit a ball yet. I don't see anything wrong with this other than the fact that this person seldom wins. But if he's having genuine fun, who cares?

The Defense Mechanics

Although it's difficult to find defense mechanisms that work around intelligent people, some players will go to desperate lengths to save face. Before the match begins, they will try to set the stage with something like, "I didn't get any sleep last night so I probably won't play well," or "I don't mean to complain but I haven't played much in six months." When play begins, their "ego outs" may have nothing to do with reality. They'll complain, "Why does the sun only shine on my side?" Or, "The wind keeps blowing in my face." Or, "They only washed your side of the court — I keep slipping over here." But the same excuses will go on even after you switch courts. These people never let up. If they beat you, they add a little more pain by saying, "Gee, I didn't think I could beat you with this bum leg."

The Player with "Two-Inch Eyes"

We all run across the player who has unbelievable eyesight. When he calls shots that land close to a line he's always telling you, "Sorry — your shot was out by two inches."

PSYCHOLOGICAL PLOYS

I've always liked what Rod Laver said: "Keep your mouth shut and let your racket do the talking." Yet some players also find that part of the fun in tennis is trying to probe psychological weaknesses in their opponents.

If, for example, you sense that your opponent is fearful of winning — she hasn't beaten you in 12 years — then try to remind her of the score, just to keep the thought of winning in her mind. "Well, Bertha, all you have to do is hold serve and you win the match." Or, if she has masochistic tendencies, you want to sink your hooks into every break that goes against her. Comments like, "Tough luck, Bertha, you almost made a great save," or "Jeez, the calls are really going against you," will give her exactly the kind of encouragement she needs to keep losing.

Don't forget, however, that your opponent will also be searching for your weaknesses. So if you're a miserable loser, keep it to yourself because you'll begin to telegraph your fears near the end of a tight match. Conversely, if your opponent knows that you fight for every point, no matter what the score, this will influence his thinking as the match drags on, and he may feel he has to hit high-risk shots in order to win. (The women on the pro tour would always talk about Billie Jean King's "will to win" and how impressed they were with her ability to dominate. Obviously these thoughts helped give her a psychological edge week in and week out. But I always wondered, "Why do they all dwell on her will? Why not work on the strokes that can beat her?")

A primary objective in psychological tennis is that you want to increase the number of variables with which your opponent is dealing. Thus, if you are losing, you have to get your opponent's mind off the things he's using to beat you. Just to have him begin to self-doubt, to worry that he may start to lose his touch, to brood over a couple of bad breaks, may be enough to turn the match around.

Over the years, a great many players were manipulated by Bobby Riggs, myself included. I once played him in a pro tournament in Cleveland in 1951 and I thought I had him cold. I was playing well and leading 6–5 in the first set when we switched courts. As we toweled off, Bobby said, "Jeez, kid, too bad your backhand's not too good. But if you hang in there it'll get better." Well, I was just killing him off the backhand — but that got me thinking. "What's wrong with this guy? Doesn't he realize he can't handle my backhand?" But I was only 21 and Riggs was a big-name player and a very nice guy so I thought he was just trying to help me. Naturally I went out and tried to give my backhand a little extra juice to impress him, and naturally I lost everything. He had said something that wasn't even true but he got me thinking about it, instead of just concentrating on stroke production and sticking with my game plan. Until Bobby's death, he would remind me of this event and get the biggest laugh out of it. After becoming a licensed psychologist, so did I.

Another way to disrupt your opponent's concentration — if you're losing — is to increase the external stimuli so that he takes his eyes off the ball. Try making a flourish as you follow a shot to the net so that he is more likely to watch you out of the corner of his eye as he makes his hit. Even if you can't volley well, just the fact that you are going to the net will bother most people. They don't like to be attacked; they want to sit back at the baseline and play chess, for when you come to the net you force them into an immediate win-or-lose situation.

At the University of Toledo one year, I was an assistant coach for the basketball team and then I coached the tennis team. We didn't have many tennis players in school, so I talked most of the basketball players into going out for tennis as an off-season conditioner. Most of them had never played competitively and we only had six weeks to get ready, so I concentrated on having them attack the net whenever possible. I wanted their opponents to see those 6'8" guys charging down on them, and to hear those size 14 feet pounding the court. This strategy worked so well that we won over half our matches.

If you are winning and playing well, you don't want to change your rhythm or the pace of the game. But if you are losing you want to do whatever you can to break up your opponent's tempo. Pancho Gonzales would buy time by squatting down and getting up very slowly as you were getting ready to serve, and Riggs's shoe always seemed to come untied when he needed to stall. But the best way to frustrate a short-fused opponent, as I pointed out earlier in the book, is to start slowing down the ball, hitting it over the net with less speed, or just lobbing deep. When you increase the time the ball is in the air, you increase anxiety levels in most players by giving them more time to think about their next shot. As Jack Kramer was advised early in his career — don't panic, keep the ball in play, and most people will find a way to lose.

Finally, if you can't beat your opponent physically, you have to beat him mentally. Don't be afraid to go way out if that's your only hope. You might even try my "last resort strategy."

If somebody is beating you 6–0, 5–0, 3–0 in the final set, you're in deep trouble, right? Whatever you've been doing is wrong, but you want to at least avoid a whitewash and salvage a little self-respect. So on your opponent's next shot, turn and run the wrong way and take a perfect swing at an imaginary ball. This should shake him up enough to help you win a game or two because he just won't be able to get that picture of absurdity out of his mind.

A similar trick was played on me in college. I was beating this fellow from Michigan, something like 6–2, 5–0, 40-love, and I was serving. Suddenly he held up his hand and said, "Hold it, hold it." He started walking up to the net and I was thinking, "What's wrong? Is he going to question a line call?"

When he got to the net he looked me square in the eye and said, "Give up?"

I think I lost the next three games, I was laughing so hard.

Making Sense out of Doubles

F YOU'RE NOT having fun playing doubles, then you should find a new partner, search out different opponents, or see your shrink. Doubles is a tremendous adventure when you know certain key points about strategy and teamwork, and then play with enthusiasm and a lot of laughs. It certainly doesn't have to be slow and boring, with everybody standing around waiting for the ball to come their way. In fact, you can never afford to fall asleep in good doubles; the point will last an exciting 9 to 12 seconds and it's over. You should be moving all the time — running, stretching, anticipating, and using a far greater variety of strokes than you do in an ordinary game of singles. To be a good doubles partner you need to know how to volley and play the net, how to hit overheads and lobs, how to hit service returns with pinpoint accuracy, how to anticipate your opponent's shot, and how to work as a team with your partner. You'll win together and you'll lose together; if you're playing crummy but your partner is terrific, you can still have a lot of fun. And the longer you play together, the more you will discover how you can manipulate, and literally control, a team that has better players, but no teamwork.

That's why it doesn't surprise me that Martina Hingis, a young star who clearly loves to play the game of tennis, is an unabashed doubles player in addition to singles. As she told *Tennis* magazine after winning both championships at the Australian Open and Wimbledon in 1997, "'I would never give up playing doubles. It has helped me in so many ways. . . . I practice all the shots I don't get a chance to in singles, like my volleys, serve-and-volley, service returns, angled ground strokes, lobs and approach shots. I've become more aggressive in singles because of my doubles play. I don't hesitate to come in to net now, when I get the right opportu-

When both teams play hard and enjoy the competition, it's hard to tell which team is the winner. (Photo: Lisa Marie Greenia)

nity. The best part is competing with a partner. . . . Tennis is such an individualized sport that it's fun to have someone else on my side to help win the points.'"

Before talking about who plays where and how, here are the key concepts you should keep in mind about doubles.

1. In top competition, your goal is to gain the proper net position before your opponents — or drive them away from that stronghold — because the team that gains the net controls the point 95 out of 100 times. Your team may still lose the point, but this is primarily the result of weak strokes.

2. Force your opponents to hit up, so that you can hit down and give them an early lunch. You can't get pushed around by opponents who are always lifting the ball. But if you finally get to the net and they are hitting down, you can get killed.

3. Learn to move in tandem with your partner, approximately 11 to 12 feet apart — up, back, and horizontally.

4. Unless you have a certain put-away shot, always try to hit down the middle. Don't be fooled by a myth of intermediate doubles: "Watch your alley." That's an early sign to sharp opponents that you can't really play.

5. The person closer to the net has priority on any shot that he can reach. If

you want to win, dump a partner who tries to tell you before the match, "See that center stripe? That's your side and this is my side. Never get on my side."

6. The best system in doubles is both players up at the net. The second-best system is both players at the baseline. The worst system of all — but the worldwide system in club tennis — is one player up and one player back. You might be saying, "Hey look, we've been playing 'one up and one back' at our club for 20 years and we're always successful." That may be true, but that's why you're still playing at your club, and not out on the tournament circuit. You're playing a system that is relegated to club tennis and can succeed only if the other team promises to play it too. If they don't, you die. Not only do you leave a wide gap between you and your partner for a diagonal shot by your opponents, but they will both come to the net, and whoever is up there on your team is going to have a Wilson logo tattooed onto his or her body.

SELECTING A PARTNER

Choosing a partner can become a very complex issue, drawing on personality issues as much as playing ability, so it amazes me how people seldom reflect upon

The team that gains control of the net is usually just a shot away from winning the point.

The player closer to the net always has priority on the volleys from net post to net post, even if it means invading her partner's territory.

this subject. A scene I have witnessed many times is two friends busting up a long-term relationship shortly after they start playing doubles together, for there's no hiding the fact that competitive tennis causes childhood emotions and experiences to surface as fast as anything I know. With that in mind, here are a few hints on choosing a partner that you plan to play with on a regular basis.

1. Determine your own personality. Do you like to play for the sheer enjoyment of tennis or do you have a killer instinct when you walk on the court? How seriously do you take losses and how important is it to win? Do you like to poach at the net or stay back and play it safe? Do you consider yourself to have "fast hands" at the net or does the net scare you? Do you like to play with a drill sergeant or someone who is rather "soft" in her speaking mannerisms?

Make a list of things you like about playing doubles and have your potential partner do the same thing. Then exchange notes. Potential conflicts will surface immediately and they need to be discussed, for seldom will deep-rooted problems resolve themselves as you play together.

2. Your particular skills may be the opposite of your partner's, but this might be advantageous. For example, I've seen doubles players who won't go to the net until it's time to shake hands, yet their partner is one who loves to have the net all to himself. That's a great match-up.

3. Remember that the right-court player throughout tennis history has often

The worst doubles system in the world is "one up and one back" on both teams. It's called "singles doubles."

An aggressive team can be deadly when volleying from close to the net against a team that has one player up and one player back.

Here's a good starting position for all four players at the beginning of a point: the server, the server's partner on his imaginary "X," the receiver, and the partner of the receiver, who stands just behind the service line, halfway between the singles sideline and the center stripe.

As the serve passes, the partner of the server should rise up on his toes in anticipation of the return coming his way. He wants to be ready to move quickly to any ball within his range.

been an introvert and the left-court player an extrovert. When you are trying to break an opponent's serve, the score is often deuce and it's up to the right-court player to get the service return into play and for the left-court player to knock off the fourth shot of the rally. That calls for a right-court player who can focus and normally not do silly things returning the serve. If the right-court player wins her point, the pressure shifts from the receiver to the server, who is now down game point. Most extrovert left-court players really enjoy returning serve in that situation.

4. If you don't like an organized approach to choosing a partner, at least have a brief discussion and tell that potential partner who you think you are and how you like to play doubles. This will save a lot of friendships and painful moments on the court, for it's easier to say in the beginning that this potential doubles team could find itself in jeopardy and you prefer to enjoy your friendship over playing doubles together.

When you're playing with a new partner and you feel a little uncomfortable and don't know why, back off. It's the best cue I know to generate some reflective thinking and future discussions with the new partner.

COURT POSITIONS TO START A POINT

The Server

When serving from the right (deuce) court, his goal is to stand as far from the center stripe as possible, while still being able to hit into his opponent's backhand corner. Pancho Gonzales, in fact, would stand right next to the stripe because he placed his primary emphasis on hitting to the backhand. You can stand a little farther away when serving from the left court.

The Partner of the Server

He should stand in the middle of the service court, where the diagonals cross. Most beginning and intermediate players hate to stand that close to the center because they're afraid their partner's serve will hit them in the back of the head. This can lead to gigantic arguments, where the net man turns and says, "You dummy, you hit me in the head," and the server replies, "You toad, you wrecked my best serve." If you're afraid of being hit, just bend over so that your head won't be a target. Then if you get hit in the rear end, at least you know it's a service fault.

The Service Receiver

A pro will stand on or very near the singles sideline, because this is halfway between where the server can run him to his forehand and to his backhand. If your opponent can't break his serve that wide to your forehand, then you can stand closer to the center stripe.

The Partner of the Receiver

Players with especially quick hands and reflexes should stand just in front of the service line. Those with slower reactions should stand behind the line. Stand on the line if you're undecided, but realize that this may block the view of the line judge in tournament tennis. With the introduction of ultralight but strong rackets in the 1990s, players are able to get a little closer to the net because they can manipulate the racket more easily.

THE BASIC ROLE OF EACH PLAYER

The Server

His main goal is to consistently get his first serve in play — deep and hopefully with some pace, so that the service receiver can't take the offensive. Then he strives to serve to the opponent's side that will produce the highest and longest ball. With the great improvement of the two-handed backhand service return, the server must now spend more time analyzing the receiver's talents. The goal is to produce the highest and longest service return so that short angles are difficult to hit by the receiver and the partner of the server can have more fun poaching. The two-handed backhand service return has become so much better that it has forced a new level of communication between the server and his partner. There should be no surprises.

The Partner of the Server

This person plays a key role in helping his partner hold serve. The last thing he can be is a passive spectator. First, assuming he and the server each understand where the server will try to place the ball, he must learn to study the service receiver's racket in order to anticipate a drive or a lob. If the racket is on the same level as the intended point of impact with the ball, it's normally going to be a drive (nobody is talented enough to suddenly lower the racket and hit a lob) and he will break forward on the diagonal to try to cut off the shot near the net. If he sees his opponent's racket head drop below the oncoming ball with a beveled face, then it's going to be a lob and he turns and tries to get three quick steps back. Famed UCLA motor-learning specialist Dr. Richard Schmidt and I made a video on the relationship between the brain and motor skills. In it, we discuss the fact that the brain needs at least 150 milliseconds to make a change in direction. There aren't 150 milliseconds left when a person is moving into the ball with the racket. So what you see is what you get. When players at every level try to make a last-second change in stroke production, the result is almost always a missed shot.

Second, as the partner of the server studies his opponent's racket he has just one other thing on his mind: "The next ball that's hit is mine. I don't care where it is — I'm going to get it." He should always be surprised that he can't actually reach the ball, never surprised that he makes the play. He wants to be thinking that he owns that fortress from net post to net post. He's not embarrassed about thinking

Ideally, the service returner moves aggressively forward and nails the ball cross-court at the server's feet.

that way, or that he could be accused of being a ball hog. He knows he has the advantage over his partner by being able to hit a much sharper volley, closer to the net. But to gain that edge, the strong volleyer is always concentrating, ready to get that first step forward so that he can hopefully close out the point. Weak volleyers, on the other hand, never think about getting a jump on the ball; they just stay rooted in their ready position until the ball has been hit by the service receiver, hopefully to the server.

Remember, in advanced tennis, you and your partner have to be determined to play an attacking game — to rush the net as a team at every opportunity. If your partner serves and doesn't come to the net to join you, that will limit how far you can advance, but not your dental bills; you'll be pulling yellow fuzz out of your teeth all day. Your only options are to dump your partner or come back to the baseline as he prepares to serve. If he says indignantly, "What are you doing here?" simply tell him, "I want to live."

The classic challenge for every service returner is to lay the ball back at the feet of the onrushing server and then follow the path of that shot to the net, ready to volley the server's shot, which is usually hit from below the net tape.

The Service Receiver

He has two major goals in good tennis: (1) to hit the ball away from the net man, and (2) to hit at the feet of the onrushing server (which forces him to hit up) or to move him as far laterally as possible in order to open up the court.

If the service receiver can land his shot at the server's feet, he must attack the net with his partner because the server is going to have to play the ball defensively. A ball hit from well below the tape of the net is impossible to hit hard and accurately. Yet I'm often asked, "What happens if you go charging in and the server hits a good lob off the half-volley?" My answer is, "I've only seen two or three players in my life who could do that. It's a unique kind of ability, so don't let it keep you from storming the net." If the server does get the ball over your heads, then remember that each player is responsible for his own lane — from the net to the baseline. When each player is always ready to cover anything that goes over his head, then that team is always going to take care of itself on lobs.

The Partner of the Receiver

If the receiver can return the serve away from the net man, everything now depends on the receiver's partner. He's the one who has a chance to make his team famous, depending on how well he can "read" his opponents and make his move to the ball. In fact, he should try to emulate the good basketball player who learns to move without the ball — suddenly the pass goes to him and he lays it in for two points.

When the point begins, the first duty of the receiver's partner is to turn enough to see where the serve lands, and to call "out" if it is long or wide. If the ball lands in, he quickly turns back and studies the movements of the other team. If he sees an opponent coming in, going "AHHHaaa! AHHHaaa!" and waving his racket over his head as he prepares to deck the ball, then he knows his partner has hit a lousy return, and it's time to retreat for his life.

However, if either one of his opponents is bending down to hit the ball, then he knows the ball will be coming back up and he can move safely to the net in order to volley down. This is where he earns his keep, by his ability to watch his opponent's racket move on the half-volley. If the racket head is parallel to the net, then he jumps forward to volley; if it is angled cross-court, then he rushes diago-

The partner of the receiver is in the best position to call the service line for his partner, but then he can waste no time in repositioning his eyes toward his opponents as he prepares to play his position.

nally in to his partner's territory. He wants to learn to react instinctively so that he doesn't stay glued to his X trying to make a decision. He knows he must move toward the ball on the very next shot.

Like his rival across the net, the partner of the receiver has priority from net post to net post since he is closer to the net. He is obligated to get anything within his reach, and to try to increase that reach by learning to anticipate and to get a quick jump on the ball — much like a clever base stealer gradually lengthening his lead off first base by "reading" the pitcher's move. In fact, I think the day will come when we actually measure the partner of the receiver by his ability to lengthen his range, because he's absolutely lethal up at the net when he does.

In 1997, I was a guest speaker with former base stealer Maury Wills and pro basketball star Karl Malone at the Senior Games in St. George, Utah. I had a chance to talk baseball with Wills and he told me that some of the movement and anticipation skills I emphasize can be taught, but he has also found that certain people can smell an opportunity while others just never get the picture, even with excellent coaching.

Most players have never thought much about their role as the partner of the receiver, let alone broken it down into specific steps. But just knowing these duties or concepts will be meaningless if you don't get out and practice. Work against an opponent who's hitting half-volleys and try to analyze whether he's going down the line or cross-court, then practice cutting off his shot. If you can learn to end the point like this, you will have a tremendous future in doubles. You will be sought out by everybody around because this is really a special talent.

Unfortunately, the role I have just described is not what you see in typical club tennis. The partner of the receiver feels he has nothing to do except watch his partner rally back and forth with the server until one of them makes an error. This is the essence of "one up and one back" doubles, with the server and the receiver playing singles while their partners talk across the net and offer encouragement — "Hang in there, George." The only thing these net persons get is a stiff neck and a suntan on one side of their face; if a shot suddenly comes their way, they dump it —"Oh, I wasn't expecting that one"— because they aren't prepared.

People laugh when I point this out to them, but somebody always says, "Wait a minute, Vic. You're telling us to serve and attack, volley, play the net, run back for lobs — but we can't do all that stuff. We're just happy to be alive."

Don't get me wrong. I'm not knocking "one up and one back" doubles. If that's what everybody at your club plays, and you're having a great time, don't feel guilty. You're supposed to be happy out there. But remember, "one up and one back" is fun only if the other team promises to play it too.

TACTICS IN GOOD DOUBLES

Controlling the Net

The net is the battlefield in good doubles, the area where the point is going to be won or lost. Storm the barrier, take over the fortress, and don't let yourself be pushed off except by a great lob. In pro tennis, the first team to gain the net controls the point nearly every time. They may miss an overhead or a volley when they get there, but basically they get the opportunity to win the point. Intermediates gain the same advantage but their chances of winning the point are about 50-50 because they make so many errors. And beginners rush up there in order to lose at a faster rate.

Intermediates might say, "We can't volley, so we'll just stay back and lob and keep our opponents away from the net." But remember, very few teams can lob well enough from the baseline to beat good net players. Not even the pros can lob deep three times in a row. So going to the net is still your best shot at winning — providing you also work on the weapons that will get you there. (Although it's usually a losing proposition, I always encourage beginners to attack the net, since they want to end up playing there eventually. But at their level, if they can just learn to lob, they can win from the baseline against other beginners who take the net.)

Just as in singles, the reason your team wants to control the net is that you can be crummy volleyers but still win the point. If you get really close to the net,

The targets are tight and dangerous when hitting from the baseline against a team that closes off the middle. But when a team is overly concerned about "guarding the alleys," a hitter from the baseline has an easy drive right up the middle.

you can hit down on the ball — which is the natural tendency on the volley anyway — and you can hit at very sharp angles. Even little dinky shots can close out the point. But the farther back you get from the net, the more talent you must have. If you volley halfway between the net and the serve line, and you pull down on your volley even slightly, the ball will catch the net. If you hit from the service line, where many intermediates and beginners volley in doubles, you almost have to lift the ball in order to keep it deep and thus maintain distance between you and your opponents. (Also, the closer you get to the net, the more difficult it is for anyone to pass you on any angle, since you are much closer to the line of flight of the ball.)

If your opponents lob successfully and drive you back from the net to the baseline, they should match you step for step and take over the net. In that case you should try to lob right back and regain the fortress, or try to end the point immediately by driving an overhead down the middle. Your odds are better with the lob, but most people begin to balk at this point. "We don't want to go all the way back to the net again," they say. "Then they'll lob over our heads and we'll have to

run back and we'll die." But this isn't going to happen because club players don't lob well two times in a row. Very often your opponents' second lob — if not the first — will be short and will give you an easy overhead to end the point. So don't be pushed away from the fortress that easily. Try desperately to get it back and let your opponents know they're not going to scare you off with one good lob.

It's that determination to get the net and control the net, and your desperate efforts to get it back should you lose it, that will make you and your partner a great doubles team. If you lob once but stay back, that's a tip-off to your opponents that you're afraid — or too lazy to regain the net. The next time you look up they will be perched at the net, knowing they have nothing to fear but their own errors. Your only hope then of winning from the baseline will be to have a great lob, a lot of patience, and a willingness to eat plenty of "fuzz" because the other team is going to be blasting overheads off your weak lobs all day.

Overcoming Fears of the Fuzz Sandwich

When the ball is put into play, two players are already in a position to move quickly to the net — the partner of the server and the partner of the receiver. Both of them should have hot-dog tendencies, eagerly anticipating their chance to make a play at the net that could win the point. Unfortunately, many players only have a feeling of panic mixed with fear: they don't want that kind of pressure placed on their weak volley, and/or they're afraid of getting hurt by the ball. The latter is especially true with women who find themselves in a game of mixed doubles where "everything goes." There are a lot of male chauvinists around who love to try to intimidate the woman at the net with a few hard shots at her navel, all in the guise of giving the woman fair and equal treatment in sports. Thus, it's more important than ever for women to learn to be aggressive at the net and not simply stand there with a racket in front of their face. Morever, as I point out in the section on mixed doubles, the woman — and not the man — is very often the person who makes her team famous since she usually gets far more shots directed her way.

I have to be honest with my women readers. Many of you want to play in the big leagues but you don't want anybody to hit the ball at you. You cannot have it both ways. If you don't want anybody deliberately giving you the fuzz sandwich, you have to establish a social relationship with your opponents where this is understood from the very beginning and everybody agrees to it. Then if somebody hits you he's a dirty rat, and he's fair game for your husband or boyfriend. But if there's any kind of competitive effort involved (if you're playing in a team tennis league, for example), then the sky's the limit. As a matter of fact, trying to produce fear in the opposing team is a legitimate part of the game. If you want to play tennis the right way, be prepared to have a ball zeroing in on your body, and don't get mad if it hits you. It's your job to know how to volley or how to scream, one or the other.

Even when women are determined to play the net, I know that fear can still take over and force them — and many men, especially in men's doubles — to do some strange things. I talked earlier about people who run up to the net and catch the ball when they mean to volley. Very often they will make fantastic mental decisions ("That ball is going to hit me") but have no physical response, and the ball bounces off their forehead. All I can suggest, if you're truly afraid of playing the net, is to keep your racket in front of your body, ready for action. When the ball comes at your head, put the racket in front of your face, then move your head to the side. But don't do like some people, who get mixed up and move their racket away instead of their face. The ball hurts, and besides you lose the point.

Over the last two decades, in my opinion, women have made greater strides than men in doubles play. Women's doubles leagues have been fierce, and crisp volleys are the rule, rather than the exception. It is now a very common sight to see four women slugging it out at the net when that was a rare sight in the 1950s and 1960s.

Protecting the Middle

I've long been fascinated by the intermediates who say, "Watch your alley," while the pros are always talking about protecting the middle. Intermediates are so afraid of their opponents hitting down the line that one of them plays wide to the left side and the other wide to the right. Unfortunately, they're one man short. You could drive a truck between them. They're so intent on guarding their alleys that when a ball is hit down the middle they both automatically turn and say, "Yours."

In good doubles, there are three reasons why you normally want to try to hit down the middle: (l) the net is lower in the center than it is at the doubles sidelines by about 4½ inches, (2) you reduce the angle at which opponents can hit back at you over a low net, and (3) there's a chance your opponents will come together and clash rackets.

Conversely, you always want to entice your opponents to try those difficult, low-percentage shots to your outside. Pros will only drive the alleys if they think you are breaking too early for a ball down the center (i.e., poaching) or if they want to keep you from overplaying the middle.

When a player must bend low to volley the ball from below the level of the net tape, he must raise the ball, giving the opponents a high-volley opportunity.

Emily is having to hit a very low shot near the net and is in a vulnerable position. Her opponents, Melanie (left) and Robin, are moving forward for the midcourt volley.

Learning to Anticipate

You can't have an indecisive approach to this game. You have to learn to react instinctively to your opponent's shot, and then break for the ball. Yet the average player can't seem to do this.

Some players become immobilized in their ready position because they are scared to death of making the wrong move. They may be thinking correctly, asking themselves, "Drive or lob? Drive or lob?" as they study their opponent's racket. But they don't want to look bad by starting forward for a drive just as their opponent lobs over their head, so they don't move either way. Suddenly the ball goes over their head and they have to turn and run like crazy to make the play. But they're always too late.

I try to tell all my students: don't be afraid to make mistakes in judgment. If you guess wrong, don't get upset. Very often your opponent doesn't even know where the ball is going when he swings. The point of the game is to have some fun, and if you can make yourself experiment and take some chances, you're going to learn to play with the right responses. But first you have to commit yourself one way or the other. Motor learning experts tell us that we will continually vacillate between the old motor program and the desired one when learning a new motor skill. Gradually, the old motor program disappears, and you're left with the new one when permanent learning takes effect. But the point is that you'll continue to make mistakes for a while, even if you are a hard worker and want to make a major change. You can't learn a skill without making a lot of mistakes, so don't beat up on yourself when you're trying something new.

When you're in that momentary ready position near the service line, or halfway between that line and the net, stay on your toes, ready to break in any direction, and keep telling yourself, "Drive or lob, drive or lob," as you study your opponent's racket. At first everybody has trouble judging before impact where the ball might go. Fortunately, tennis balls are round and they travel right where the racket aims them. So if the racket head is tilted up, the ball is going up, and you can retreat for a lob. If it's tilted down, your opponent will have to hit under the net. If the racket face is vertical, and moving straight across, the ball's going on a horizontal level and you want to take off and crowd the net. The key is to watch your opponent's racket — and don't let yourself be distracted by his body movements. Prior charting will help give you an even better sense of what he is going to do.

Given the speed of the ball and the emphasis on quick reflexes, I'm often asked, "At what point should you actually guess in doubles?" My advice is that if your team is down love-40 in any game, your chances of winning the next point are better if you guess and take off for your opponent's anticipated shot than if you simply stay in the same place and do what you've been doing.

Moving Together as a Team

If you and your partner can learn to move as a team in the direction of the ball, approximately 11 to 12 feet apart, you will rarely be passed, either down the line or between you.

For example, on a 27-foot-wide singles court, it's hard to pass a player who knows how to follow his shot to that side of the center stripe to which he hit and who knows how to shift with the ball. It's even more difficult in doubles, where the court is 36 feet wide and each player only has to cover 18 feet laterally — if he or she moves in tandem with his or her partner.

Learn to shift with the ball: forward and diagonally for a drive, and back for a lob. If you hit the ball to the right side of the court, overload that side to cut off the angle of your opponent's return. If the ball goes down the center, come back to the center, and if it goes to the left side, move to the left — and few teams will get the ball past you on purpose. You may feel you're leaving yourself unprotected on one flank when you shift far to the left. But if you ever find a player who can consistently hit the ball in that narrow target area on the diagonal, I'll show you a player in white robes.

Always maintain that 11- to 12-foot distance apart. If your partner shifts and you fail to move, this obviously leaves a gaping hole between the two of you for your opponent's return shot. Get the feeling of being connected to your partner by an invisible rope as you practice shifting together. But don't use a real rope. I once

Moving aggressively to the ball, this player has the right idea on the backhand volley. He takes a short back-swing (controlled by the non-hitting hand) and volleys from the shoulder, letting his body provide the power, so that his swing can be short and accurate. Notice how his eyes are focused on the ball (below) and that his follow-through remains high with no forearm movement as he closes in on the net for a possible follow-up shot.

tried this trick with an intermediate tennis team and both persons got rope burns when they tugged — one going east, the other going west.

Communicating out loud with your partner is the best method I know to help coordinate reactions and movements as a team. Both of you should learn to call out, "It's a drive!" or "It's a lob!" while breaking for the ball. At first you may be a little self-conscious, and there will be times when your partner calls out, "Drive" just as you yell, "Lob" and you run in different directions. But after you've played together a while you should begin to react instinctively so that when the ball is hit — boom — you're both going as a team. To develop this teamwork, however, neither of you can be reluctant to call out advice or instructions that can help the other partner. This requires a conscious effort. Basketball players think nothing about yelling to a teammate on defense — such as "Switch, I've got this man." But tennis players have somehow gained the impression over the years that they're not supposed to talk to their partner while the point is being played. Thus I see many teams where both players are silent, each of them absorbed in their own game of singles. I've also found that when people forget to even talk to their partner during the point — at least in a strategic or tactical sense — they each feel less of a responsibility to get that quick jump on the ball. Nor do I give much hope to the team where one player is talking and the other one is quiet. But when both players are yelling and forcing themselves to call out the shot, the player who tends to react later than his partner will start working harder at anticipating a drive or a lob, providing he has the barest sense of teamwork.

Both players should stay focused on the ball and be ready to move.

Reacting to the Ball

On a drive (any shot that you can volley) your team wants to get that fast first step toward the net. Attack — don't wait for the ball to come to you. The closer you can get to the net, the higher above the net you can volley and the sharper can be your angle. The ball drops rapidly and if you let it sink below the tape of the net, you place yourself on the defensive and all you can do is try to punch the ball deep. I used to watch Jack Kramer go nuts in the stands when he saw a player with good position hesitate and let the ball fall below the level of the net, then try to hit an offensive volley. Jack has seen few players in the history of the game who could take a low ball and convert it into an offensive volley with any real success.

If you and your partner see a lob coming, turn and run back three steps. If you can reach the service line before the ball reaches the net, nobody will ever lob over your head successfully. You will always have good position, either to lob back or to hit an overhead smash out in front of your body.

There are two ways to retrieve well-hit lobs that are definitely going over your head. The one I prefer is to look at the lob as you're turning to run, in order to see to which side of you the ball will land. Run full speed, facing the back fence, until you hear the ball land. Then turn and go for the ball. I've seen very slow people learn to reach balls near the back fence using this system because you don't slow up watching the flight of the ball. My second choice is to look over your shoulder at the ball as you run, since most people can get back faster that way than by backpedaling. (If you prefer to backpedal, put me to the test. Go out on the court and try all three ways to see which is actually faster for you.)

Another question I always get is "What happens if I can get to the ball for an overhead smash, but I may have run too far?" That's a beautiful problem, for you simply run back into the right spot and hit your overhead while your weight is carrying you forward. The key is to be there early enough to hit up at about eight degrees with a vertical racket face.

Many doubles teams are afraid to react quickly up at the net even if they smell a lob coming. They think their opponent is going to trick them by faking a lob to get them going back, then leveling off and smacking a drive. Fortunately, people can't hit the two shots with uninterrupted stroke production. Remember how I said earlier in the book that a hitter must have a full half-second to effectively change the motor program from the brain to the muscular to effect a smooth change in stroke production. In doubles, if the opponent strikes the ball in one manner, it's asking too much for him to switch to a second approach all in one swing. Let him try, of course, but don't worry about the result.

Good Doubles Is Organized Chaos

Doubles action is pretty slow the way most people play. When a player gets to the net, he often says, "Made it!" He's so happy about landing on the X that he's not about to budge. But in good doubles, if you're standing still for two shots, you've probably committed a serious error. You should always be moving in unison with your partner — up, back, or laterally — and committing yourself almost automatically.

In fact, at the pro level today there's a trend for a kamikaze type of approach to doubles, where very often the team receiving serve is blindly going to the net because they've discovered that to stay back and try to win from the baseline is a losing proposition. Thus you see all four players attacking each other near the net, and "the first chicken loses." There's a lot of chaos in their exchanges as they rely on quick hands and reflexes.

However, I don't buy the theory that it's impossible to win from a deep position. The "gain the net" system hasn't been tested well enough by two players who have the strokes to really keep the team at the net under constant pressure: by lobbing well consistently, by retrieving overhead smashes and returning them with well-placed lobs, and by hitting strong overheads from behind the baseline. But if a team doesn't have these strokes, then it might as well go kamikaze because to stay back is sheer folly.

For professional players the common thinking is everyone attack each other. However, in 1997 Davis Cup play against the United States, I watched the Netherlands' top team of Paul Harhuis and Jacco Eltingh stay back very effectively for a few shots. They used this to disrupt the rhythm and shot-making selection of their opponents. Then, they were right back at rushing the net. In that match, they defeated Rick Leach and Jonathan Stark, a fine doubles team.

"Who Has Priority on Shots Down the Middle?"

Intermediates around the world have never been able to resolve the question of who takes the ball down the middle. Thus you either see both of them saying, "I've got it," and then crashing into each other, or both of them saying, "Yours," and then looking at each other with an angry stare as the ball passes between them.

Smart teams, however, can work out this decision before the match by basing it on two fundamental considerations: (1) which player is closer to the net, and (2) who has the stronger shot down the center?

When your team is at the net, the player closer to the net always has priority. He should have the freedom to run right in front of his partner to volley because his angle is better and he can end the point quicker. The player who's deep has a greater chance of missing his volley and he can't hit volleys on as sharp an angle.

If both players are the same distance from the net, then the person with the stronger volley down the middle should make the play. It's not automatic that the forehand volleyer takes the shot, since some players actually have a better backhand volley than their partner's forehand volley. Ken Rosewall, for instance, had such a fantastic backhand that you wouldn't dream of getting in his way. In 1996, I gave a clinic with Rosewell (and Roy Emerson) and I was stunned at how well he still plays on the backhand side. Even in his sixties his backhand is as good as that of almost every pro on the circuit.

The best way to prevent confusion and hesitation when the ball comes down the middle is to work out a 5/8-3/8 system with your partner. Decide ahead of time — objectively — who has the best volley at the net and near the service line, and the best groundstroke at the baseline. Then that person will take the ball within 5/8 of the distance between you if you are playing side by side. If you both have crummy volleys, then flip a coin to decide, but never feel guilty about negotiating over who has the stronger volley (and the stronger groundstroke). It isn't simply that you might let a ball get between you, but that the slightest bit of timidity by the player going for the ball can result in a weaker volley. This person needs to go after the ball with all the confidence in the world, his mind free to really crunch a volley without worrying about clashing rackets or getting cracked in the head by his partner's racket. This kind of mix-up can create unbelievable fear and hesitation the next time a ball comes down the middle, so try to eliminate the confusion beforehand.

"What Are You Doing on My Side of the Court?"

One of the most common arguments in tennis starts with the accusation, "Hey, you took my shot." This stems from the predominant understanding in doubles the world over: "This is my side and that's your side. Don't get on my side." But if you have a partner who wants to play this way — and you want to win — then you'd better dump this person fast. If it's your mom, then try to have her realize that the player closer to the net has priority.

Teammates should retreat quickly together to cover a lob by running versus backpedaling.

There's no such thing as "my side, your side" in big-time tennis. It's zoom, zoom, crossing back and forth in front of one another. If a player is caught back, he wants his partner to jump across and take away his volley at the net. He knows that his partner has priority from net post to net post if he can make the play.

You can never get mad at your partner for running in front to steal your shot. Basically he is hitting the volley where you were supposed to have been if your tail had been in gear. Plus your team has a better chance of winning the point. In fact, the person who takes the volley up close should turn around and say to his lagging partner, in a joking manner, "Get your rear end up to the net and take your own shots — I'm going to wear out."

I used to play some doubles around southern California with Louise Brough, who was U.S. National doubles champion twelve times, and I know what it's like to have your partner keep handling your case. When we first started playing together, Louise had a faster first step than I did, and thus she would beat me to every volley between us. She was better than me, but it still hurt my ego to see a skirt run in front and say, "Mine, mine," while I just went, "Terrific, terrific," all day long. I literally had to get out on the court early in the morning before a match just to practice my first step so that I could learn to hold my own.

Another warning: when you cross the center stripe on the dead run, you now own that side and your partner is obligated to take your side of the court. Don't cross the line and suddenly think, "Oh, oh, I shouldn't have gone," and then jump back, because you'll leave your partner in the lurch. You made a decision to go for the ball, and now you're responsible.

"Who Takes the Lobs?"

Some players think that when their team is at the net and a lob goes over one partner's head, his partner should run back and try to make the play. That is wrong. In every category of doubles, you are responsible for your own side of the court from net to baseline when a ball goes over your head. Don't automatically turn around and say, "Yours," because your partner may be saying the same thing. You must both retreat together and you should make the play unless for some reason you are completely out of position.

Think of yourself as being responsible for a sidewalk that is exactly 18 feet wide and 39 feet long. Your primary responsibility starts there. The only time your partner should come into that area is when he has priority on the shot, or you have lunged for a ball and haven't recovered your balance yet.

"What Side Should the Lefty Play?"

I get this question all the time from righthanders. The key factor is to understand who you're playing. If your opponents are intermediates who always try to hit down the alley, then the lefthander should be on the left side so that you have forehands down each alley. But against good players, who are always trying to hit down the middle, the lefthander may play the right side, which gives your team two forehands down the center. Also, the lefthander can swing across with his backhand on the service return and pull the ball away from the net man. The righthander does that automatically from the left side.

Over the years, I have seen more lefthanders playing the right side. However, it's what each player is comfortable doing. If a professional has always played the right side and is looking for a partner, she will search for a great left-court player, regardless of whether that person is righthanded or lefthanded.

TIPS TO KEEP YOU ALIVE

1. Never try to watch your partner serve. Not only is it dangerous, it contaminates your reactions and movements at the net. Besides, you can tell exactly where the serve has gone by simply watching the receiver.

2. When your partner is behind you and is going to hit an overhead smash, don't turn around to watch him. He may mis-hit and give you the fuzz sandwich.

3. In fact, it's unnecessary to see what your partner is doing — you don't play

your partner. Concentrate instead on studying your opponents and learn to sense what type of shot they're going to hit.

4. If your opponent is winding up to deck an overhead, and you're at the net, don't be a hot dog by standing in front and trying to fake him out or return his shot. That's a good way to risk serious injury. It's your responsibility to get out of the way or to turn your back as a sign of submission. Your opponent does not have to try to hit around you and thus risk missing his shot, unless you turn away. Then his job is to simply try to hit a clean winner away from your body. If he still accidentally hits you, he will hold up his hand when you turn around, meaning that he's sorry about the accident. You have to accept that. But if his hand isn't up when you turn around, then it's war — and the next time you have an overhead near the net, your opponent's first move will be to take off in the opposite direction.

OTHER PLAYING TIPS

1. People who have trouble in doubles are those who hero-worship their partner or who are dependent thinkers. They're always thinking, "My partner will get it." But if you want to help form a winning team, you must be ready for every situation that occurs. Your only thought should be, "I'm going to get the next ball." If your partner gets it, fine, but already you're anticipating the very next shot.

2. In good doubles everywhere, the point is going to end very quickly. The

Naaki will be aiming for the high targets to ensure a nice deep shot for her opponent.

Susan has anticipated the next shot and is ahead of her partner, Emily. Thus, Susan has priority on the volley because she has a far greater potential angle.

ball will seldom cross the net more than two or three times, so take good care of the shot you're on, because statistically it's your last. You can rest between points.

3. Just because you are playing doubles, don't forget good volleying form. Work on having fast hands and quick feet so that you can contact the ball properly off your front shoulder. Keep your racket head up as you go for the ball and finish with a high follow-through to keep from chopping down. Remember that most volleys in doubles, especially on quick exchanges, wind up in the net because people under pressure tend to face the net and pull down, instead of keeping their side to the net, hitting through the ball, and carrying it out deep. Even if you're angling the ball sharply, don't try to make a little play with the racket head or you will dump your shot into the net or beyond the sidelines. Wherever you volley on the court, work to be aggressive in getting to the ball and then making your hit.

Even if you're a raw beginner, volleying is obviously crucial in doubles, since you're at the net half the match. Some people, in fact, have good volleys but weak groundstrokes, so developing sound groundstrokes doesn't necessarily lead to a good volley, nor must groundstrokes come first.

Susan again from the rear on a second shot where she has gained priority on the volley as she is the closer player to the net.

4. Think about your different responsibilities and practice them; get them ingrained in your mind so you don't have to think during a point. Each little concept that's important in doubles must be practiced, yet most people tell me, "Jeez, I don't have time to practice — I'll think about it at home and then just do it in the match." But you're not going to pull it off in the match without some prior rehearsal on the court. If you wait to try out all of your new tricks when you're playing a big match, you're going to run out of partners.

Now don't get me wrong. You never want to be afraid to experiment and makes mistakes as you play; you want to learn something from every match. But first set up a practice session where you have specific goals in mind. For instance, "Today I will practice taking balls down the center and I will work on getting close to the net. I'm going to keep my feet moving. I'm going to work on anticipating my opponent's shot. I'm going to keep my eyes down on the ball when I make my hit, and try to block out my opponents. Then I am going to work on getting my first serve in play so that my partner doesn't have to wear a helmet."

5. Psychologically, always try to enhance your partner's position by making

him (or her) feel good, not lousy. Your partner's not a masochist and hopefully you're not a sadist, although it's a great combination if you also have the strokes. Great players always try to talk positively to their partners; they have respect for one another and they know they win or lose as a team. Recalling what it was like to play doubles with Martina Navratilova, normally her singles rival, Chris Evert said, "It was great to play with Martina. She never got down on her partner; she was always encouraging and supportive." You should take the same approach. Sure it's frustrating to see your partner play poorly or dump crucial shots, but once a person starts feeling that he (or she) is the weak link on the team — and is constantly reminded of that fact — he can't do anything right. When you or your partner is in trouble, you need support, not criticism. Or as John McEnroe said, after a career as one of the greatest doubles players ever, "There's no sense in berating your partner — it only makes the situation worse."

Tennis is supposed to be fun, and nobody should be having a miserable time. So if your partner is getting down on you all the time and ruining your fun — or vice versa — then dump that person, or give him the chance to find a more congenial partner. If you're thinking, "Well, I can't — it's my husband," then the two of you should just try to be realistic. If you have a clear understanding of each other's strengths and weaknesses, and your objectives are well known, then this tends to prevent hostile feelings from building up.

POACHING

Poaching means to intentionally enter your partner's territory, normally when your partner is serving and you are at the net. This enables you to cut off your opponent's service return if it heads for your partner. If the ball goes into your former side of the court, your partner moves over to make the play. A second objective is to distract the service receiver by your movements at the net and thus force him into errors.

Most people don't realize how valuable, and how much fun, poaching can be. But it adds three important ingredients to your strategy: (1) By increasing the external stimuli, you make it more difficult for your opponents to focus attention on key fundamentals, such as "Eyes on the ball" and "Head down through impact." (2) It establishes you immediately as the offensive team. (3) You can literally control your opponents by forcing them to hit in the direction you have preselected by your ability to poach or fake a poach.

Let's say that your opponents are always returning serve at your partner's feet when he rushes the net, which forces him to bend down and hit weak half-volleys. This in turn enables your opponents to bombard you at the net. You finally get tired of taking that kind of punishment, so poaching becomes your means of retaliation.

Using hand signals worked out ahead of time with your partner, hide your hand behind your back and signal your intentions just before the first serve. Many secret signals can be used, but normally one finger means you're going to cut across the court on the first serve only, two fingers mean you're going on the second serve only, a clenched fist means you're not going on either serve, and an open hand means, "We've been partners for 11 years and I'm not getting any action up here — I'm going on anything that lands in."

Experience in playing together will help you overcome two common problems in poaching. The first is that while you are busy signaling, your partner is so wrapped up in his own serve ("Dear God, let this go in") that he doesn't even notice your signals. Second, some people forget that they must conceal their intention to poach. Thus you see them turn around, with their signal still in place behind their back, and say, "Did you get that, Bertha?"

Now that big bucks are on the line in professional doubles, many players prefer to talk between points and not signal. One of their fears is that a pal of your opponents' might be sitting behind them and relaying your signal to your opponents.

Once your signaling is coordinated, then the instant your partner's serve crosses the net, and your opponent is committed to a shot, take off across the center stripe to intercept his return, while your partner rushes in to cover your old territory. However make sure that the service receiver is committed to hit in the direction you want before you make your break. Even if you break when the ball crosses the net toward him, there might be enough time for the receiver to actually change the direction of the ball.

The same ruling applies to the server. He must wait until both direct and peripheral vision has been taken off him by the receiver — when it's too late for the receiver to change his swing — before he breaks and takes the opposite court. He should actually take his two or three steps forward after his follow-through, and then run cross-court. If he's too eager to get to the other side, he will tip off the poach by taking just one step forward and then breaking across.

When the receiver detects a poach, he doesn't have to panic. He can hit a fairly soft return toward the net man's vacated position (where the server is heading) — or he can lob, since both opponents are moving, and in awkward positions. Yet to show you the real value of poaching, even when many service receivers "read" the poach, they're still so bothered that they miss their shot. Similarly, you might poach and flub your own shot, but you will worry your opponents on future shots. By always threatening to poach — instead of just camping at the net on every serve — you make your team infinitely more effective. In a sport where few players keep their eyes focused on the ball to begin with, any distraction you can throw at people to force them to start looking your way will increase the number of stimuli with which they are dealing, and thus improve your chances of winning. But when you assume the same ready position at the net that you've had since '78, then you decrease your opponents' anxiety because they know right away you're never going to poach. We coaches often have to counsel the conservative doubles players who get visibly angry when their partner misses a poach, reminding them that seldom are poachers properly rewarded for the missed service returns they cause.

Learn to poach effectively and you can easily manipulate people mentally. You can make a person hit the ball where you want, and even get him so bugged that if you just give a little knee movement or a shoulder fake, he'll drop his racket. But to learn how to poach, you must practice. Play one match where you poach on every point, or on all the odd points, or all the even points, and you'll be amazed at how many more balls you get to hit up at the net, and how much more fun you have.

To defend against poaching when you see it coming, try to lob, go down the middle as the two players are shifting, or hit behind the poacher down the alley. But pick your shot and hit it — don't suddenly second-guess yourself. And know how far the poacher can come across before he is vulnerable to a passing shot behind him. When I try to anticipate poaching by my opponents, I don't watch for head or shoulder movements — they can be fakes. I watch the belt buckle, because a man never runs without his pants. If a woman is poaching, I try to find another piece of clothing. In professional tennis, the serve is normally being hit too hard for the receiver to make any last-minute changes.

PLAYING MIXED DOUBLES

If you're the woman in mixed doubles, and you know how to volley, you're going to make your partner famous — if his ego doesn't interfere.

Yet we all know what happens on the typical husband-and-wife team when the man goes to serve. He takes his wife up to the net and says, "Darling, big match today, right? If we win, we'll be king and queen of Pismo Beach. You are so valuable and you volley so well that I'm going to put you in this all-time important spot" — a four-foot cubicle in the alley, right in front of the net. When he walks away he says, "And don't forget, hold the racket up in front of your face." Subconsciously, what he is really saying to her is: "Look, I can play these guys alone. If I could, I would put you on the bench but it wouldn't look too good to our neighbors."

This scenario is still true around the country, but in the last twenty years I have seen women turn the tables and put their husbands in the cubicle. Unfortunately, this is not a good plan for any team, since sharp opponents will quickly go after the weaker player — and confidence by this player is necessary right from the start. Remember, the name of the game is for both players to have the freedom to make the play, based on the fundamental principle that *the player closer to the net has priority.* Thus, if you have position on your partner — and the quickness — jump right in front and take his volley. Don't let him scare you off by saying, "Stay on your side," because as I pointed out earlier, that's a losing syndrome. What he's really saying is, "Look, darling, the closer you come to my side, the more our chances of losing increase."

Tennis is one of the few sports where men and women can compete together — if not always harmoniously. In club and league tennis, the physical strength aspects encourage macho male partners to try to crowd and take the woman's shots, while displaying subconscious hostilities by aiming at the woman across the net. It's only natural to fear getting hit by the ball. I'm afraid it's your responsibility to get out of the way, but a strong volley is the best method I know to even the score — by winning the point. One scene I love to see in pro tennis these days comes when a male player volleys as hard as he can at the woman playing the net and the woman hits a volley so hard that it hits the man's body. My joy is not in seeing the man get hit by the ball, but to know that certain women pros are no longer intimidated by the man's speed.

So, women, don't let men push you off to the side and make you so fearful to move and cover your shots that you simply settle into that classic ready position, racket held in front of your face like a gun sight. Neither can you leave the volleying to your partner and still win in good mixed doubles competition. You must learn how to volley, how to react quickly, and how to overcome your fears up at the net — three requirements that are closely intertwined. Not until you learn to defend yourself — and to attack — with an adequate volley will you develop the confidence to react instinctively, and either crowd the net, lunge for a passing shot, or retreat for a lob.

The biggest gain I've seen in women's tennis the past 20 years is their amazing ability to handle a high backhand volley and service return, both critical skills in mixed doubles. In addition to the right technique, developing a strong backhand volley requires strong extensor muscles on your hitting arm (see drill, page 97), so that you can keep the ball deep. For example, smart players will test your strength immediately by hitting high to your backhand volley; if you don't have a strong arm you'll hit the ball short and give them an easy put-away shot. But if you can "muscle" that ball and keep the head of your racket up so that the volley goes deep, then your opponents will know they are in trouble.

Positioning

When it comes to deciding who plays on which side of the court, the man very often perpetuates another myth. He plays an unfair role by trying to convince the woman that he's giving her the easier of the two sides. If they are both righthanded, he will say, "Look, darling, I'm giving you the easy right side to receive serve and I'll take that tough left side." This is a lie, but the woman sometimes falls for it. When she plays the right court — especially in good tennis — she is in a challenging spot in its own right. She will invariably receive serves to the backhand side, and she must be able to hit inside-out in order to keep the ball away from the net man. Her partner, however, never sees it this way.

Let's say play begins and the opposing team serves to the woman's backhand. The tendency by nearly everybody is to swing across on the backhand, and the woman is no exception: she pulls her shot right to the net man and he gives her husband the fuzz sandwich. The husband then turns around and says, "Dummy, I've told you for 15 years — keep the ball away from the net man. Now look, I'm going to show you one more time how to do this." He goes back to receive serve, it comes to his backhand, and he swings the exact same way as the woman. Except that when he swings across, the ball goes away from the net and right at the server. The man looks great only because he happens to be on the side which facilitates making a nice shot with his weakness. So, women, don't let the man get away with being an impostor. Remember, the great doubles teams in history have been made by a right-court player who can return serve. This is the pressure point — at

30-all and deuce — and if the woman can get the serve back and help win the point here, then all the pressure goes on the server to hold serve.

In club tennis, when the woman has a decent backhand, it pays to have her play the right court — providing her partner understands the situation. First, a righthanded man is faster poaching from left to right across the net. Second, he can move from left to right to chase down a lob over his partner's head. (Although the ideal is for each player to cover his own lane, from net to baseline, the reality is that many women are slower getting back on lobs.) Third, the man is hitting forehand volleys down the middle, which helps compensate for the fact that most women don't have the strong extensor muscles needed to attack the high backhand volley.

When the man arbitrarily puts the woman in the right court, a check-and-balance system fortunately exists that helps the woman get even at the end of the day. When she serves, the man loves to poach at the net and he wins lots of points, which helps her hold serve. But when the man serves, if the woman doesn't like to volley and is afraid to poach, her partner usually loses his serve. Now they're driving home and they start having a gigantic argument about who was to blame for their loss. But the woman flattens the man immediately. "Don't look at me," she says. "I won every serve."

Improving Your Game through Conditioning, Lessons, and Practice

WHETHER YOUR GOAL is the singles title in Pacific Palisades — or the finals at Wimbledon — I've emphasized throughout this book that your game must be built upon basic stroke production and the mental and physical tenacity to keep getting the ball back over the net. Then you can start worrying about match-play psychology, strategy, fancy shots, and how to jump over the net without breaking your leg.

However, building a sound tennis game assumes a dedication greater than simply playing once or twice a week. You must devote time to physical conditioning, you have to learn how to practice your strokes, and you must have the ability to break comfortable old stroking habits and groove what are at first uncomfortable but proper new habits — with or without the aid of a good teaching pro.

Remember, there's a learning sequence in tennis, as in any other sport, and you have to master certain skills before you can move up to higher playing levels. Nearly all players can reach a certain level of proficiency where they can keep the ball in play well enough to be identified as "tennis players." But when they get about halfway to their goal of being good players (on the 3.0 level, let's say) they tend to peel off because they fail to realize that good tennis is built on the shot you hit prior to the one you are hitting. For example, you'll be a much better volleyer if you have a good approach shot that keeps your opponent deep, but you won't get the first approach shot if you fail to hit a deep groundstroke that keeps your opponent away from the net.

Think about what a little improvement can mean to your game: if you can improve by one ball over the net per point, you'll beat nearly everybody you play today. We all tend to play people near us in ability, and statistics show that the ball fails to cross the net more than four times on most points. So if you can improve your average by one ball per point, you stand to increase your chances of winning that point by 25 percent. Unfortunately, this improvement is easy to talk about, tough to execute — but that's why tennis is such a fascinating challenge.

PHYSICAL CONDITIONING

A superbly fit tennis player is considered to be that individual who can play aggressive or defensive tennis on a competitive basis for from 90 to 120 minutes on a daily workout program. On the opposite end of the spectrum are those players who take three trips around the refrigerator and then need a nap. How then to make that quantum leap to physical respectability, whatever your age, occupation, or ability level?

Everybody can start by trying to play the game correctly, once or twice a week. Instead of camping on the baseline and working on your tan, try to chase down every shot and move quickly into hitting position so that you can swing easily once you get there. Then concentrate on playing with your body instead of standing flat-footed and "arming" the ball. By lowering your body properly on every groundstroke, and lifting up and stretching out toward your intended target, you give your thighs and stomach muscles a real workout. Add a lot of hustle and you won't find yourself complaining, "I played two sets of tennis and I gained a pound."

Although a set or two of good, vigorous tennis can be a conditioner in itself, you also need to devise a program of general conditioning exercises and specific drills that will help develop the muscles and reflexes you need to play the game right. But before you set out to whip your body into playing shape, remember that proper conditioning is a slow process that demands intelligent planning. If you are over 35, then you should have a physical examination under stress conditions, which may turn up special warning signs about the heart. Exercise physiologists also point out that it's better to exercise 15 minutes a day — every day — than to have only one or two long workouts on the weekend. You cannot make up for lost time with body conditioning by adding workout hours at the end of the week.

Arm and Back Muscles

1. Traditional push-ups strengthen back and arm muscles used in practically every stroke. Doing the push-ups on your fingertips will help your wrists and forearms, but this takes strong fingers.

2. Although I've argued during the book that the strength of your arm is relatively unimportant to good strokes if you utilize the power in your body, strong arm muscles will help give you a more solid stroke. My experience has been, as a player and as a coach, that strength is needed because we don't always hit the ball while well balanced. Often, having to reach, we find ourselves in awkward positions and just swinging with our arms, which overloads the muscles in our muscular system. So often we hear about an injury in this fashion: "I was just stretching for one of his short angles and I could feel the pain immediately." Strong muscles are also needed because we don't always hit the ball on the comfortable "sweet

spot" of the racket and the muscles take a bigger beating while trying to stabilize the racket. I often demonstrate the drill where I take a good racket and simply let it fall using gravity on my forehand. Using very little muscle, I can hit the ball 78 feet. The problem is that we seldom get in the position to make life easy on our muscles. The ball-in-the-racket-cover drill (see page 97) is excellent for developing the extensor muscles that are crucial on the backhand. Another popular exercise device can be built and used at home. Take a cut-off broom handle, drill a hole in the middle, and attach a piece of four-foot rope or cord with a small weight (one or two pounds) tied to the end. Hold the stick straight out from your body and slowly roll the weight up, then roll it back down. This slow rolling action creates the most continuous exertion on the forearms. Remember to do it with palms up and then palms down.

Stomach Muscles

Jack Kramer placed much of his conditioning emphasis upon developing strong stomach muscles. He felt that in getting low and then having to lift up up as he stroked the ball, his stomach was as important as his thighs. Thus he would work with a medicine ball, and do a lot of sit-ups, although exercise physiologists tell us today that sit-ups are not the most practical exercise you can do for the stomach. Some exercise physiologists believe there is sufficient evidence to prove that there's potential damage to one's back doing full sit-ups. The modern-day choice in the gym is slow "crunches."

Thigh Muscles

Personally, I feel the "sit-and-hit" chair drill (see page 60) can be one of the most valuable exercises in tennis. Not only does it develop the muscles actually used on proper groundstrokes — particularly the thighs — it enables you to practice the stroking patterns which I seek. Sitting down and touching a bench while practicing your stroke will also work.

Deep knee bends are good for the thighs, providing you go only halfway down. When you try to bend all the way down, you risk knee injuries (especially in adults) by placing excess demands on undeveloped muscles and ligaments around the knee.

Developing Good Footwork, Quickness, and Stamina

Most people forget about their feet as they play and very few players practice moving to the ball and covering the court. They just get out and hit the ball. Yet even without natural speed afoot, you'll have time to get into proper hitting position for nearly every shot if you will work on several specific drills — and your concentration. Today, a number of popular experts teach power and speed movements, responding to the fact that an explosive first step is a major factor in playing good tennis. Also take note that the top players are now running on their toes as they cover the court. We studied Steffi Graf on film and we realized that once she starts

The server practices his footwork to the net. His back foot comes across the line first as he moves forward, and when he takes his check step, he's flying. However, I don't recommend getting airborne like this because a player can't break in any direction until he lands.

for the ball, her heels hardly ever touch the court and she plays most of the game on her toes.

First of all, remind yourself that thinking about good footwork will improve your footwork. Learn to anticipate your opponent's shot and get that fast first step the instant you detect where the ball is going. This alone will give you nearly all the "quickness" you've been told you need to play this game properly. One player, who had the slowest first step, was the best anticipator and it helped him win Wimbledon. But don't let me mislead you: it's tough to learn to play with this degree of intensity. You have to work at it constantly.

Second, the following exercises should help you prepare for the stop-and-go type of action in tennis:

1. Shadow tennis, promulgated by former Davis Cup captain Dennis Ralston, is the single best drill I know to get your body ready for a match while giving your heart, lungs, and legs an excellent workout — all in five minutes or less. What you want to do is simulate actual match play by "shadowboxing" imaginary points on an empty court, without actually hitting a ball. (You can even do this at home if you have a piece of lawn half as long — 39 feet — as a tennis court.) Work out your own sequence of strokes, but concentrate on the shots you need to beat an opponent by working your way up to the net. For example, serve and fall in, take

your three steps forward, and then slow down with your stutter-step. While moving slowly forward, suddenly break left or right for an approach volley or bend down for a half-volley, but keep moving forward as you hit. Stretch out for an imaginary volley at the net, then retreat quickly for a lob. Reach up and hit an overhead back near the baseline, then run in again for a low forehand approach shot or a high backhand volley, before racing back again for another lob. Always keep your feet moving, and bend low, lift up, and stretch out exactly as you would in a match. If you think this all sounds easy, try playing an imaginary point for one minute and see how exhausted you become. "Do this drill two or three times a week," says Ralston, "and I guarantee, you'll improve your quickness and your conditioning." And it will certainly pay off in a tough match. In the 1997 Davis Cup match against the Netherlands, Andre Agassi played a point that was over 20 strokes long. He had to run from one corner to the next, hit off balance, hit a slice and then a flat shot — all from the baseline. He won the point and the crowd went crazy. But what seemed more important to me was that Andre appeared to gain strength from that point, going on from there to win his match.

If you regard yourself as a "baseline player" and you think Ralston's drill is rather meaningless to your game, consider these two points: (1) You're a baseline player only as long as you play intermediates. But when you go up against somebody who knows how to play, that person will force you to come to the net and volley. (2) Even from the baseline you have to run left and right for low and high backhands and forehands; you have to serve, and hit service returns, lobs, and overheads. "Shadowbox" a sequence of these strokes but always come back to the center stripe after each shot, and see how quickly you become winded.

2. Rope jumping will improve your footwork as well as your stamina. The drill I like best is to simulate a boxing match by jumping rope for three minutes, resting for one minute, then jumping again for another three minutes. Go slowly at first, one or two rounds a day, but as your "wind" improves, see how many rounds you can last. When Jack Kramer was on his way to becoming the number one player in the world, he went looking for the best-conditioned athletes to see what they did. He felt that boxers had the greatest demands placed on their bodies in a concentrated period of time and the boxers spent a great deal of time jumping rope. He used the drill described here, and when he could go 15 rounds and still feel fresh enough to play, he knew he was ready for Wimbledon.

3. I believe in practicing pretty much as you must perform. Thus the "coin footwork" drill, on the court or in your living room, can help you develop the proper footwork on your groundstrokes while making you more agile on your feet. Toss a coin out in front of you, then run to the coin and make your back foot always land right on it, with your side to the imaginary or actual net. This enables the front foot to step toward your target. Remember that I like the front foot to go forward so that your center of gravity is ahead of your front foot and can help you get to the net sooner. More than likely you will have to take little skipping steps as you get closer to the coin in order to land on it with the back foot, but these skip-steps will keep you from hitting off the "wrong foot."

Warming-Up Exercises

I talked earlier in the book about the importance of hitting all of your possible shots while warming up. One reason, of course, is that you want to be ready to play your best tennis from the first point on. But more important is the fact that most people get hurt during a match by doing things they haven't done in practice. On the serve, especially, they can pull a shoulder muscle by failing to warm up sufficiently. Or take the low volley. Very often people will be forced to hit their first low backhand volley in the middle of a key point. As a result, they haven't stretched the muscles they need for that shot, and they're awkward and uncomfortable trying to make the play.

That's why, in my opinion, Ralston's "shadowboxing" drill is the best way I know to get your brain, body — and your strokes — ready for a match. By taking every stroke you can imagine and rehearsing each as you run to the right, to the left, diagonally forward, and then back to the baseline, you'll be puffing hard and you'll be properly loosened up.

Another excellent tune-up drill is Jack Kramer's old trick of never letting yourself be out of proper hitting position for any ball during the warm-up. This requires you to be up on your toes, watching your opponent like a hawk to anticipate the direction of his next shot, and then running — sometimes sprinting — so that you reach the ball in plenty of time for the first bounce.

I know several people who like to run long distances for aerobic conditioning. However, I rarely see a match where I feel aerobic conditioning comes into play. Tennis is primarily an anaerobic sport — short bursts of speed and great energy expenditures in short time frames. At Wimbledon, for example, the ball crosses the net from 2.6 to 3.3 times per point. That's about nine seconds of play. A player has to anticipate and move at full speed to be effective. I still treasure the moment in a televised match when Andre Agassi hit a blazing forehand to Pete Sampras's forehand corner, but Andre's blast caught the net and the point was "stop framed." While the ball was shown touching the net, little attention was paid to Sampras, who was already in position for his forehand in the corner of his court. Pete looks frail, but he is one of the strongest, best-conditioned, and fastest players on the tour.

The following statistics from two pro matches in the late 1980s help illustrate why tennis must be approached as an anaerobic sport. My staff and I recorded every ball hit in a match between Andre Agassi and Paul Annacone and a match on clay courts between Gabriela Sabatini and Steffi Graf.

Let's begin with the match in which Agassi defeated Annacone 6–2, 6–4. This was a classic confrontation between a constant net-rusher (Annacone), who would force the point to end quickly, and a counterpuncher (Agassi), who happily refused to go to the net. The breakdown:

Total playing time: 4.95 minutes
Average playing time per set: 2.47 minutes
Total points in match: 92
Average seconds per point: 3.25
Average hits per person/per point: 1.59
Two-stroke rallies (42.40%): 39 points
Three-stroke rallies (26.01%): 24 points
Four-stroke rallies or more (17.40%): 16 points

Now let's take a look at the women's match, which resulted in a rare defeat for Graf early in her career (Sabatini winning 6–3, 4–6, 7–5):

Total playing time: 37.69 minutes
Average playing time per set: 12.56 minutes
Total points in match: 213
Average seconds per point: 10.8

Thus, even on clay courts, one can see that points don't last too long and the warm-up plays a major role for the quick burst of action to follow. In fact, Agassi's warm-up period with Annacone was longer than the actual playing time of their match.

Most people fail to take advantage of the backboard as a useful practice companion, or to review their strokes before a match. They use the backboard either to get a fast workout by pounding the ball back or to pass the time until they play —"I hope somebody comes soon because I'm getting tired of slugging this thing against the wall." Either way, they simply ingrain bad habits by failing to pay attention to what they're doing.

The real value of a backboard is that it gives you the chance to individualize your own instruction without being distracted by your opponent. By concentrating on one concept at a time, you can check out your forehand and backhand groundstrokes, work on timing and synchronization problems, practice your serve, and improve your reactions and footwork on the volley. And, as much as we would like to say that we can hit the same shot off the backboard every time, we can't. So, using the backboard can be a little bit closer to "random" practice than ball machines.

When you hit against a backboard — even if it is 39 feet away (the distance from the baseline to the net) — let every ball bounce twice so that you have time to check out your rhythm. One reason people end up slugging the ball is that backboards are built improperly; instead of being slanted back 5 to 15 degrees so that the ball hits and comes back naturally, backboards are vertical, and thus the angle of deflection brings the ball down. This forces people to keep moving closer to the board as they try to return the ball on the first bounce, and thus they never have a chance to check what they are doing on their swing. But when you let the ball bounce twice, and get into that slower-paced rhythm, you have the time to analyze key elements in your forehand

and backhand, such as: Is your front foot stepping toward the board? Are you coming through with your body, and not simply "arming" the ball? Are you staying over the ball through contact? Are you remembering to follow through properly? Are the knuckles on your backhand and the palm on your forehand going out toward the intended target?

If you have 39 feet to play with, your eyes should remain fixed on the point of ball/racket impact until you hear the ball pop against the backboard. You'll still have plenty of time to reach the ball on the second bounce. This 39-foot distance will also enable you to work on your serve. Have a piece of chalk along so that you can draw target circles one to two feet above the net; if the backboard hasn't been marked with a net, draw in the center stripe and a net line three feet above the ground at that point. To practice serving to your opponent's backhand corner from the right side of the court, place your target circle just to the left of the center stripe and above the net line, and then stand just to the right of the stripe, 39 feet from the backboard.

When you go to practice your volley, do so at close range — unlike your groundstrokes. Try to keep hitting the board without letting the ball bounce and this will force you to learn how to change grips quickly, while sharpening your reactions, anticipation, and eye contact on the ball.

Although the backboard will never replace a court for warming up before a match, it can certainly help you review the key fundamentals of your swing before you get absorbed in rallying with your opponent. But keep in mind that you're not trying to beat the backboard; you only want to check out the strokes you hope will beat your opponent.

FINDING A TEACHING PRO

It's difficult for anybody to learn to play tennis, or to make significant improvement, by operating in a vacuum. The self-evaluation techniques I've described in this book can certainly be helpful, but you still need another person to periodically analyze your swing and point out problems. Unfortunately, most people don't know what to look for; their eyes aren't trained to study technique. They can notice that something is wrong with your swing but they're not sure what. Another problem here is that the self-perception of what one is doing versus the reality of the situation is often quite different. For example, I'll often ask a student to freeze her body at a particular point in the swing and we go through an analysis. The student is usually amazed to find the racket is nowhere near where she thought it was.

Therefore, unless you can basically teach yourself, or unless you have friends with knowledgeable eyes for good tennis technique, you should rely on a series of lessons with a qualified teaching pro or periodic crash-course instruction at a tennis college or camp. Having worked both sides of the net — as a teaching pro and, from 1971 to 1997 as Director of the Vic Braden Tennis College in southern California — I know what each route can offer to players at every ability level.

The Tennis College Approach

The reason that a tennis college was so important to me was that I was frustrated by the limitations of weekly half-hour and hour-long lessons. A lesson could end just as the student was beginning to effect the desired changes. When that student left the court, there was almost no tracking of his or her progress. The process of sending and receiving information is very complex and the research involves experts from many disciplines. Even if you gather in the correct information, converting it to the proper use of muscles is another issue. I found that most people wanted a lot of information in a short period of time, so I preferred to get them into a setting where they could eat and sleep tennis for a few days. In addition, I now would have the time to track their daily progress. At best, tennis lessons produce temporary learning. Permanent learning doesn't take place until a person can consistently hit the new stroke under stress. Usually, the coach finds herself working with a student who last week took a half-hour lesson, and her feeling is that she has to start all over again from the beginning. It doesn't mean that it can't be done, it only means to me that I prefer to have students in my school for a longer period. When I do teach private lessons, I like the students to write down or tell me how they practiced between lessons.

Evaluating the Pro before Signing Up for Lessons

The primary goal of most teaching pros is to help you maximize your performance and enjoyment of tennis in the shortest period of time. Qualified pros should welcome the chance to have you sit near the court and evaluate their instruction during an actual lesson — before you commit your own money. Many pros feel that prior inspection is an insult to their teaching ability, but if your prospective pro appears threatened in this way, keep searching for the instructor with the right self-confidence.

Watching a pro give a lesson should help you decide whether the chemistry would be right between the two of you; perhaps there's something about the pro's coaching patter, his manner, or his approach to technique that strikes you wrong. Remember, talented pros never offer their students a get-rich-quick approach to the game. Teaching tennis and learning to play tennis are very complex operations involving the brain and the rest of your body. Learning seldom comes fast and one must learn new motor programs while erasing others. When you take a lesson, there is only temporary learning, and permanent learning will have to be measured at a later date and under stress conditions. While you're learning to play, you need support from your coach, not criticism and uncomfortable feelings.

You also want to discover, either in prior conversations with the pro or as you observe one of his lessons, whether or not he makes sense. If, deep inside, you really don't believe what he has to say about technique, then you won't try to work on his suggestions once the lesson is over. He might say, "You're starting to improve. I can see you're trying to make the right changes in your swing." But the moment you begin to play a match, you look over your shoulder to see if the pro is around, and you're thinking, "I know what Vic said, but I've got this little shot that I can beat Bertha with every time." Some people go so far as to tell their pro, in effect: "That's terrific what you teach, I really like you, and here's your twenty bucks. But don't horse around with my strokes."

TAKING LESSONS

Several references in the literature refer to the Learner's Bill of Rights. For example, each student has a right to be happy, to be treated with respect, to be listened to, to be taught intelligently, and to be able to question the coach. I completely agree with these rights; however, we seldom hear about the responsibilities of the student. For instance, each student should try his best at all times, listen carefully to the coach, provide honest feedback to the coach, and alert the coach when instruction is unclear.

Before going out on the court for the first lesson, the coach should try to learn something about your athletic background, any fears you might have about the game, or persistent problems you are trying to work out with your strokes. He'll want to know how you learn best. Are you a kinesthetic learner, who likes to have the instructor guide you through the proper stroking movements to give you a feel for the proper sensations? Or do you learn best by imitation? Here are some other questions I've learned to ask students to help me facilitate learning, beginning with the query "How do you like to be taught?"

- A little information at a time . . . or lots of information?
- Lots of technical data . . . or keep it very simple?
- Lots of rationale . . . or very little explanation?
- A drill-sergeant approach . . . or soft and gentle responses?

I must say, I have been surprised over the years how many students want a "drill-sergeant" approach, even though research indicates that "overguidance" is not an effective tool for producing permanent learning.

Once the lesson begins, a talented coach will help you feel comfortable right away on how to enjoy and learn from your mistakes. He will not put you into embarrassing situations or demean your talents in any way. His job is to take a student where he or she is at the moment and carefully nurture a healthy growth pattern. A good coach will continually inform you of your gains and caringly inform you of areas which still need work. A true professional understands that shouting and screaming orders doesn't guarantee learning. In most cases, it inhibits learning.

In addition, you should want an instructor who judges you by your swing, and not the results of that swing. Don't let yourself — or the pro — be ball direction–oriented. If you have a faulty swing and the pro tries to suggest a correction, the tendency is to answer, "Yeah, but that ball landed in." A confident pro, however, won't weaken. His objective will always be to keep you from repeating — and thus reinforcing — an incorrect stroke, even if the ball lands in play occasionally.

A good pro tries to get you into rhythmical patterns as you swing, but he also knows that anxiety can sap out any rhythm you might have. So he'll try to reduce your anxiety level by taking a positive approach to instruction. If he has to slug you with a concept that's hard for you to accept or to grasp, he'll throw support your way for the trying. He'll always reward your willingness to experiment with new — and correct — stroking sensations, even if the ball keeps going out.

Another sign of good instruction is the coach who doesn't want any shot to be wasted during the lesson. Students will sometimes complain, "Coach, I don't want to run for that volley — it's going out anyway." But so what? You can still stretch for the ball, try to keep your racket head up, and then punch the shot deep. You'll squeeze everything possible out of a lesson by taking this approach to every shot.

A real professional won't waste time. She won't spend 20 minutes on instruction and 40 minutes picking up balls. And, you can always tell a pro who hasn't thought about you at all between lessons when he asks at the beginning of each lesson, "Let's see, what did we work on last week?"

In Defense of Ball Machines

Many teaching pros are opposed to ball machines. They argue that nothing can replace the live "feel" of hitting against a coach, and that a person who learns using a ball machine will be thrown off in an actual match when every ball is hit with different pace and bounce. However, I feel that ball machines are of great value — if properly used. No machine can replace the good coach, but if the goal is to improve one's response to a particular shot, few coaches can match the accuracy of a ball machine.

The research on ball machines actually comes from motor-learning experts, who emphasize that to develop the proper strokes and to be able to use them properly when playing, the student must learn to position himself in the same situations as match play. This means the hitter must position himself so that he varies his shots. For example, hitting a fine forehand drive from waist height and then getting out of position and being forced to hit a low backhand so that you practice just as you would be expected to perform in a match. That's why many new ball-machine manufacturers have produced machines that vary the nature of the shot. However, I have found that most students learn the pattern set by the machine and arrive early for every shot, which doesn't happen in a match. So make sure that you work yourself out of position in order to get the tough shot you want from the ball machine. Nearly everyone can stand in one position and become an expert. But tennis is played with random shots.

There are plenty of ball machines with computer chips, but the machine of the future will actually have chips for the playing style of current leading pros. Because the data will be available, due to sophisticated monitoring devices, the actual speed and shot selection of pros will be programmed for your practice session. That will also include the exact duplication of the serve, which includes speed, spin, direction, and trajectory.

Improving Your Anticipation Skills

In singles and doubles alike, as you move up in this game, reaction time shrinks. The ball comes faster (especially as rackets continue to improve) and experienced opponents know how to take the ball on the rise at the baseline and how to move in and volley shoulder-high balls in the midcourt area. This demands greater anticipation skills on your part so that you can break for the ball with a fast first step and get into position to hit the ball aggressively.

As I discussed earlier, when your opponent goes to hit, learn to look for racket and body cues. In pro tennis, players rely more on experience and instinct because the racket face is moving too fast and players have the strength to change directions more easily in the hitting zone. But club and league players are locked in; they have a racket position that will not allow them to make a last-second change, and thus their movements are very revealing. At the tennis college, for example, the first thing I ask people to do is become an expert at reading the racket face, because the racket face hits the ball. When we get people in one-on-one volley drills and they focus on the opponent's racket, suddenly they start anticipating much better.

I also encourage my students to look for that giveaway grimace when a player is going to drive the ball, or the exaggerated facial expression when he's about to throw up a lob. In fact, the way the game is going, future pros may need to hire a body language coach. Or members of a player's entourage may be assigned to study an opponent's specific body parts and what these cues may reveal about the resulting shot. Video cameras could also help the investigation. In that vein, if you're thinking about playing the pro tour, you should keep in mind your own body language and learn to have noncommittal facial features as you swing.

Statistical tendencies are already part of the pro game. If I still played, I would have a person help me keep a detailed book about all my major opponents so that we could determine, through charting, just what a person tends to do in a particular circumstance. In doubles, for example, I would want to know: "When he was down the ad, receiving serve, and we served high into the backhand, did he hit ten out of ten cross-court or just five out of ten?" If he mixes it up, 50-50, we're going to hold our ground. But if it's nine out of ten, our net person is going to poach cross-court because there's only a 10 percent chance that the receiver will go down the line. This is no different from baseball, in which teams keep exacting records of what pitch a person pitches in a particular situation against a particular batter (lefty or righty) and a particular individual (Ken Griffey or Barry Bonds).

Jack Kramer was a keen observer when he played and he did his homework when he watched a match. He always felt that a certain part of a player's game would eventually break down if he could just keep attacking that weakness by playing his own game — and it almost always happened. John McEnroe also paid attention to the tiny details. When he played doubles with Peter Fleming, I would see John make a fairly unique play and win the point when they were in a critical tie-breaker because he had been logging data and he knew the probability of his opponent's attempting a particular shot.

The important lesson here isn't that you necessarily score a tremendous number of points by scouting, being observant as you play, and keeping records, but that you win the key point in a set because you knew the probabilities and you anticipated correctly. If you have a particular rival and you're smart, you'll become increasingly aware of his motor program — that is, the way his software package works — and the longer the two of you play, the more you should be in the right position at the right time. But, of course, remember: he should be logging the same data about you.

The Role of Your Muscles in Motor Programming

There is a memory involved in controlling muscle movements, but the memory is located in the brain and not the muscle. The goal is to make the muscles work in a way that produces the shot you're seeking. Thanks to motor-learning experts, we're beginning to get a handle on what has to be done to get a person to change his or her motor program, which is directed by the brain.

Effective coaches seem to understand that each student is the owner of his motor program and only he can change it. We as coaches are only information providers and motivators; the student calls the shots. Therefore, our goal is to provide that information and motivation which will encourage the student to begin the complex task of changing a motor program.

Though we lack definitive research to show exactly how long it will take to change a motor program, there are some cues. For example, in a project I started at my tennis college, we looked at beginners and intermediate players. If the student was convinced that a change would be in his best interest and was willing to work hard to make the change, we found that it took about eight weeks to acquire a new stroke and be able to use it effectively in match play. Then the question surfaced: "How many times do I have to practice each of those eight weeks to make good things happen?" It turned out that some players only played once a week and others played four times a week. But the players who worked out only once a week also spent time just swinging the proper stroke (without a racket) in their office or living room.

As a student, you have to be convinced that a change will be in your best interest, and that the pro's basic job is to help you understand the physical laws which rule the game and to tell you what it is you're doing in relation to those laws. He'll try to provide you with an idea of what the correct sensation should be, and he'll help you recognize what you are doing right and wrong.

When Drs. Gideon Ariel and Ann Penny and I were doing some EMG (electromyography) studies in the Coto Research Center in the early 1980s, we found that we could intercept the signal from the brain to the muscular and detect the confusion the brain was experiencing trying to adapt to a new motor program. And under stress, the brain would want to go back to the old motor program. This often occurs when a player is really beginning to make substantial changes in her game, but suddenly reverts back to the old pattern during the tie-breaker.

A well-trained coach will have you swing very slowly at times to see if you can gather some feedback through your joints, ligaments, tendons, and muscles. The faster one swings, the less feedback is available. Also, the process of learning is exciting if the proper atmosphere is generated. In the right environment, the fastest discovery is not made by trial and error, as that system has proved to be rather ineffective. The student can spend too much time involved in trials that have no relationship to effecting the proper swing. Good information and isolating key parts of the swing and patient information delivery systems will go a long way to speeding up the learning process.

In every learning curve there are progress, learning plateaus, and even regression. That is to be expected, but eventually the new motor program disappears less frequently and for shorter durations. Then, one day the student finds the old motor program has disappeared. The student who is prepared for the joys and disappointments of changing a motor program will be more apt to speed up the learning process. As usual, the coach is completely dependent upon the student to do his part to effect the proper software change in his brain.

A related problem that inhibits learning — especially by adults — is that very often they have an image of themselves which is very different from reality. They don't look the way they think they look when they swing and they can get pretty defensive when the pro points this out. That's why videotaping can be so effective if people will give it a chance. The television screen shows you exactly what the pro is seeing, and there's no hiding from that reality. So no matter how high your self-esteem, remember to have an open mind when it comes to your tennis swing.

Most research seems to indicate that it's better to video players from the rear so that they don't have to make a visual reversal when viewing the action. When we video from the front, the viewer must try to imagine what it's like after making the reversal in the brain.

The following are other reminders to help you learn to improve your game at a faster rate, with or without a teaching pro:

1. Be objective about your strengths and weaknesses. Have a friend chart your matches and put your different strokes to the test so that you'll have a realis-

Children learn early to aim for air targets over the net in order to produce deep shots.

tic idea of what you can actually do out on the court. This will keep you from attacking the pro for giving you the bad news about your tennis game.

2. Don't be afraid to experiment, as this will help you reach your goal sooner. Also, don't be afraid to confront any anxieties about learning this sport, or showing your lack of expertise in particular areas.

3. Remember that tennis is a mistake center for everybody. Enjoy learning what your mistakes are and discovering appropriate cures. Your goal should be to strive for improvement; winning matches will follow in a natural sequence. Every tennis player on the pro tour started out as a beginner. They know what it's like to start a new sport.

4. When it comes to improving, your goal should be to understand the rationale for every stroke, practice intelligently, and then go out and just hit the ball. We know from research that you don't want to be out there thinking about your last lesson and dwelling on all the components of a particular shot. In fact, when you tell yourself to just hit the doggone ball, you're usually going to be closer to the desired stroke than when you try to incorporate all the little checkpoints from practice sessions. But let's not forget: you can't develop the right kind of hit until you've gone through all the correct stages in practice. Not surprisingly, most people don't practice effectively and they try to develop these pieces in a match — which is too late.

5. Since we have a tendency to perform whatever we visualize, try to develop a positive mental image of yourself playing the game right — even if you haven't yet developed the correct strokes. Most people try so hard not to look bad that they visualize potential problems and thus reinforce what it is they do wrong, rather than visualize what is right. Billie Jean King once told me that when she went to the net to volley, "All I imagine is the ball going right through my opponent." She never imagined herself missing or even coming close to missing — only that she made the successful play.

6. We always have people going through the tennis college who dearly enjoy learning, while others struggle and fight back and work very hard not to learn. That's why I stress a philosophy that learning to play a better game of tennis can be fun, not drudgery, and that when you enjoy playing you have more incentive to improve your strokes. This increases your chances of winning, which increases your enjoyment level, so it's a beautiful circle. If, however, the game is providing more stress than relaxation, then you have the wrong sport or the wrong teaching pro. It might be helpful to remember that if 30 million people play tennis today, 15 million people will lose.

Evaluating the Coach-Student Relationship

Many people try to blame the pro for their lack of improvement. They go from lesson to lesson without really listening to the pro or working on making specific corrections in their swing, and yet they complain, "Gee, the pro isn't very good," or "This pro can't coach me." Perhaps the pro is an ineffective teacher, but oftentimes people are simply shopping around for a pro who will tell them what they want to hear.

Every pro, therefore, should develop an evaluative technique on paper that will objectively outline the student's specific improvements and the old problems that still exist. The pro can say, "We've been together a month and here's what I've told you (checklist, checklist) and here's what you're doing (checklist, checklist). You've improved here, here, and here, but you're still making the same mistakes here and here. Perhaps we should change my approach a little." Another of my suggestions to teaching pros is that they videotape their student's strokes at the first lesson — and then again in three months or six months or whatever. The pro should try to see what improvements have been made, and ask himself, "Was this instruction really worth $500?" Some pros would say, "It's worth $500 just to be with me every week," but I doubt that they're going to last long in this business.

GETTING THE MOST OUT OF PRACTICE

Dr. Richard Schmidt, a UCLA motor-learning expert, discusses three types of practice. The first is "blocked" practice, in which the student hits the same shot over and over again. The second type is "variable" practice, in which the student hits the same stroke but varies the height and other conditions with which he hits the ball. And three, "random" practice, in which a player only hits one shot of each stroke. The different subjects utilizing these three systems are tested for accuracy at the end of the instruction and the results often show that the best scores hitting for targets belong to the blocked practice system. In second place are those who learn with the variable approach, and third is random practice. However, when all subjects are tested again at a later date — to determine the amount of permanent learning that has taken place — the random system normally places first, variable second and blocked third.

There is an explanation for this turnaround. In an actual match, for example, a net-rusher often serves, moves in to volley the service return, tries to hit a low volley to the backhand corner, and then lunges down the line for a forehand volley. No two strokes in this sequence are alike. The shots come in random fashion. Thus, the player who practices with a random system usually has a big edge, and that edge is based upon the word "retrieval". When a person hits a high forehand, the brain must call up a high forehand software package to recruit the appropriate muscles. However, the opponent's next shot is to the person's low backhand. Now the player must give up that high forehand package and retrieve a low backhand package. This goes on the entire match. The player who works a blocked practice system rarely practices retrieving any new software packages.

The name of the game is to practice in the same manner as you're expected to perform, and that also goes for drills. Any drill that does not simulate actual playing conditions is normally worth very little. Some drills are employed to help people have fun, which is fine in small doses, but these drills usually have nothing to do with learning and playing tennis.

Players at every ability level invariably tell me, "Jeez, I was better before I started taking lessons" (or tried to improve a particular stroke). And very often it's true, for when you're trying to break old motor-program patterns, the tendency is to retrogress before you finally begin to improve. Unfortunately, most people lack the patience or the willingess to keep concentrating on key changes in their swing while their ego takes a beating, and thus when they find themselves under stress they invariably revert to what's comfortable, even if it's a losing style of play.

That's why I urge you to avoid competition when you are working to change your technique, unless you can block out your desire to win as you concentrate on effecting your new or adjusted swing. But whenever your ego interferes, remove the stress by simply rallying with people until you feel comfortable with the changes you have made. If you need to play six points to keep yourself from getting sloppy or to make practice more fun, then don't keep a cumulative score. Serve, receive, and play out the point to get your adrenaline flowing, but don't fall in the trap of seeing who can win ten points first.

I realize it's hard to find people who are willing to be your backboard and your ball machine for an hour; they'd rather play two sets. But a good club pro will always know members who simply want to work on their game in a noncompetitive situation and what these people are looking for in a practice partner. For example, Joe Jones only wants to work on groundstrokes, or John Smith is working on his service return and wants somebody to hit serves. To practice your overhead, find the person who wants to practice his lobs.

Try to avoid rallying with somebody who just wants to slug the ball; instead of relaxing and working on your own strokes, you'll worry more about matching this person's power. Better to seek out a dinker who just keeps the ball in play. Even if the ball is hit softly, get your racket back and move into position quickly, then practice swinging slowly and easily. Don't try to power the ball back — you're working on your stroke, not the speed of your shot.

However you practice, always have a purpose in mind for every shot. Know your weak strokes and where you are making your errors on the court, then get out and practice these shots; don't simply hone your strengths (though you should never stop practicing your strengths). Try to isolate what the pro told you at your previous lesson so that you can actually improve between lessons. If you have specific weaknesses during a match, practice before you play again and concentrate on your errors. The shot you're most afraid to hit in a match is the shot you should be practicing between matches. Whenever Jack Kramer had trouble with a particular stroke — such as his low backhand volley — he would go out on a practice court immediately after the match and hit that shot 100 or 150 times . . . or until he knew he could sleep well that night. Contrast this to the average player, who simply takes a shower after a match and thinks, "Maybe next week I'll play a little better."

To get the most out of practice, learn to become target-oriented on every shot, since targets point out weaknesses faster than any other method. You'll be frustrated by the fact that you seldom land the ball where you are aiming, but this will help you become much more objective about your game and what really needs work. For example, to improve the depth on your groundstrokes, stretch a piece of cord across the court five feet inside the baseline, and try to land every shot inside that area. This will give you a graphic reminder of just how short most of your shots land. To work on approach shots, set up a four-foot square inside your opponent's backhand corner and try to hit every approach shot there. For the serve, place one or two tennis ball cans in your opponent's backhand corner and see if you can knock them over. On service returns, aim for cans that are set up down the sideline, and others which are set up cross-court, away from the onrushing server.

If you are rallying without specific targets, envision a target area and don't be satisfied with your stroke unless you can produce a shot that lands within three feet of that target. Another way to improve your accuracy from the baseline is to imagine that you're playing a 4½-foot alley (which is the width of the doubles alley) and that you want to land every groundstroke inside this alley. Strive to keep the ball down the middle and deep at first and then, with experience, you can shift your "alley" down-the-line or cross-court.

You may think that playing tennis with targets in mind — rather than concentrating on just keeping the ball in play — will give you too much to think about ("Who can think and hit at the same time?"). But I've found over the years that when you fail to become target-oriented as you move into a shot, you tend to do your thinking in the middle of your stroke. I've heard it a thousand times in my 50-plus years of teaching: "I can't hit the targets in practice, but I can do it in a match." Unfortunately, I will pass away never having witnessed one of these phenomenons.

A final reminder about practicing: everybody needs it to improve. Some people think that simply playing a lot of tennis will improve their game because they'll gain a better "feel" for their strokes. But if you have improper strokes, playing all the time will simply help you solidify a lousy game. Of course, if your only goal is to just play five days a week without really worrying about improving, then I'm with you all the way. The idea is to enjoy yourself out there. But if you've also set improvement as your goal and you don't improve (because you refuse to take lessons and/or you fail to practice) then you're going to be pretty frustrated because playing five times a week, you get more chances than the average player to recognize and review your failure.

In the end, I like to measure tennis players not by how many matches they win, but by how hard they work to improve their game. Many top players set a good example by using stroke production and intelligent and creative approaches to solving competitive problems to judge their progress, while the average player only sees progress in terms of competition: "I won, so I'm playing well . . . I lost, so I'm playing lousy." Therefore, when you're practicing with a friend — or instead of playing a match — try drills in which you compete but the reward is not based upon winning the point. For example, gather up all the balls and serve until you're tired, while your friend practices service returns. Then have your friend serve until he's tired while you work on returning the ball. Instead of keeping track of who wins the most points, see who can get the best percentage of first serves in play, or who can return the most serves. You'll still have fun, and you'll improve.

People often challenge me when I talk about winning not being the only thing in tennis — or any sport, for that matter. They say, "What else really counts?" And I tell them: "It's the striving to win and striving to improve that's important. Learn to judge yourself by your own improvement during a match — and between matches. That's the real reward. No matter what your level of play, give it your best shot, have some fun, and you'll enjoy this great game for a lifetime."